CORVETTE C4
HOW TO BUILD & MODIFY
1984–1996

Chris Petris

S-A DESIGN

CarTech®

CarTech®

CarTech®, Inc.
6118 Main Street
North Branch, MN 55056
Phone: 651-277-1200 or 800-551-4754
Fax: 651-277-1203
www.cartechbooks.com

Edit by Wes Eisenschenk
Layout by Connie DeFlorin

ISBN 978-1-61325-795-1
Item No. SA542

Library of Congress Cataloging-in-Publication Data Available

Written, edited, and designed in the U.S.A.
Printed in China
10 9 8 7 6 5 4 3 2 1

DISTRIBUTION BY:

Europe
PGUK
63 Hatton Garden
London EC1N 8LE, England
Phone: 020 7061 1980 • Fax: 020 7242 3725
www.pguk.co.uk

Australia
Renniks Publications Ltd.
3/37-39 Green Street
Banksmeadow, NSW 2109, Australia
Phone: 2 9695 7055 • Fax: 2 9695 7355
www.renniks.com

Canada
Login Canada
300 Saulteaux Crescent
Winnipeg, MB, R3J 3T2 Canada
Phone: 800 665 1148 • Fax: 800 665 0103
www.lb.ca

CONTENTS

History and Inspection

The C4 Corvette's 12-year production run began during a low-performance era in automotive history. Despite this, the 1984 C4, which produced 205 hp and 290 ft-lbs of torque, was the fastest US-made production car. For 1985, a new L98 tuned port-injection (TPI) engine delivered 230 hp. The TPI system's eight molded aluminum tubes provided 330 ft-lbs of torque, although high-end RPM and horsepower remained limited.

General Motors released the 1990 wide-bodied ZR1 LT-5 option, which produced 380 hp at 6,200 rpm and 370 ft-lbs of torque at 4,500 rpm, although its $27,000 price tag limited its appeal. This technological leap featured a Lotus-designed, Mercury Marine–built engine with four overhead camshafts, sequential fuel injection, a distributor-less ignition, and dual fuel injectors and intake runners per cylinder. The Formula One–inspired marvel was pure joy, as it spun effortlessly to 6,200 rpm.

Eight years into production, General Motors reintroduced the LT1 engine for 1992 with 300 hp and 330 ft-lbs of torque at 5,700 rpm. Based on Chevrolet's small-block design, it featured reverse-flow cooling and a front-mounted ignition distributor that was driven by the camshaft. The long L98 intake runners were replaced with short runners and a large plenum, raising the power band. The reverse-flow cooling system directed coolant to the cylinder heads before the engine case, enabling a 10.4:1 compression ratio that increased horsepower.

The 1992–1996 LT1 and 1996 LT4 engines were the top power producers of the C4 era (excluding the ZR1), with 2¾-inch inside-diameter exhaust systems and dual catalytic converters. The 1994–1996 powertrain control modules (PCMs) have sequential fuel-injection, a first for the base Corvette engine, making these PCMs ideal for bolt-on upgrades. The 1996 LT4 option ($1,450) increased power to 330 hp and 340 ft-lbs of torque, offering beefed-up internals and the mandatory ZF 6-speed manual transmission. There was no more ZF reverse lockout knob to pull up, which eliminated the awkward reverse gear selection from earlier models.

The 1984 transmission options

Lance Miller drives while the* Corvette Challenge 65 *provides the smoke during the inaugural burnout competition at Carlisle. This 1984–1996 C4 Corvette book focuses on performance.

included the 4L60 4-speed automatic and the innovative 4+3 manual gearbox. The latter provided seven forward gear ratios through a BorgWarner T-10 4-speed transmission with an electronically shifted overdrive. In 1989, the hybrid BorgWarner T-10 4+3 transmission was outdated and the superior ZF 6-speed manual was offered. The 4L60 automatic improved yearly and handled factory torque loads effectively. For 1994, C4s received the electronically shifted 4L65E automatic transmission.

The down-and-dirty part of a project's completion can be frustrating. Loose fasteners, electrical problems, and leaks can quickly reduce enthusiasm. Poor choices waste time and money, while choosing the appropriate parts and undergoing thorough planning will result in a high-performing C4. However, expect issues regardless of preparation. Your ability to assess problems and implement solutions separates success from failure. Careful planning helps you save time and money that is otherwise spent on trial and error.

Paperwork is crucial. The job isn't complete until the documents are finalized. During car hunts, I've frequently encountered questionable documentation from owners who never properly transferred titles. Always verify with local authorities before making a purchase to avoid spending thousands of dollars on a car that you can't legally own.

Your most important performance investment is attending a driving school. That's a cold, hard fact. Most drivers can't approach the C4's handling limits. In novice hands, a factory C4 often outperforms modified ones with an experienced driver behind the wheel. Schools, such as the Ron Fellows Performance Driving School, teach cornering, braking, and car control—skills that lower lap times far more than bolt-on parts. During a Michelin media event, I rode along with Fellows and calmly chatted while he masterfully navigated the course at Spring Mountain Motor Resort and Country Club in Pahrump, Nevada.

The Van Steel 67 C4 Corvette carves up an autocross course with race-inspired suspension components. The driver's side of the vehicle has minimal drop powering through a right-hand corner. The passenger-side front tire surface contact is excellent due to Van Steel's anti-roll-bar components.

You can also enjoy your C4 in the Eastern region of the United States at non-stressful track events. The National Corvette Museum has a myriad of fun and competition track days available annually. It also offers driver education. There are plenty of opportunities to drive a new Corvette or your C4 Corvette, so that should get your blood pumping. This is an excellent reason to give your C4

This 1984 C4 Corvette has participated in the annual Brock Yates' One Lap of America event and local track-day events. Dr. Charles Lovelady of Scottsboro, Alabama, recruited Throwback Automotive (doing business as Petris Enterprises) to prepare and inspect the C4 for the rigorous event.

a comprehensive checkup and enjoy the track time. You may discover that you're a natural racer and that you want to pursue a career in motorsports. Your C4 is an excellent place to start the journey.

If you want a real test, participate in the Brock Yates' One Lap of America event. Participants are required to drive their performance car to each event, and tire changes are acceptable—for those looking for the best lap times. You can pull a small trailer or have a support vehicle throughout the event for tire changes, repairs, and maintenance. Typically, it's 7 days and 3,500 miles of testing your C4's stamina and measuring your hard work. Cruise to each event, set up, race, change back into street attire, and then go to the next event.

Powertrain Options

Throughout the C4's production run, several engine options were offered, and technological advancements continually built performance across the nameplate.

L83

The L83 Crossfire used a dual "shower head" fuel-injection system that sprayed fuel onto throttle blades (similar to a carburetor). Its unique read-only memory (ROM) chip and transmission-specific engine control modules further limited performance potential. With low compression, poor airflow, and limited fuel management, the L83 remains challenging for significant power enhancement.

Some enthusiasts have developed improved L83 intake manifolds with dual injectors and better airflow, but those remain scarce with uncertain future availability due to high production costs for a limited market. When upgrading the intake, the cylinder heads should also be replaced. Despite its limitations, the L83's decent torque makes it enjoyable for street driving and even competitive in autocross events, particularly when exiting corners.

L98

The 1985–1991 L98 TPI engine featured 17-inch intake runners, delivering excellent torque. Cost-conscious engineering resulted in batch-fired fuel injection that alternated between cylinder banks (1, 3, 5, 7 and then 2, 4, 6, 8), spraying fuel regardless of valve position. This system worked best at higher RPM but limited the camshaft options, as long-duration camshafts caused excess fuel delivery at lower RPM.

For 1990–1991, General Motors made controversial changes to the engine control system. It replaced the reliable under-dash engine control module (ECM) with a problematic under-hood unit and abandoned the failure-prone mass airflow (MAF) sensor system in favor of speed-density fuel control.

On a positive note, stock 1985–1991 L98 TPI engines excel in gymkhana, autocross, and twisty road courses with limited long-distance straights. Long-duration camshaft upgrades require sophisticated fuel management and updated engine control modules.

Gen II LT1

The 1992 Gen II LT1 engine refreshed the 37-year-old small-block design. Its Optispark ignition system provided cylinder position data to the ECM, although General Motors didn't fully utilize its capabilities until 1994. The 1994 ECM introduced sequential fuel injection, ending bank-to-bank fuel-injector control, while the 1994–1996 MAF sensor significantly improved upon earlier units. Reliability issues arose from placing the new Optispark distributor between the water pump and engine block, and an updated ventilated version was introduced in 1995. For 1996, Chevrolet added a crankshaft position sensor for OBD-II misfire detection. These LT engines accommodate longer-duration camshafts better than previous generations.

The factory service manual cautions that the balancer and flywheel have weights placed into the circumference of the outer perimeter. The weights are to be removed and then placed into their replacement balancers or flywheels. With the flywheel, the locating hole or dowel for the flywheel ensures replacement in the same position on the crankshaft. Theoretically, when flywheels are replaced with aftermarket pieces that do not provide balance-weight retention holes, the crankshaft balance would be off. Automatic transmission flexplates do not adhere to this procedure.

The balancer hub has no keyway to ensure hub replacement is in the same location. Did they balance the crankshaft on an engine stand with the timing cover and hub/balancer assembly in place? They would have to spin the complete rotating assembly for a dynamic balance. Or, did they mark the crankshaft hub location after balancing the crankshaft so that they could install the hub in the same location? If they did have a plan, that means when the balancer hub is removed, it must be placed in the exact location from which it came or there is the risk of vibration.

So, if you decide to replace your

The large box-like-plenum intake manifold with opposing throttle bodies sprays fuel directly into the plenum. Throttle-body syncing requires a manometer (vacuum-gauge set) to balance the vacuum between the units. The two idle air control (IAC) valves increase the cost of maintenance and are complex for the simple showerhead-fuel delivery system.

Obstacles restrict airflow, and the throttle body and extended runner length add to the restriction. The L83 cylinder head-to-intake port's rectangular shape is shortened, which is another bottleneck to add to the already-poor airflow numbers. It's a great conversation piece, but it is not smart to use on a high-performing engine.

This L98 tuned port injection (TPI) intake manifold base requires intake air to flow across it before entering the cylinders. Intake velocity builds and flows from the opposing runner-attachment side to the cylinder head, which unfortunately slows as RPM increases due to tube diameter.

The LT1 intake manifold's short runner length and large plenum promote high flow at engine speeds that the stock L98 engine could never attain. This is a dream to work with over the L98 TPI. Easy access to the fuel system and intake-manifold gasket reduced replacement time by five hours.

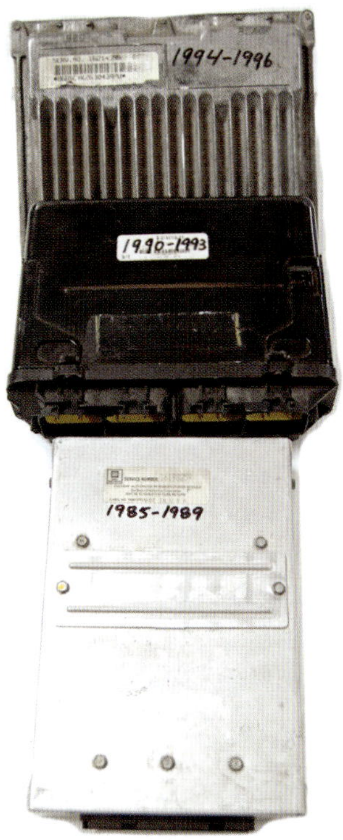

The 1984–1989 ECMs were durable and reliable units. The 1985–1989 ECM (bottom) is shown. The 1984 ECM is similar but has an edge board connector. The 1990–1993 ECMs (middle) had a black metal case and were prone to failure from poor solder joints and underhood heat. They commonly shut down without warning. A hand slap brings them back to life. The 1994–1996 ECMs (top) became powertrain control modules (PCMs), controlling the engine and transmission. These finned PCMs rarely fail.

manual transmission flywheel and the engine is apart, have the crankshaft and flywheel balanced.

Significant engine main case and cylinder head changes occurred when the Gen I small-block received important upgrades. This started in 1986, when convertibles featured D-shaped exhaust-port aluminum heads. By 1987, all C4s had aluminum heads with hydraulic-roller-lifter camshafts and low-drag piston rings, boosting the L98 to 240 hp. Chronic oil leaks were addressed with one-piece rear main seals and center-bolt valve covers with raised mounting rails. These changes finally eliminated the trademark oil spots that had plagued small-block Chevrolet (SBC) engines for 32 years.

Handling

To maximize your C4's performance, thoroughly study vehicle handling fundamentals. Understeer often precedes an impact when steering becomes ineffective, while oversteer occurs when the rear wheels attempt to overtake the front. Driving preferences differ based on the individual. Find what feels comfortable for you. Every great race car driver has lost control many times on the quest for the ultimate lowest track time, as the margin between grip and spinning is remarkably thin.

Decide whether you want ultimate handling, weekend track performance, or street enjoyment. The best-handling C4 will be a rough ride on city streets. Weekend warriors require balanced suspension and driveline setups, allowing quick adjustments for track competitiveness. Street-focused C4s remain enjoyable and can confidently participate in gymkhana and autocross events.

Workspace

Assess your abilities and workspace realistically. A standard two-car garage fills quickly during drivetrain removal, while even a 24x24-foot space becomes cramped during engine work with limited storage for components. Consider whether a major overhaul matches your skills because professionals complete such work efficiently and reliably. Specialty tools, which are rentable, are another consideration. The factory service manual is essential, and it is complemented by this book. Keep detailed notes via digital or paper methods to track progress and maintain direction.

Project Car Inspection

This section covers the typical C4s that can be found online or perhaps the vehicle you've been eyeing in someone's yard. This will prepare you for proper inspection and safe testing of a dormant C4, including the underhood components and support systems.

The first part to inspect is the removable roof panel. Replacing this is a significant cost if the panel is damaged. Used examples are $400 to $900 and more for a perfect panel. Three roof panels were used (1984–1986E, 1986L–1988, and 1989–1996), and bargain hunting can be difficult. The roof panel plays a role in overall body rigidity. An aluminum frame supports either an acrylic or composite panel. Composite body-color roof panels add support to the frame. Their acrylic counterparts do as well, but they are prone to cracking from ultraviolet (UV) rays. The composite panel can be re-bonded if required.

If you find a convertible C4 with a hardtop that is in decent shape, that can be quite a deal. The convertible top has rigid mounting points at the front, sides, and through the rear deck. I believe the hardtop C4 is as robust as the removable roof panel when secretly bolted in place. Used tops cost thousands of dollars if you

I found this 1991 triple-black convertible 150 miles from the shop. It's best viewed from a distance. It's one of my favorite C4s, with the round front and rear bumpers, being a convertible with the removable hardtop, and the 6-speed ZF manual transmission. It has better airbag and dashboard electronics than the 1990 model year, plus the L98 engine provides the perfect excuse for an LS swap.

Loosen the top at all four corners before jacking or lifting the vehicle. Remember to tighten the top before test driving and check it before heading to the track.

Place a jack cup under the vertical seam, which is the strongest point under the C4. It consists of three main frame and interior panels that are spot-welded together. Ensure that the jack cup is centered on the vertical seam. Don't lift on composite or steel floor sections. The jack location is critical. It must be 3 to 4 inches rearward of the mirror to lift the entire side evenly.

The jack is raised to maximum height with jack stands placed on the vertical seam (front and rear). This rear jack-stand placement area has a triangulated recess with three seams in front of the rear wheel inner liner. The flat band above the jack stand is a parking-brake cable guide that is unaffected when the C4 is lowered. The jack stand placement allows for convertible top X-frame removal.

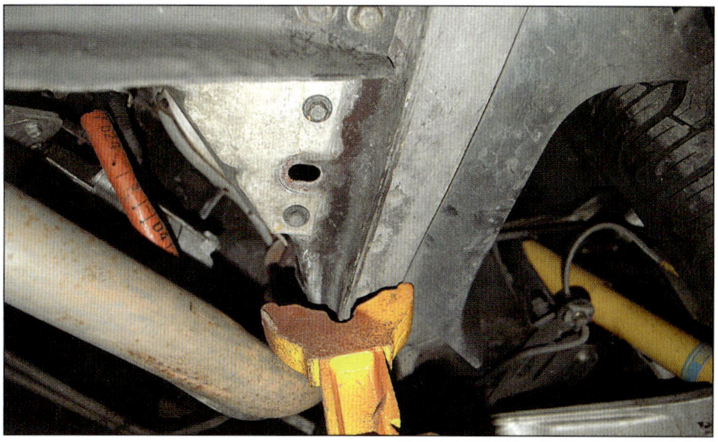

The front jackstand is placed on the three-rib seam that is close to the exhaust downpipe. This allows for the removal of the convertible C4 X-frame and provides fuel filter access. The two 10-mm screws on either side of the oval hole retain the fuel-filter shield. Once the stands are properly placed, take your time lowering the jack. NASCAR drops aren't recommended. Move to the other side and repeat.

This area draws air from the road surface and is often damaged from road debris and parking-lot stop bumpers. The A/C condenser is in poor condition. Expect the radiator to be similar or worse. Another sign of an impending cost is the wire harness being out of place from accident damage, improper installation without the original retainers, or worse, a cobbled-together C4 from multiple donors.

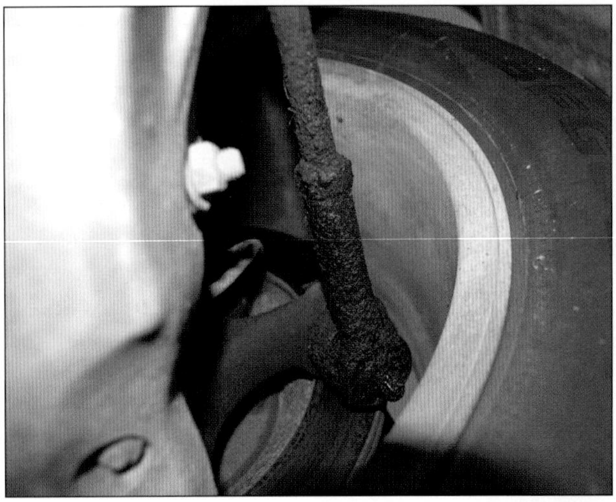

This is a common leak point. The power-steering fluid has leaked for a long time and coated the outer tie-rod with grease. Fluid from a power-steering hose leak could be dripping onto the steering rack. This should be a high priority and requires deeper investigation into the power-steering hydraulic system.

can find them in decent condition. Convertible roll-bar installation and interior work is easier. It is more troublesome, though, if you decide to remove the hardtop for soft-top use. You'll need a storage area for the hardtop when it is not installed on the car.

The C4 floor is hybrid composite up front with a stamped-steel rear section. Look under the lower valence between the front and rear wheels for damage. Floor-panel damage from improperly placed jacks is common, so there will likely be jack cup impressions at the rear and/or cracked composite floor panels. Immovable objects tear up the floor also. Major damage can require significant time and money to repair.

I know that jacking up a vehicle may seem rudimentary, but the jack points on C4s are limited and front and rear access is difficult. Incorrect techniques can result in suspension damage. The floor jack must roll inward as the C4 is lifted. Having your C4 in the jacked-up position allows easier access to the underside and under-hood projects. Leaning over the tires is rough on your back, so removing the front wheels allows the best possible access.

The rear spindle links have cracked rubber bushings that are still intact. This should be a high priority on your to-do list. It requires replacement but not immediately.

Take out your notepad, phone, or tablet and evaluate what you have to work with. Starting at the front, look at the condition of the underside and all of the attaching pieces. If you're working with a tight budget, there are support pieces that may not make your C4 perform better but are must-have safety items. C4s ride low, so there are often bent and damaged suspension and steering items that are of concern.

Look over the entire underside for worn components. The next step is to remove all four wheels, for a complete brake inspection. Many of these C4 projects have been sitting in the dirt or sand for years. The plan is to make sure that your C4 is safe enough for a road-test evaluation. A road test is next if you have a decent brake pedal. Check the steering and the brakes before trying any wide-open throttle (WOT) action and note any changes that are needed.

Engine Inspection

For a simple engine health check, remove the positive crankcase ventilation (PCV) valve after the engine reaches operating temperature. If blue smoke billows out of the valve cover like a steam locomotive, expect problems. High crankcase pressure from worn/broken piston rings is common in the 1986–1996 aluminum-head engines. Warning signs include the dipstick pushed upward out of the dipstick tube, oil seeping from the oil-filler cap, and poor performance. The damage typically stems from spark knock (preignition) that creates extreme cylinder pressure and cracks piston ring lands, which often occurs from the cooling system overheating.

Cylinder balance testing is often avoided in lieu of a relatively quick compression test. Cylinder balance testing effectively reveals piston, ring, and valve condition by measuring power output equality. Cylinders wear more at the top where ring pressure is highest during compression. For an accurate assessment, perform leak-down tests with the pistons at top dead center (TDC). Uneven readings (for example, 5-percent versus 20-percent leakage) cause rough running, while measurements exceeding 30 percent indicate need for engine replacement or a major overhaul.

The procedure requires a shop air supply with an air compressor that has at least a 20-gallon tank. You must securely prevent the crankshaft from rotating off TDC after the compression stroke. Three methods can be utilized:

1) Leave all but one spark plug in. It takes less effort to hold the crankshaft, but the downside is that it takes a lot of effort to rotate the engine as you test each cylinder.
2) Remove all the spark plugs. The engine rotates much easier, but more effort is required to secure crankshaft rotation.
3) My favorite method is to remove both valve covers, all of the rocker arms, and all of the spark plugs. When pressure is applied, the crankshaft will move the piston to bottom dead center (BDC) without concern of any valve being open. Check for leaks at the intake and exhaust if the leakage is greater than 20 percent. If not, disconnect your air-pressure coupling and move the piston to TDC and check it again. You may be surprised by the cylinder leakage percent at TDC. More effort is required for total engine health evaluation.

After the rocker arms and spark plugs are removed, rotate the crankshaft until number-1 piston is at TDC. Rotate it by using a long breaker bar or ratchet with 5/8-inch medium-length socket to access the crankshaft-balancer bolt. As the number-1 cylinder approaches TDC, use a short pick to feel the piston approaching TDC. Record each cylinder's pressure differential. We're looking for balance.

With the L83/L98 timing marks aligned on the number-1 cylinder at TDC, connect your air supply. Each cylinder can be tested after rotating the engine 90 degrees in the 1-8-4-3-6-5-7-2 firing order. You must strictly adhere to the 90-degree rotation sequence. A shorter or longer rotation will alter every cylinder's TDC position. Rotate the LT engine similarly. The crankshaft must be held during testing, so an assistant is valuable. When air pressure is applied, your assistant must be prepared for possible crankshaft movement.

By now, you should have a clear engine health assessment. If leakdown tests show under 20 percent, start with a basic tune-up. For engines with fewer than 80,000 miles, replace the spark plugs, distributor components, and fuel filter. For engines with more than 80,000 miles, add oxygen sensors to the list, as they become difficult to remove with age and compromise fuel control as mileage approaches 100,000.

If your leakdown test showed bubbles in the radiator or surge tank and your engine is approaching 100,000 miles, it has detected a head-gasket combustion leak reverse pressurizing the cooling system. Further testing requires running the engine to operating temperature, letting it cool, and pulling the spark plugs. The following morning, spin the engine over and watching for coolant coming out of the spark-plug holes. If coolant sprays out, a head-gasket replacement is required.

Commonly with L98 LT1 and LT4 aluminum heads, the rubberized coating around the coolant ports gradually deteriorates due to different thermal expansion rates between materials. This subtle coolant seepage typically begins around 85,000 to 100,000 miles and worsens over time. Early symptoms are difficult to detect but eventually trigger oxygen-sensor codes. In severe cases, the cylinders fill with coolant, causing catastrophic engine failure (bent connecting rods).

This intake gasket has oil and coolant leaks. An obvious leak is usually neglected until coolant or oil has dripped on the ground. At that point, the whole engine is likely coated with it.

Some 1987–1991 engine blocks are prone to cracking above the lifter bores. However, it is a somewhat rare issue. If you remove the intake and find blobs of apparent carbon buildup, the case is likely cracked. I've seen blocks with cracks running across hydraulic valve lifters from front to back on both engine banks.

Head-gasket sealing ring damage is shown. Loose carbon is a telltale sign on the piston top at the cylinder bottom. This engine requires a complete teardown and overhaul. Only replacing the head gaskets will result in disappointment within a few miles if the engine is not overhauled.

Combustion leakage can be verified with a combustion leak solution. The solution is placed in a specific clear cylinder that allows any combustion gases to pass through the solution. While testing, no liquid coolant can contact the testing solution. If the solution turns yellow,

Intake Manifold Leaks

All C4 (1984–1996) small-block Chevrolet (SBC) intake manifolds will leak oil.

The 1984–1991 intake manifolds will eventually leak coolant internally and externally. The 1992–1996 intake manifolds have no coolant coursing through them, and the cylinder heads do not have ports for coolant flow.

The intake manifold is wedged on top of the cylinder heads with gaskets separating them. Thermal expansion works slowly at the gaskets, tearing away at them. Often, at the front and rear rail (often called the China wall), the silicone sealer is not applied correctly, resulting in an oil leak. Coolant leaks cause cooling-system corrosion from constant air intrusion as the engine cools down. ■

Vacuum Gauge Testing

Vacuum gauges are capable of checking vacuum and mechanical fuel-pump fuel-pressure output. The output side of the vacuum gauge will be in the exhaust section, checking for clogged exhaust systems, primarily catalytic converters. Bumping or dropping a vacuum gauge can knock off its calibration quite easily. Take care to avoid major shock to the gauge and always make sure that the pointer needle is at zero. ■

My main concern when performing a vacuum-gauge test is a wildly fluttering gauge needle, which indicates a sticking intake or exhaust valve or a broken valve spring. Low vacuum indicates late or retarded ignition timing.

combustion gases are present. There's no turning back when the solution changes to yellow, as extensive repairs are required. Combustion leak testers are available at a moderate cost from major automotive parts suppliers.

When mentioning an intake-manifold oil leak to the seller of a C4, a common reaction is for the seller to say, "There is little to no oil on my driveway." However, the leaked oil blows back to the rear of the car, behind the transmission and torque tube, coating the differential.

A seller also might say, "The engine oil level is never *that* low between changes." Well, how many of us check our engine oil frequently today? If the low oil level light doesn't come on or oil pressure falls, we change the oil and go on.

A thick coating of oil and grease attracts dust and dirt. The coating keeps the engine hotter, and in the case of 1992–1996 C4s, the Optispark gets coated. You can either continually wash the engine and add oil or seal it correctly. I do not recommend constant engine cleaning with an Optispark-equipped engine.

The exhaust manifold has been removed for clarity. This multiple ground wire and cable connection can become loose and cause poor engine performance and random service engine soon (SES) codes. Follow the flat braided cable to the frame and check for cleanliness and proper retention.

The alternator output cable shows prolonged overheating. The cable's insulation has retreated from the terminal's strain relief. It is likely that the alternator's output terminal stud is loose internally, which causes more heat and resistance.

The 1986–1992 C4s use this battery junction block for the alternator's output lead wire battery connection. The 1984–1985 C4s have a dedicated wire lead from the alternator to the starter. The 1993–1996 models connect the alternator to underhood fuse panels near the battery. This junction block behind the battery feeds the entire 1984–1993 C4, which is important.

The most common high-energy ignition (HEI) distributor problem is a worn upper bushing. If you plan to rebuild your unit, be aware that HEI ignition coils and pickup coils require polarity synchronization. There are two pickup coils: one with a clear or black connector and another with a yellow connector. The red and yellow wires and corresponding pickup coil connectors connect as shown.

The red and white ignition-coil wires pair with the clear or black pickup coil. The ignition coil and pickup coil connectors are rotated 180 degrees, criss-crossing the wire when installing. A mismatch will result in poor low-RPM performance and high-RPM misfire. ACDelco part number 19207437 replaces the often-cooked 1985–1991 internal wiring harness.

The 1992–1994 spline-drive unventilated Optispark distributors were prone to moisture and condensation degradation. No matter how carefully you avoid water splashing on the exterior, rust forms on all of the shielding and internal components. Expect an erratic ignition system operation followed by no spark or fuel-injector pulse. It is more pronounced when the unit reaches operating temperature. Replacement is the best solution because the shaft support bearing has typically failed or is failing.

The 1992–1996 Optispark systems demand maintenance with coolant temperatures below 225°F. Front intake manifold oil leaks are particularly destructive, contaminating the distributor externally before penetrating internally. The 1992–1994 distributors lacked vacuum venting, making them prone to internal corrosion. However, with proper care, Optispark distributors can last 200,000 miles in daily-driven Corvettes.

The 1992–1996 Optispark distributors also depend on proper voltage and tight, clean engine grounds. If Optispark supply voltage drops below 10.6 volts while cranking, many LT engine ECMs/PCMs will trigger "code 16." Disconnecting the battery and thoroughly cleaning the terminals with a wire brush will improve the electrical system performance. Corroded or loose ground wires, cables, and ground straps are common maladies for Corvettes. Multiple grounds are located on the engine block (above the oil filter and at the transmission bellhousing directly behind the oil filter). These ground wires should receive regular maintenance—at least a glance to check for corrosion.

This engine was disassembled for cylinder-head work. The spark-plug wire supports were removed and probably discarded. Locating the spark-plug wire retainers and supports is difficult due to limited availability. Spark-plug wires will be susceptible to damage if left off, so suitable replacements should be used. Expect misfiring from this spark-plug wiring mess.

Owners could spend hundreds (if not thousands) of dollars on diagnosis and repairs. The alternator is often upgraded with one that has a higher-amperage output, but the original output wire lead is often left to handle the already-overloaded system wiring. It's highly recommended to increase the gauge of the wire going from the alternator to the junction block, starter positive cable stud, and fuse panel. The alternator cable gauge requirement is commensurate with amperage output: a 140-amp alternator requires a 6-gauge cable, whereas a 200-amp

This original C4 L98 spark-plug wire and factory wire retainer assembly (pulled up for a photo with all of the supports intact) shows the correct number-5 and number-7 spark-plug wire routing. General Motors crossed the number-5 and number-7 spark-plug wires instead of running parallel. The number-1 and number-3 spark-plug wires should always separate the number-5 and number-7 spark-plug wires. After ignition service, I often discover that the number-5 and number-7 spark-plug wires are routed parallel to each other, which causes a misfire.

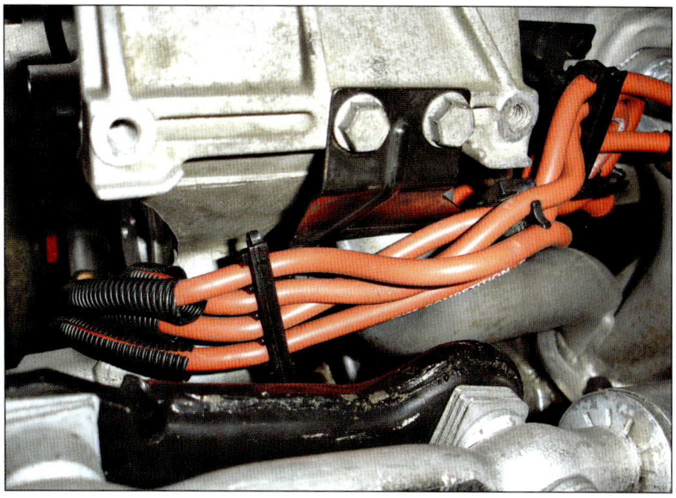

The A/C compressor, belt tensioner, and idler pulley have been removed for clarity. The LT1 driver-side spark-plug wire routing is a challenge. The plug wires are routed between the belt tensioner and above the spindle for the belt idler. The number-5 spark-plug wire is on the top outside, and the number-7 spark-plug wire is on the bottom inside to prevent cross-firing. The 3/8-inch convoluted tubing prevents plug-wire chafing. Retainers keep the plug wires off the A/C compressor and crossmember's upper control-arm-mount area.

alternator requires a 4-gauge cable. Distance also matter, and always increase the cable gauge size when lengthening cables.

Check the spark-plug wires for thermal damage. Plug wires that lie on hot exhaust manifolds and hot air injection reaction (AIR) tubes crack and burn. Engine misfire complaints are commonly caused by unsupported, improperly routed plug wires. Poor performance complaints occur after a so-called tune-up if the spark plugs are not gapped correctly or if a platinum chip breaks off when attempting to gap a non-gappable plug, new spark-plug wires are burned through from poor routing or support, or the spark-plug wires are zip-tied into a clump, causing crossfire as the high-current spark voltage courses through the adjacent wires. C4 spark-plug-wire retainers are available, but you may have to be resourceful, ensuring correct routing and retention.

Performance spark plugs, ignition coils, and fuel-filter choices will be covered in the following chapters.

Tuning

The L83 and L98 ignition timing is adjustable and should be checked for top performance. A handy distributor wrench with a 9/16-inch, 12-point box end and a 90-degree handle is available from auto parts stores. To set base timing, the engine should be at operating temperature with the thermostat open. General Motors set the base engine timing at 6 degrees before top dead center (BTDC).

You can advance the timing up to 12 degrees when using 92- or 93-octane fuel, depending on your terrain. If you hear spark knock (also known as "ping"), back off the timing 2 degrees (8 degrees BTDC) incrementally until it is not audible. The timing set bypass must be enabled, and the check-engine light will illuminate and trigger "code 42." After the timing procedure is completed, use a scanner to clear the code or disconnect the battery for 10 seconds.

After setting the base timing, the throttle-position sensor (TPS) voltage can be set. The throttle-body blades and bores must be clean before setting minimum idle air. Minimum idle air can be set at operating temperature. Balancing TPS settings with minimum idle air requires patience to find the optimal performance. For longer-duration camshafts needing additional fuel, increasing the idle TPS voltage can improve idle quality.

Locate the single wire connector with a tan/black stripe near the driver-side valve cover (as shown). Setting the base timing to 10 degrees before top dead center (BTDC) is a good starting point. It's a balance that you can work with for best power outcome. Reduced spark timing at wide-open throttle (WOT) sometimes increases horsepower. A trip to the drag strip or dynamometer will prove what strategy works best. Once the base timing has been set, reconnect the connector and restart the engine for the computed ignition timing to take over.

After setting ignition timing, connect the ignition-timing disconnect. Insert two pins alongside the throttle-position sensor (TPS) connectors (the black and dark blue wires) until they touch the inner terminals (as shown). Set the multimeter on "DC volts" and start the engine. Adjust the idle air blade stop screw until a 450- to 500-rpm idle speed is achieved. Factory idle TPS voltage is then set at 0.54 volts. Balance now comes into play. Increased-duration camshafts require a higher minimum idle air to raise the TPS voltage and increase fuel flow. The TPS can be raised to 0.70 volts and still be considered in "idle" position. You may need to raise or lower TPS voltage and/or minimum idle air to obtain best idle.

Minimum idle air is also a factor to prevent stalling. Try raising the minimum idle air speed to 550 to 700 rpm. The actual idle speed is controlled by the ECM and requires programmable read-only memory (PROM) chip programming to raise idle speeds.

If you raise the TPS voltage too high, it will not be in idle mode. This will be recognized by a delayed return to idle after holding the throttle above 1,500 rpm for a minute or longer. The 1984–1989 C4 used adjustable TPSs with consistent connectors and wiring. For 1990–1991 models with a non-adjustable TPS, you can retrofit the earlier ACDelco number 213-905 sensor. Adjustable units allow positioning and rotation modifications that affect fuel control.

Counterintuitively, reducing the TPS's wide-open throttle (WOT) voltage can boost performance. Manufacturers typically enrich the fuel mixture at WOT as a protective measure. Adjusting WOT TPS to 4.20–4.60 volts may unlock power while maintaining safety margins. Never compromise with low-octane fuel. If you detect a knock or ping, increase TPS WOT voltage or reduce timing advance to 6 degrees BTDC or less.

CHAPTER 2

Bolt-on Components and Engine Modification

What's your performance goal? For autocross, gymkhana, or short road courses, horsepower isn't the primary factor. Drag racing, however, demands high torque and horsepower numbers to maximize acceleration. Committing to a specific racing discipline will yield the most satisfying results.

Intake/Exhaust Airflow

Performance improvements include enhancing intake and exhaust airflow, camshaft swaps, compression increases, and optimal cylinder-head selection. Exercise restraint because excessive camshaft duration requires engine fuel-control upgrades, particularly for 1985–1993 models. Note that the performance claims of aftermarket speed manufacturers typically reflect perfect conditions with ideal engines, temperatures, and premium fuels, and some claims are just not true.

Air-filter elements, assemblies, and air foils offer affordable entry-level enhancements . . . or do they? K&N oiled filters were popular early upgrades, but they require careful maintenance. The 1985–1989 and 1994–1996 C4s utilize MAF sensors for fuel metering, and excess oil during filter reconditioning can contaminate sensor elements, causing a lean running condition. While 1985–1989 Bosch MAF sensors included a burn-off cleaning cycle, the more reliable 1994–1996 sensors lack this feature and are more susceptible to oil contamination. Don't expect dramatic performance differences; these filters primarily benefit those seeking lifetime filtration.

Performance air-filter assemblies complement other engine modifications but won't deliver noticeable

After the 1985 C4 was introduced, the first order of business for buyers was to cut out the center of the air-filter cover. This practice continued until 1996. This 1990 model had the cover cut to maximum size. It's simple and easy to do, but does it make a difference? It makes the front lighter. Cold air is the most important factor.

The Vortex air filter is available for 1990–1996 C4s. The concept is sound. Incoming air is forced into the air-filter box that is mounted on top of the radiator housing. Since air flows through the path of least resistance, is there less resistance through the air cleaner or radiator? What I don't like is that the radiator housing and air-filter box material is thin, which makes complete sealing to each other difficult.

The Vortex Rammer cold-air filter assembly is ready for action. The exposed hose clamp retains the filter to the ductwork. This means that to service the oil-gauze filter element, you need a helper to remove the cover to reach the filter. The cover isn't too difficult to remove, and you can clean the A/C condenser while you're at it.

standalone gains. The 1985–1989 C4s have limited options—only the Vortex Rammer cold-air system is currently available. Despite advertised gains of 15 to 22 hp (claims that appear to be overstated), note that it lacks California Air Resources Board (CARB) certification, potentially limiting its legality to off-road use in some states. The 1990–1996 C4s fare better with two options: the Street Legal Performance (SLP) cold-air induction package (using triple cone filters) and the Vortex Rammer.

Power coupler air-cleaner intake ducts are available for 1985–1989 and 1994–1996 C4s. Smooth air ducts and couplers will have minimal effects or horsepower gain. The idea is that the convoluted (ribbed) pieces interfere with airflow. To avoid tube collapse, General Motors opted for ribbing. They may be the only choice as an OEM replacement, and used replacements become available. Replace any torn air intake ductwork to keep grit out of the engine.

Air foils were among the earliest C4 performance products. They were marketed to reduce intake turbulence by placing a blended aluminum filler between throttle-body bores. For L98 tuned port injection (TPI) engines that peak at 4,200 rpm, these provide a minimal benefit. Your wallet gets lighter without meaningful performance gains. If these truly offered 10 hp, General Motors would have incorporated them from the factory. Real-world gains are negligible. Meaningful improvements require larger throttle bodies that incorporate blended air entry.

Intake air-temperature sensor relocation kits were popular for 1985–1991

A bit of alcohol wiped on the inside helps to ease the smooth tube over the flanges. The challenging part is pushing it over the throttle body, especially with a performance replacement piece.

Catch Cans

This Mishimoto oil catch can's provided bracket requires minor modifications to attach to the inner fender for a simple installation. Push-on hose fittings with the appropriate hoses were used to prevent hose collapse. Do not use a vacuum hose. It will collapse from internal engine oil exposure. All of the connections, except push-on hose fittings, require clamping.

Oil catch cans deliver actual performance benefits by reducing intake-tract oil contamination. This is especially valuable in high-performance applications, such as the 383-ci, 500-hp small-block Chevy (SBC).

Modern thinner piston rings reduce friction, but compression gases can be greater, increasing blowby. Products such as the Mishimoto catch can be installed inline with the positive crankcase ventilation (PCV) valve, and the included sight tube allows oil-level monitoring. Even General Motors has incorporated this technology in its Gen V LT engines. Ensure that the PCV system's vent side remains open to atmosphere and filtered (ideally positioned across from the PCV valve side). ■

C4s. Since this sensor significantly influences air-fuel ratios (cooler air demands more fuel), relocating it from the underside of the intake plenum to the incoming airstream initially registers cooler temperatures. However, once airflow stabilizes during operation, this advantage diminishes. The drawback is that after heat-soak conditions, the relocated sensor misleads the ECM about actual temperatures, causing excessive fuel enrichment during hot starts.

Gaining 25 to 30-Plus Horsepower

Cast-iron cylinder-head intake manifolds used six inline bolts per side, while aluminum cylinder-head intake manifolds positioned the four center bolts at different angles. Most aftermarket manifolds accommodate this variation. The specific 1992–1996 LT1/LT4 manifolds eliminated coolant crossflow passages.

The later Fast Burn heads (never offered on C4 Corvettes) used vertical bolts with the omission of center bolts, allowing a raised intake tract that increased power. However, this design's fewer, smaller bolts (downsized from 3/8-16 to 5/16-18) led to sealing problems. Even with the thicker, rubber-core gaskets that these heads required, they were prone to leaking compared to traditional fiber gaskets.

The Fast Burn (Vortec) TPI intake manifold has higher airflow numbers than any other aftermarket TPI intake manifold. Fast Burn cylinder heads must be used in conjunction with the intake manifold. The Fast

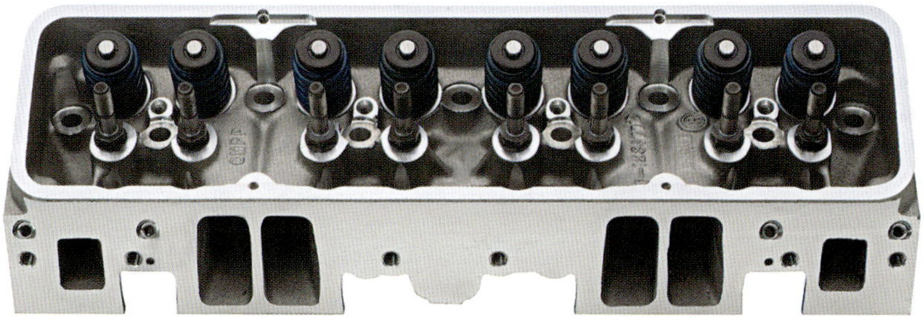

Make sure that your intake manifold has provisions for the Vortec eight-bolt retention pattern. Fast Burn cylinder heads offer 12- and 8-bolt retention patterns. The Vortec intake-manifold bolts are installed vertically, and the center four bolts were omitted. The intake-air tract and reduced combustion volume make them a proven power adder. However, cost may be a factor when all the required ancillary items are added up. (Photo Courtesy Fast Burn)

Burn cylinder-head combustion chamber and intake-runner design is the best out-of-the-box General Motors cylinder head. The initial cost of the intake manifold is reasonable, but adding the cylinder heads makes a noticeable dent in the budget. The cost of the conversion is justified for someone who wants a somewhat-OEM look with a significant airflow gain.

During my latest search, there are no new high-flow aftermarket TPI intake manifold bases available. Edelbrock and Accel discontinued the intake-manifold bases due to low sales volume. A 2025 eBay search shows multiple options that are available for used aftermarket intake-manifold bases and runners. They're pricey for a used manifold, but high demand and limited availability may explain the price surge.

Two designs of intake runners were used: the 1985–1988 design with a cold-start injector port and the 1989–1991 design with no cold-start injector port. Always check the runner tube to the plenum and runner to make sure they match the intake base ports. Arizona Speed and Marine is currently the only supplier of 1985–1991 C4 large-tube intake runners. Edelbrock, SLP, and TPIS runners are no longer available unless they have been stored away in someone's parts stash.

SLP offered siamese blended intake runners on sequentially firing engine cylinders to avoid choking opposing cylinders. TPIS went the other route and applied the siamese blending to all intake runners for more airflow volume.

Siamese hands-on porting requires significant dedication, and it often costs as much as an LS swap when considering labor. While I question the cost-effectiveness, that determination ultimately remains yours. There are also a few TPI pioneers that made their own siamese intake runners with welded aluminum sheet-metal panels for maximum airflow. My search found some siamese runners available at an astonishingly high cost (an average of $850 on eBay).

When tuned port injection (TPI) was popular, many attempts were made to increase high-RPM airflow, including using siamese intake runners. Street Legal Performance (SLP) offered siamese intake runners for TPI owners.

This is as good as it gets for a stealth look while increasing intake airflow to the new Golen crate engine. These Arizona Speed and Marine large-diameter intake runners are bolted to an Edelbrock-base intake manifold for maximum flow.

Budget-conscious C4 owners can open up the intake manifold, which is not an easy task. The aluminum runners require grinding from one side of the intake to the other. Be cautious because using a high-speed die grinder with extended bits can be dangerous. At high speeds, the cutters bend from centrifugal force.

If you have the time, a follow-up siamese porting of the dividers on the runner side of the intake manifold allows maximum airflow. The ultimate TPI consists of the Fast Burn Vortec intake that has the center port dividers removed and matches a pair of siamese runners.

Once a high-flow intake base and runners are utilized, a die grinder can open the plenum and port match all of the connecting pieces. The plenum throttle body opening also requires port matching. Until then,

Port matching the large runner tubes or siamese intake runners is necessary for maximum flow. The throttle-body plenum requires machining to fit your increased-diameter throttle-body blades. Place your gaskets of choice on the plenum, mark the plenum, and begin grinding.

This Accel Lingenfelter Super Ram intake manifold assembly looks impressive. The controversial design aids airflow and horsepower numbers. Some say that it's better than a mini ram intake style with minimal runners. The extra effort that is required to install and maintain it makes it a dinosaur. The wiper motor removal and installation is difficult but possible.

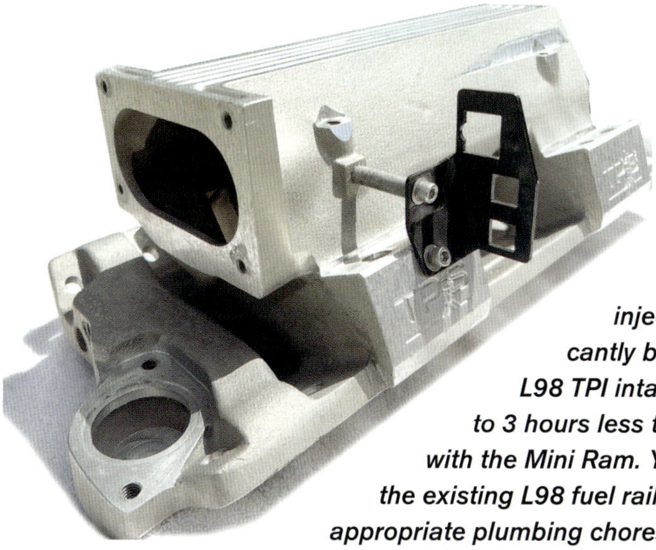

The TPIS Mini Ram intake manifold allows easy access to the fuel injectors and distributor. Fuel injector access is significantly better than it is for the L98 TPI intake manifold. It takes 2 to 3 hours less to replace fuel injectors with the Mini Ram. You will need to replace the existing L98 fuel rail and perform the appropriate plumbing chores for the connection.

don't waste your time port matching the intake pieces.

The Accel-Lingenfelter Super Ram intake manifold provides better low and midrange torque than a stock TPI. The use of abbreviated intake runners boosts high-RPM horsepower output. Factory TPI fuel rails work and are as difficult to access as the original TPI intake-manifold system. They are the top dog for the C4 Corvette TPI application when using stock differential gearing. The large plenum makes a statement, overwhelming the top of the engine. They are available used, but the cost will be in the thousands. Your exhaust system should be upgraded along with a set of $1^{7}/_{8}$-inch primary tube headers.

The 1985–1991 TPIS Mini Ram intake manifold is an excellent choice to upgrade the airflow. The short-runner, large-plenum manifold checks all of the boxes: high airflow for a major horsepower increase and a large plenum that maintains low-end torque numbers. Low-RPM torque versus the TPI intake will be reduced, requiring a differential gear change to utilize the higher-RPM horsepower. The cost is noticeable ($2,000 or more) for the required intake manifold, fuel rails, and fuel injectors. Plumbing skills are also required to connect to the existing fuel supply and return lines. This upgrade allows a wide selection of camshaft choices. Exhaust headers are also recommended to achieve the engine's potential.

The LT1 intake-manifold design, which is similar to the TPIS intake, promoted additional airflow, while the large plenum enhanced low-engine-RPM torque. The LT4's unique intake manifold matches the LT4's higher intake runners, which

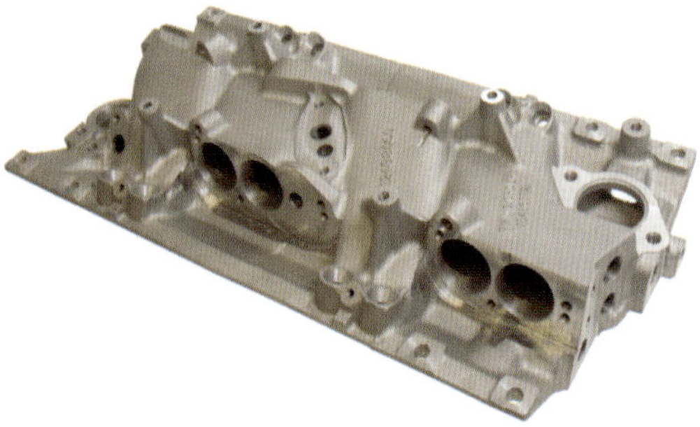

Another option is this Scoggin Dickey TPI high-flow intake manifold base. Later Vortec cylinder heads are required to match the intake ports to the cylinder heads. (Photo Courtesy Chevrolet Performance)

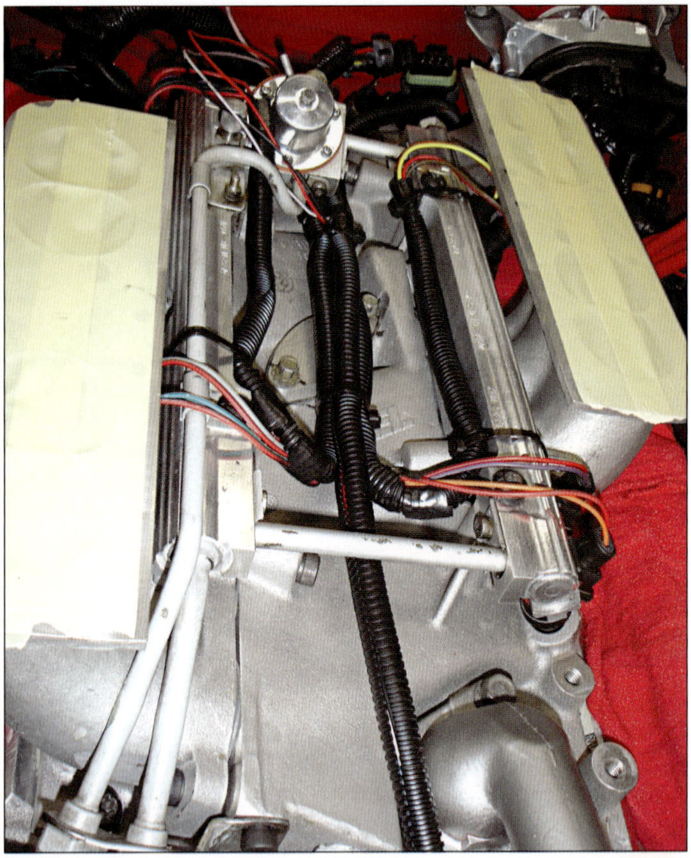

The in-depth assembly requires even more patience than the original TPI intake manifold installation. The intake plenum top is the only easy-to-remove part, which requires the removal of 17 screws. The intake runner-to-plenum screw installation is challenging to install and tighten. One design has all of the inner screws installed from the bottom. Another design has the same screws installed from inside the plenum with a safety wire to avoid ingestion.

A variety of throttle cable versions are available for early and late C4s. There are provisions for the automatic-transmission throttle valve (TV) and cruise-control cables. Tighten the throttle-body bolts incrementally in a crisscross pattern and then torque them to 120 in-lbs. Overtightening can distort the throttle shaft and cause binding.

were painted red to stand out. The LT4 cylinder heads' higher intake-port floor enhanced the cylinder-head airflow numbers. Ironically, the LT4 intake manifold requires extra machine work to achieve the same airflow numbers that the LT1 flows. Port match the intake runners and throttle body, bolt it on, and it's ready to run.

Installing 1,000-cfm throttle bodies on stock L98, LT1, or LT4 engines won't add power without port matching and additional modifications. The plenum inlet requires enlargement to match the bigger throttle blades. On L98s, even with this modification, the restricted intake runners prevent power increases due to airflow restrictions. LT1/LT4 manifolds do flow better with larger throttle bodies, but they require port matching and intake porting to utilize the additional air capacity. Simply dumping more air into a flow-restricted engine yields no power gains.

BBK has the most comprehensive coverage of all 1985–1996 C4 throttle bodies, including reconditioned units that will help you save some money. The original 48-mm throttle body flows 650 to 675 cfm. That's plenty of air for 350-ci TPI large-tube runners, aftermarket intake manifolds, and camshaft durations under 230 to 240 at 0.050-inch lift. If you decide on the TPIS Mini Ram, Accel Super Ram, or a major ported siamese treated intake manifold, a 52-mm (750-cfm) throttle body is recommended up to 383 ci. The next step up for a boosted 383-ci (and above) engine is 58 mm (1,000 cfm), which is more than adequate for the majority of 383-ci L98 and LT1 C4 highly modified engines.

Intake Manifold Preparation and Installation

When replacing the intake-manifold gasket, cleanliness is important. Clean all of the silicone sealer and gasket material off the engine case, cylinder heads, and front and rear of the intake manifold. Place a few shop towels in the valley as close to the cylinder heads as possible, covering the entire area. Tightly stuff paper towels into the intake ports before using a sharp scraper to remove the material.

Installing the Intake Manifold

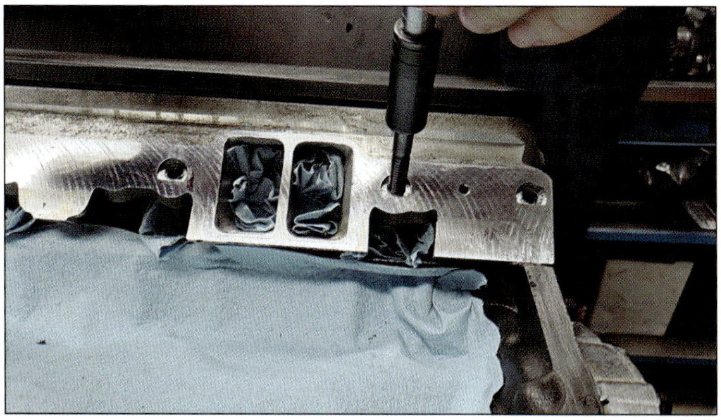

1 *The LT1 intake manifold has been removed, and protective shop towels are in place to avoid debris from getting into the oil-pump pickup tube assembly. A 3/8-16 tap is used to chase the intake-manifold bolt-hole threads. The four outer intake-manifold bolts are blind-threaded holes that do not require oil sealing.*

2 *This Matco blunt-blade scraper works well to remove the gasket without gouging the soft aluminum surfaces. Many opt for high-speed Scotch-Brite discs for gasket removal, but in many instances, catastrophic engine failure follows. The particles from the abrasive pad can get into the oil-pump pickup, and some of the grit passes through the oil filter to the crankshaft bearings.*

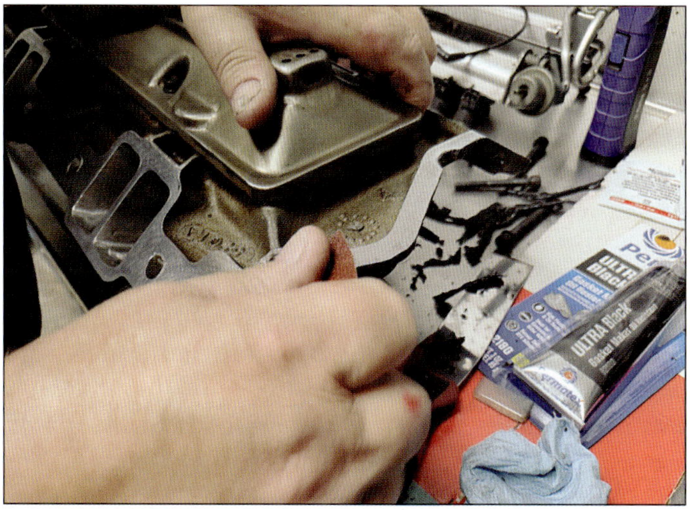

3 *The 80-grit paper is used to carefully roughen up the end-seal surfaces on the cylinder block and heads. As noted, care must be taken to prevent grit from entering the engine as the surfaces are roughed up.*

4 *The intake manifold bolts receive the same treatment, running them through a 3/8-16 die to clean the threads. Once the threads are cleaned, spray them off with brake cleaner before coating the first three threads with Teflon sealer. Coat the bolts with sealer and set them aside for installation.*

Installing the Intake Manifold *continued*

5 *Wipe down all surfaces of the intake manifold and engine block with alcohol, especially at the end rails. Do not touch these surfaces once they have been wiped down. The idea is to avoid getting any oils, even those from your fingers, on the engine, preventing silicone sealer adhesion.*

6 *When it's 65°F, you have 15 to 20 minutes before the silicone sealer skins over. If the silicone sealer skins over, start again. Notice that the silicone sealer is applied up the sides to seal the gaskets to the rails.*

7 *The intake manifold is installed straight down to avoid moving it back and forth as the bolts are started. Always start at the center of the intake manifold when tightening and torquing the bolts. Tighten the bolts to 71 in-lbs, let it sit for 1 hour, and perform the final torque at 35 ft-lbs.*

Once the major pieces of gasket and silicone are removed, use a Scotch-Brite pad to remove the residue from the silicone sealer. Roughen up the cylinder block and intake-manifold sealing rail surfaces with 180-grit sandpaper. Primarily, naphtha, brake cleaner, or alcohol should be used to remove any oil from the surfaces.

Clean the bolt threads with a 3/8-16 die (a wire wheel also works) and the intake-manifold cylinder-head bolt holes with a 3/8-16 tap or thread chaser. Apply brake cleaner or alcohol to the thread surfaces and then dry them.

Vacuum the intake-manifold ports as the paper towels are removed and remove the intake valley protective sheets. Check for debris in the intake valley and remove it as necessary. Wipe down all sealing surfaces with alcohol until the cloth that is used does not discolor after the rub down. Do not touch any sealing surfaces after the cleaner is applied.

Be prepared. Apply high-temperature Teflon pipe-thread sealer to the bolt threads, covering two to three threads completely. Have the manifold and coated bolts nearby.

Apply a 3/8-inch bead of hot-oil-resistant silicone sealer to the front and rear of the engine case, run the bead 0.500 inch up the cylinder head where the intake manifold gasket will sit, and install the gaskets. Then, apply a 1/8-inch bead to the top side of the intake-manifold gasket down to the engine case.

Set the intake in place as soon as possible, install the bolts, and hand-tighten the center bolts. Working outward, torque the bolts to 35 ft-lbs, starting at the center. The best policy is to let the sealer have at least 5 to 6 hours of cure time before starting the engine. If the silicone sealer sets up (skins over), it must be removed and the process must be started over. On a warm day (85°F plus), silicone skins over in a few minutes.

Camshaft Performance Gains

Too often, camshafts are selected solely for their idle sound, which is a characteristic that you could replicate by simply richening the idle mixture. Engine compression should dictate the camshaft selection. Low-compression engines with aggressive camshafts (230 degrees of duration at 0.050-inch lift or more) suffer further effective compression loss at low speeds.

Conversely, high-compression engines with mild camshafts (210 degrees of duration at 0.050-inch lift) provide smooth idle but sacrifice high-RPM performance and risk detonation. For example, pairing a 230-degree camshaft with stock 1985–1991 L98 intake components yields disappointing results (compromised low-end torque without high-RPM gains due to restrictive runners). Save yourself frustration by avoiding standalone camshaft swaps on L98 engines without airflow and engine control upgrades. The 1992–1993 LT1s can handle the 230-degree camshaft but not as well as the 1994–1996 LT1 engines. They respond best to camshaft upgrades. The GM LT4 hot camshaft provides excellent results with a stock rotating assembly and intake manifold.

The camshaft lobe centerline or lobe separation angle (LSA) significantly affects valve overlap and idle characteristics. A 108-degree centerline produces aggressive idle with noticeable "chop," while a 112-degree centerline provides more manageable behavior. The 1985–1993 batch-fired electronic fuel injection (EFI) systems struggle with centerlines below 112 degrees, resulting in sluggish throttle response. The 1994–1996 LT1/LT4 engines better accommodate 108- to 112-degree centerlines. Centerlines below 108 degrees create pronounced idle characteristics. Caution: Verify valve-spring coil bind clearance when valve lift exceeds 0.500 inch, particularly with increased rocker-arm ratios. Always check for binding after any camshaft change.

The 1984–1986 C4 Corvette coupes (cast-iron cylinder heads) will absolutely gain power from a roller-lifter camshaft swap. Roller lifters reduce friction while allowing steeper cam lobes. Valves open quicker, remaining at higher lift for an extended period of time. This increases airflow, so we're back to the L83 L98 intake manifold airflow restriction being the number-one obstacle. Reduced camshaft wear is another benefit. It's not common to hear technicians saying that they've replaced many roller camshafts or roller lifters.

Today's engine oils have minimal zinc due to the United States Environmental Protection Agency (EPA) regulations and catalytic converter premature failure. Flat-tappet hydraulic-lifter cam lobes require zinc to prevent premature lobe wear. Zinc additives must be used at every oil change for an engine with flat-tappet lifters. Engine oils with zinc additives (that are considered for off-road use) are available. OEM 1984–1986 cast-iron cylinder-head engines must have the zinc oil additives.

For camshaft upgrades, it is suggested to thoroughly complete the camshaft supplier's profile worksheets and provide accurate engine specifications. These detailed forms ensure appropriate recommendations. Supplying incorrect data inevitably leads to disappointing results.

Use PennGrade oil or oils that are rich in zinc dialkyldithiophosphate (ZDDP) and phosphorus. The 1984–1986 engines have a flat-tappet, hydraulic-lifter camshaft. Fresh engines that use oil with inadequate zinc content have accelerated camshaft lobe wear. Sometimes, they don't survive the break-in process. In some cases, Mobil 1 15W-50 oil isn't the best choice for roller-lifter camshafts. The higher viscosity does a poor job of cold-weather lubrication, which can damage roller lifters. Always heed your engine builder's oil recommendations.

For a bulletproof valvetrain, this 1985 C4 383-ci engine features Dart 180-cc runner, 64-cc combustion-chamber cylinder heads with Comp Cams 1.6-ratio stainless-steel rocker arms and pushrod guide plates with 3/8-inch pushrods. Flood the rocker-arm trunnions with engine assembly lube before installing the valve covers. If you decide to make a rocker-arm ratio change, check the scrub area of the rocker-arm tip on the valve stem. In most cases, longer or shorter pushrods are required to center the rocker-arm roller on the valve tip.

Does the additional cost of roller-trunnion rocker arms justify their cost over roller-tip rocker arms? Testing shows that roller-tip rockers provide minimal horsepower or durability improvements. However, roller-trunnion (pivot) rockers significantly reduce friction, making them worthwhile investments. Regarding ratio changes, increasing from 1.5 to 1.6 enhances valve lift and potential airflow. Changing the rocker-arm ratio on the L83 Crossfire and L98 TPI engines offers minimal benefits without major airflow modifications. LT1 engines show measurable improvements, although they are not necessarily perceptible improvements in driving feel. The LT4 already utilizes 1.6-ratio rockers from the factory.

Cylinder Head Replacement

The 1987–1991 L98 and 1992–1996 LT1 D-port aluminum heads are adequate but not optimal for maximum power. Porting and multi-angle valve jobs improve performance, but factory heads have inherent airflow and combustion-chamber limitations. For targets less than 400 hp, factory heads with modifications suffice and the machine work costs would exceed the benefits. Also, consider the engine's mileage. Units with less than 75,000 miles should withstand head modification or replacement, but higher-mileage engines may require additional considerations.

Cylinder-head swaps deliver maximum power gains but represent a comprehensive commitment, requiring compatible camshafts, intake manifolds, headers, and, crucially, upgraded engine management (particularly for 1984–1993 C4s). Properly selected replacement heads improve compression and optimize airflow.

Many performance cylinder heads are available online that are inexpensive and often cost less than overhauling the original L98 or LT1 cylinder heads. Watch for accessory bolt holes on the front and back of cylinder heads that are not as deep as the originals. The accessory retaining bolts can bottom out before tightening the support, the threads can strip out, or the bolts can be seized into the head. I've also had to oval the accessory-support mounting holes to fit the bolt pattern on the head.

Airflow Research, a premium manufacturer, offers numerous options: four street-series heads and five race-series heads. No intake port work is required, and all gaskets match. The cylinder heads accept center-bolt or perimeter-bolt valve covers with a tall rail at the outside, eliminating the typical SBC valve-cover gasket leaks. There are no concerns with the accessory bolt patterns or depths.

Various aftermarket suppliers provide diverse combustion chamber and intake runner designs. For more in-depth guidance, consult CarTech's *High-Performance Chevy Small-Block Cylinder Heads* book by Graham Hansen.

Air Flow Research (AFR) heads, which have proven air-flow numbers and high-quality castings, were chosen over reworking the original high-mileage LT1 cylinder heads. The 1993 C4's stroked 383-ci LT1 has a pair of 195-cc intake-runner cylinder heads that have been installed, torqued, and are ready for pushrod guide plates and new roller rocker arms.

When budgeting staged modifications, save the camshaft and cylinder-head replacements for last. Starting with radical camshaft changes leads to disappointment. Instead, accumulate all of the necessary components before beginning installation. During this planning stage, calculate total costs. You may find compelling reasons to bypass individual modifications in favor of a complete crate engine with the latest technology, proven reliability, and superior power/torque characteristics. Better yet, consider a salvage LS1, LS2, or LS3 swap.

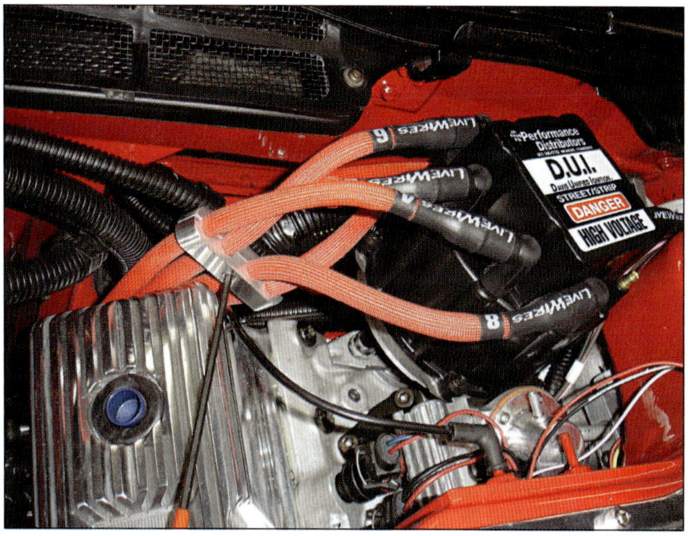

This Performance Distributor has been flawless in a 1985 L98 500-hp C4. The distributor had to be rotated out of the typical L98 position to clear the intake plenum. For these units, install them, set the base timing, and enjoy. Performance Distributor also has multiple options of spark-plug wires to complement its excellent distributors.

Ignition System

The 1984–1991 high-energy ignition (HEI) systems were exceptionally reliable, combining high-voltage in-cap coils with dependable ignition modules. For performance upgrades, Davis Unified Ignition offers its robust DUI-000333 replacement module, which delivers precise spark timing. While aftermarket distributor pickup coils and caps aren't available, performance coil options include MSD #8225 (42,000 volts) and Accel #140003 (45,000 volts). They both exceed the requirements for naturally aspirated small-blocks.

Performance Distributors's Racing or Street/Strip Mini Voltage Intensive Power (VIP) transformer will enhance any HEI distributor's spark output. The 18 volts of current to the coil's positive terminal will allow up to a 0.075-inch spark-plug gap for a massive spark flame kernel. This allows you to increase fuel pressure for more torque and high-RPM horsepower. Expect increased distributor and rotor contact wear, which is well worth the performance advantage.

The Performance Distributors Mini VIP is simple to install. It needs 12-volts in from the existing pink primary distributor connector, and it needs a ground. A wire is then inserted in the existing distributor's connector, feeding the distributor with 18 volts of energy. (Photo Courtesy Performance Distributors)

If you've surpassed 125,000 miles, chances are good that the original HEI distributor requires a full rebuild or replacement. Performance Distributors from Memphis, Tennessee, is a great choice for a new, complete, blueprinted high-performing distributor. They have multiple options and are compatible with your existing ECM. Drop it in, and you're ready to go. Each unit is hand-built to order, requiring a wait time of six to eight weeks, which is to be expected for quality custom-built products.

Throwback Automotive's Optispark replacement distributor, which is assembled in the United States, has been installed and is ready for a new water pump. The front of the engine was cleaned of all oil and grease for long-term performance and reliability. The ignition coil was replaced to obtain peak performance.

This Vortec Dyna-Module Optispark ignition control module increases dwell for better throttle response and power increases. It fits 1994–1995 LT1 C4 Corvettes. (Photo Courtesy Performance Distributors)

To get your LT1 or LT4 running like new again, these items, which are in one package, are needed. This Throwback Automotive comprehensive kit ensures long-term ignition-system reliability. Using high-mileage spark plugs and high-resistance plug wires will negate your new distributor's spark output capabilities. Servicing the cooling system is covered with the new included thermostat and water pump. (Photo Courtesy Throwback Automotive)

GM's 1992–1996 LT1/LT4 Optispark distributor represents a complete design departure that has gained a notorious reputation among Corvette owners. "Bad Optispark" becomes the default diagnosis from most technicians when confronting C4 performance issues. While legitimate concerns exist, inadequate maintenance (not inherent design flaws) typically causes failures.

Throwback Automotive Inc., formerly Petris Enterprises Inc., offers a complete Optispark replacement distributor that is assembled in the United States with the best possible pieces available. Each unit is assembled using fixtures and then tested for correct timing. Once assembled, they are real-world tested for spark, fuel-injector timing and operation, and correct low- and high-resolution pulse outputs. The 1992–1994 units are upgraded to the 1995–1996 ventilated version. All units receive a new electrical and vacuum harness for a trouble-free installation.

Optispark Replacement Options

Bailey Engineering pioneered Optispark solutions with a coil-on-plug conversion, which maintains a proven track record. Its system utilizes the Optispark's existing low- and high-resolution pulse outputs to control individual coil-on-plug ignition coils. This eliminates high-voltage routing through the distributor cap and rotor at all RPM. The conversion costs approximately $800 and requires a functional Optispark distributor.

Torqhead offers complete 1994–1996 Optispark elimination through its system, combining an external

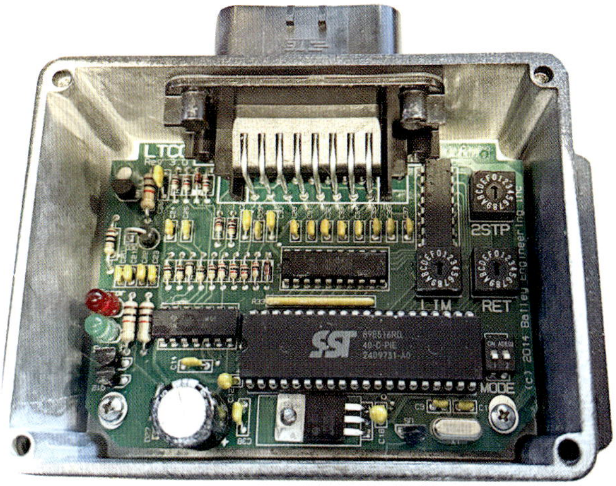

Bailey Engineering's LTCC kit includes the interface unit and harness components to connect the LTCC unit to GM's ignition-coil harnesses. The LS1, LS2, and LS7 ignition-coil assemblies are required to complete installation and can be found on eBay and at scrapyards. Custom-made spark-plug wires are also required.

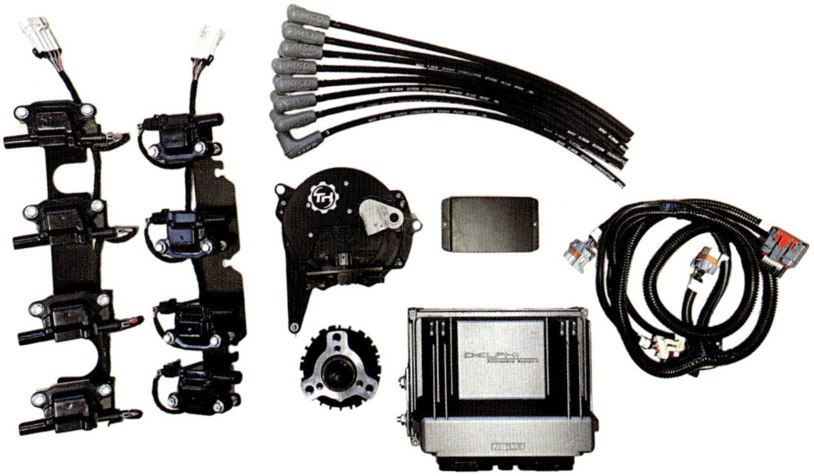

The Torqhead 24x Link the Works Kit has all of the pieces in one package to eliminate the OEM Optispark distributor. It features true crankshaft versus camshaft position sensing. The coil packs, plug wires, controller, LS Gen III PCM, and connecting harnesses for a 1994–1996 C4 are included with this package. (Photo Courtesy Paul de Boer/Torqhead)

crankshaft trigger wheel with an internal LS-based camshaft position sensor. This setup uses a 24x Gen III PCM for engine management and coil-on-plug technology. Installation requires replacing the crankshaft hub with the company's ATI unit that accommodates the 24x reluctor wheel. Package options range from a basic PCM and wiring to the comprehensive Works Package, which includes ignition coils and a preprogrammed PCM. The midrange Essentials package requires separate ignition coil and spark-plug wire purchases. A central control module (CCM) interface module maintains digital gauge functionality. The factory main engine harness remains in use.

My preferred Optispark elimination system comes from EFI Connection, which replaces both the ignition and engine management systems using the latest LS engine sensor technology and coil-on-plug ignition. Although installation requires a 1996–1997 LT1/LT4 timing cover with

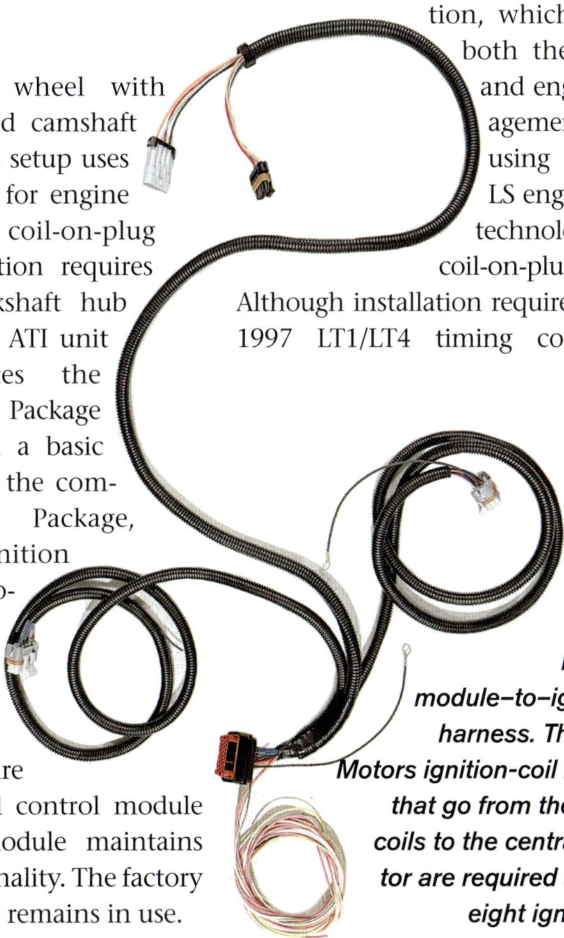

This is Bailey Engineering's LTCC module–to–ignition coil harness. The General Motors ignition-coil harnesses that go from the separate coils to the central connector are required along with eight ignition coils.

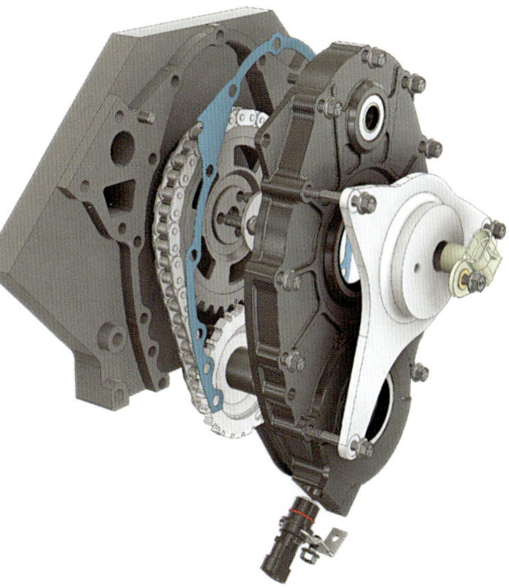

EFI Connection offers various Optispark elimination options for 1992–1996 Corvettes. Its EFI 24x and 58x conversions can be used with mechanical or electric water pumps. ATI harmonic balancers can be used with a multitude of kit options. This system can be controlled with the General Motors PCM (part number 12200411) or those from Holley, FAST, or FiTech. (Photo Courtesy EFI Connection)

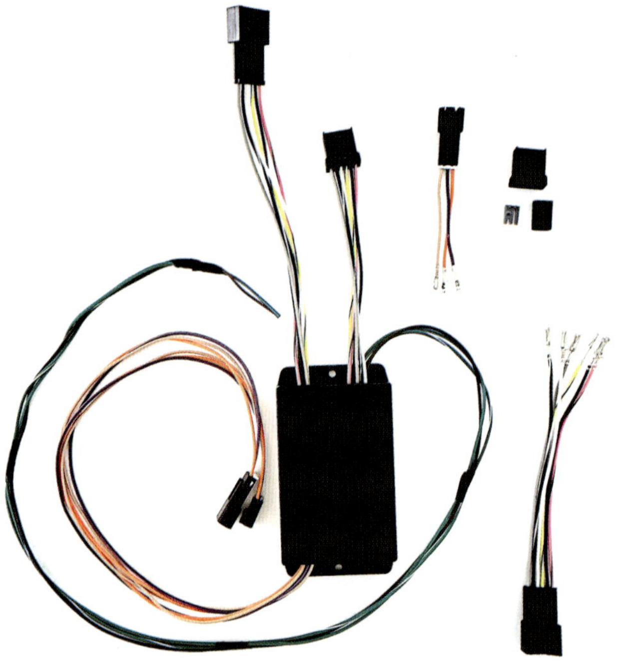

This fabulous little black box from Torqhead converts the later PCM (part number 12200411) engine data stream to the LT1 data stream. A later PCM can control an LT1 or LT4 engine, and dash functions (and more) will be available. (Photo Courtesy Paul de Boer/Torqhead)

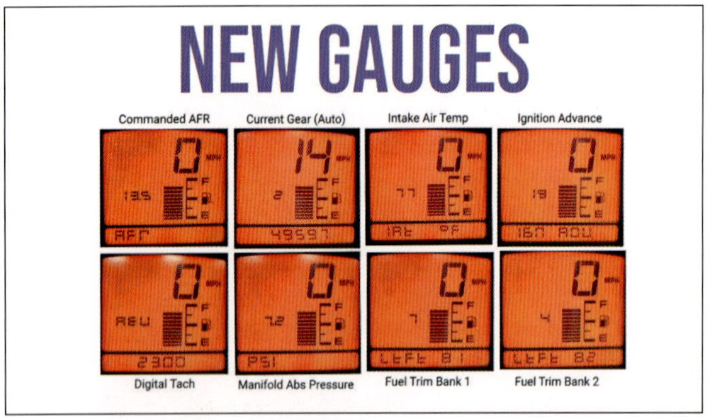

The 1995–1996 C4 gauge's function button will have more information than ever with the Torqhead black box. Readings are included for the air-fuel ratio, current gear (automatic), intake air temperature, ignition advance, the tachometer, manifold absolute pressure, and fuel trims (bank one and bank two). In addition, there's a mini scanner for those who are tweaking their LT1's performance. (Photo Courtesy Paul de Boer/Torqhead)

> **TECH TIP**
>
> **Double-Check Your Work**
>
> Be fair to your suppliers. When product failures occur, it's often due to improper installation, poor wiring, or loose ground wires.
>
> When you replace an electronic component multiple times for the same failure, there is likely an underlying cause. Pay careful attention to wire connector terminals. They may have been distorted from frequent removal and installation. In addition, vermin wreak havoc on wiring insulation. The soy content in the wire insulation is delicious to them. We all eventually pay more for the improper installation of every item that we purchase. ■

crankshaft sensor provisions (rare components), EFI Connection now offers its own new timing cover, eliminating the hunt for scarce factory parts. This system requires either a later-model ECM or aftermarket ECU, pushing total conversion costs above $2,000, depending on controller selection.

An additional EFI Connection conversion consideration is that the 1996 LT1/LT4 engines use internal crankshaft reluctor wheels, positioning their crankshaft hubs farther outward than 1992–1995 engines, which potentially causes accessory-belt alignment issues. The project also demands substantial wiring modifications when using LS-style computers or complete harness replacement with aftermarket ECUs.

Ignition Coils/Modules

The LT1/LT4 ignition coils are industry-standard pieces. They deliver 45,000 volts and are available in two versions. The 1992–1995 and 1996 had an Optispark distributor cap/plug/wire–style connection and weatherproof primary ignition coil power connector. The early ignition coils' primary connectors were internal electrical bus connector circuits. Moroso, MSD, and Accel (in this order) get the nod for aftermarket performance replacement coils.

Higher-output ignition coils allow spark-plug gaps to be opened up to 0.060 inch or more. This promotes low-speed operation more than high-RPM performance. Expect advanced distributor cap and rotor erosion. A significant part of replacement is removing the existing coil and ignition control module (ICM) for cleaning.

Leaking intake manifolds coat the ignition coil with oil, which attracts dirt and debris. The gooey oil coating acts as an insulator, trapping more heat, on the already-hot-running ICM. The ICM uses a thermal heat-sink paste, which

LT Crank Trigger Option

Some ingenuity is required to make the MSD Flying Magnet Crank Trigger Wheel Kit (part number 8610) work. The ATI Super Damper (part number 917274) replaces the LT1 engine's asymmetrical balancer and hub so that it can be used with the MSD crank trigger wheel. The Optispark low-resolution circuits are not required, while the original high-voltage distributor cap and rotor are still in use.

The crank trigger wheel required the in-house modified spacers to space the crank trigger wheel away from the balancer. The LT1/LT4 engine has the traditional lower bolts at the front of the engine, above the oil pan. The adapter was bolted to the engine. It is crucial that the crankshaft trigger sensor is mounted securely for proper timing output. After that is completed, this setup can be used with a Holley HP V5 ECU programmed to use a magnetic crank pickup and batch-fired fuel injectors. ■

We removed 0.100 inch of material from the crank trigger wheel inner bore for a snug fit on the hub. The mounting hub holes lined up with the crank trigger wheel. Timing will be handled with the crankshaft-sensor pickup assembly.

The sensor must have an air gap of 0.050 to 0.080 inch for proper signal and can be moved up or down for timing purposes. One of the round magnets must line up with the sensor when the engine is at top dead center.

The flat-head recessed studs and spacers allow clearance for the Optispark, and the ATI balancer is bolted to the hub. The 7/16-20 hardened stud is used to install the hub in a very restricted area. Throwback Automotive has an LT1/LT4 hub installer available with ball bearings to make the difficult task easier.

The balancer is ready and in the process of installation. ATI has specific assembly directions and torque specifications. This is where you want to ensure the crank trigger installation instructions were followed and the timing is close to perfect or engine damage may result.

is degrading with every mile that is accrued. Removing the ICM, washing away the thermal paste, and applying a fresh coat is an excellent idea. The ignition coil is riveted in place. Replacement coils provide screws and nuts for installation.

This MSD Blaster SS ignition-coil bracket was custom made. The coil was recommended for use with an MSD 6AL ignition box. The Holley Dual-Sync distributor (part number 565-200) was chosen to provide crankshaft- and camshaft-position pulses to the Holley HP ECU. The smaller-profile distributor cap of the Holley Dual-Sync distributor freed up much-needed space around the intake plenum.

Fuel-fouled spark plugs are coated with black, fluffy soot. It's a sure sign that the engine is over-fueling. Check the engine oil for fuel. The extra fuel washes away piston-ring lubrication. A tan or gray color is what you want to see because it indicates that the fuel control is close to perfect. The plugs decrease in heat range from left to right. The more porcelain that is showing, the hotter-burning the plug will be.

One performance ICM is available: the Performance Distributors Vortec long-dwell saturation version for 1994–1995 C4 LT1s. Long dwell saturation periods provide a longer-duration spark, completely burning the fuel in the combustion chambers. In addition, ICMs are available from other quality brands, such as ACDelco and Standard Ignition.

To wrap up items on the tuning side, do you need multi-electrode or platinum-tipped spark plugs? Regarding multi-electrode spark plugs, manufacturers claim that they keep a consistent spark-plug gap. When one electrode wears, the other ground electrodes become the dominant ground electrode. As a rule of thumb, spark plugs should be replaced at 75,000 to 80,000 miles to prevent spark-plug thread damage in aluminum cylinder heads, which makes the value of using multi-electrode spark plugs minimal. Platinum-tipped spark plugs work well to keep the flame kernel focused, and wear is minimal. They are my favorite. Note that platinum-tipped spark plugs should not be gap-checked because the platinum chip can be knocked off.

After years of shop use, Autolite spark plugs have been my go-to option for all applications. They are priced reasonably and haven't failed under extreme conditions. There's no need to send me negative input on my spark-plug choice, as we all have a favorite—and if it works for you, that's what matters. True performance engines looking for maximum power may have a set of plugs changed after every run, to check the tune and prevent failure at high engine RPM. Supercharged and nitrous-equipped engines require frequent spark-plug changes if you enjoy the racetrack. You may also have to decrease the spark-plug gap on supercharged, turbocharged, and nitrous-enhanced engines.

Multiple-spark ignition boxes can also fail. The concept is sound: amplify

This is a convenient location for an MSD digital 6A ignition box (part number 6201) in a C4. A piece of 0.125-inch aluminum plate was configured and attached to the lower side of the frame rail. The frame rail has a vertical seam connecting the two halves. This is where the plate was affixed. Always add a bypass circuit to eliminate the ignition box to get you home.

For spark-plug wire resistance, Blue Max wire reads 1,020 ohms per foot. Moroso spark-plug wires do a great job of supplying available spark voltage at the spark plug. All wires are marked for cylinder placement with well-insulated boots. Another great attribute is the correct length of the custom-fit line of plug wires.

spark voltage and provide multiple sparks per ignition event. Multiple spark events at low RPM make sense to some degree, but at high RPM, the multiple-spark benefit goes away. Spark pulse intervals are very short at wide-open throttle (WOT). Amplifying the spark via increased ignition coil operating voltage has merit. My experiences with them are mixed. Does the chance for failure outweigh the benefits? For me, an aftermarket performance ignition coil is enough. If I required supercharged or turbocharger boost timing control, I may go that route to avoid changing the harness and engine controller.

Spark-plug wires are not complicated. They come down to proper terminal retention and resistance. The General Motors OEM plug wires have 6,000 ohms per foot resistance for a reason. The top concern is radio interference—especially shielding the buffered, low-voltage engine, transmission, and body computer circuits from electromechanical interference (EMI). Performance plug wires have one aim: lower the resistance for more available spark voltage.

While this is a great plan, it can cause issues with key electronic components and hinder performance. Chances are good that lower-resistance plug wires will be of little concern if they are routed properly and not laying directly on sensor wiring. The L98 TPI spark-plug wires interact with the main engine harness on both sides of the engine, which may cause EMI interference. The LT1/LT4 plug wires are routed away from the main engine harness, except at the front of the engine. If the coil high-voltage wire is rubbing on the main engine harness as the engine is running, EMI can cause unexplained service engine soon (SES) codes. The same holds true for the 1996 LT1 or LT4 crank-position sensor wiring that is close to the coil high-voltage wire. EMI can disrupt the crank-position sensor output. Be aware that if engine performance is poor or the SES light comes on after a spark-plug wire upgrade, EMI may be the culprit.

Moroso makes my favorite set of replacement performance spark-plug wires with the correct fitment, tight-fitting terminals, and high-heat-resistant spark-plug boots. I've used them all, and correct-length plug wires are important with robust plug boots. Correct-fitting LT-engine spark-plug wire sets are difficult to find. L98 engines have more options, and semi-custom sets are available for the correct fitment and routing. Race header temperatures (1,600°F plus) and quality wire and plug boot protection is essential.

Crate Engines and Aftermarket Engine Control

Direct-fit, mass-produced C4 Corvette crate engines do not exist. They all require modification for installation. You'll typically start with a long- or short-block and add components. Expect to need a compatible intake manifold that provides adequate airflow for the cylinder heads.

The 1984 L83 Crossfire and 1985–1991 TPI intake systems severely restrict most production crate engines. For outputs less than 350 hp, the TPI intake remains usable, although it is suboptimal. The L83 Crossfire applications generally fare better with remanufactured replacement engines.

The easiest method to increase power is to install a crate engine. However, a plug-and-play option is not viable. Some fabrication is required.

A critical mistake during crate-engine installation is reusing worn ancillary components. Reinstalling old distributors and high-mileage fuel injectors compromises performance potential. Many customers reject comprehensive quotes that include engine-management sensors, spark-plug wires, distributor rebuilding/replacement, fuel-injector servicing, and cooling-system maintenance.

Competitors often provide attractive initial estimates that increase as the job is being performed, or they omit these critical replacements altogether. There's no truly economical approach to proper crate or remanufactured engine installation. False economy leads to ongoing repairs and frustration, which explains why many partially-upgraded C4s appear on sales platforms. Reliability remains paramount.

Most engine suppliers void warranties if internal modifications occur. Verify warranty requirements before making changes. Review supplier compatibility statements carefully, as many indicate incompatibility with L98 TPI or L83 Crossfire components. This may reflect legitimate concerns about intake restrictions or emissions regulations,

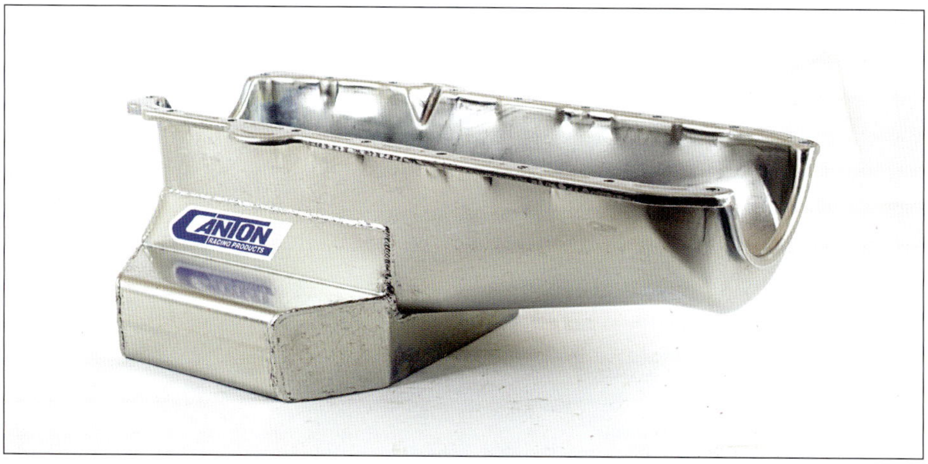

The Canton oil pan is expensive, but you don't need to worry about cracking or poor fitment and you'll never need another one. Use the recommended oil-pump pickup tube assembly. Canton provides oil drainback and temperature-sensor bungs in multiple locations for custom installations. (Photo Courtesy Canton Racing Products)

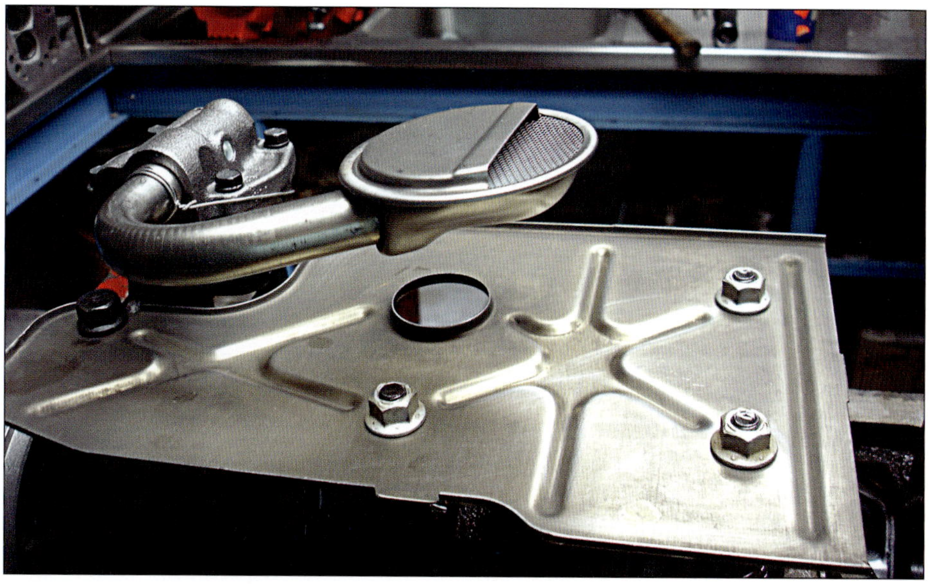

It is important that a 0.750 pickup tube, such as the one in this photo, is used. I use 0.025-diameter stainless-steel wire and wrap it around the pickup tube at the oil pump and then around the pump body to prevent the press-in tube from coming out of the oil pump.

so confirm specific reasons before proceeding.

The oil pan should be replaced with a Corvette-specific, shallow, long-sump oil pan on all Chevrolet Performance crate engines. You'll need it to avoid anything that is more than 3 to 4 inches above the road surface. Many crate engines come with a deeper pan, which is not a problem—as long as you ease over speed bumps and are mindful of the road surface. There were two- and one-piece rear main seal versions of this long, shallow oil pan. New OEM-style oil pans are difficult to find because their availability is in question, but used examples can be found in decent shape.

Aftermarket oil pans include those from Canton Racing Products or a few other contenders. Canton Racing Products part number 15-240 fits 1984–1986 L98 with a two-piece crankshaft rear main seal and the driver-side dipstick. Part number 240M fits the 1984–1986 two-piece crankshaft rear main seal and passenger-side dipstick. Part number 240T fits the one-piece crankshaft rear main seal with the passenger-side dipstick. All factory-equipped aluminum cylinder-head engines use the 15-240T. The pan holds 6 quarts of oil, prevents oil starvation under extreme cornering, and provides adequate ground clearance. Ports are provided for oil-level sensors, oil-temperature sensors, and the turbo and supercharger oil return.

Small-block Chevy engines are not known for high oil pressure (15 psi at idle is common at 200°F). Many crate engines are equipped with 0.625-inch oil-pump pickup tubes. To avoid oil starvation at high RPM, General Motors used 0.750-inch oil-pump pickup tubes on all 1986-and-newer C4s. I highly recommend replacing the 0.625 tube assembly.

The 1984–1986 C4 two-piece rear main seal (internal balance) crankshafts require a non-weighted flywheel and harmonic balancer. The 1987–1996 C4s with one-piece rear main seal (external balance) crankshafts require an external weight on the flywheel and a non-weighted harmonic balancer. Increased-engine-stroke configurations, such as the 383 and up, may require an internal- or external-balance crankshaft.

To avoid constant vibration, adhere to the crate-engine supplier's flexplate and harmonic-balancer recommendations. The flexplate on the right is externally balanced, with added weight welded to the flexplate at the bottom. The smaller flange on the flexplate that is on the right side denotes a one-piece rear main seal.

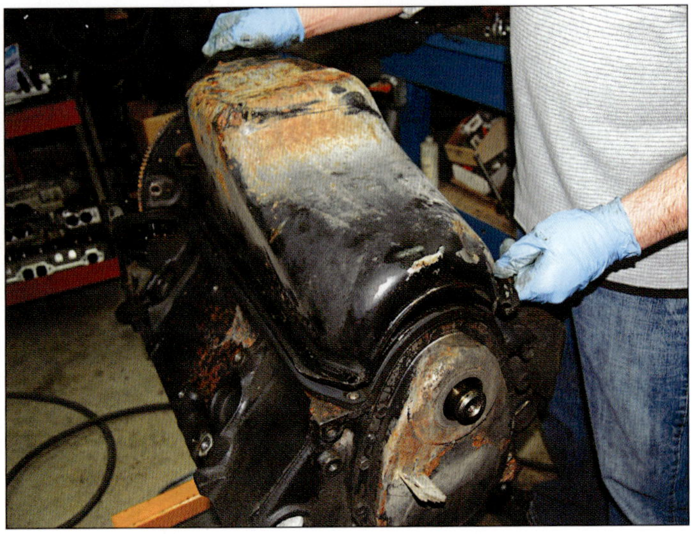

A replacement crate engine will most likely be the later 1986-and-up one-piece rear main seal type that requires a later oil pan. Be aware that there are different dipstick locations. The 1974 Corvette dipstick was on the driver's side, and 1986-and-up dipstick is on the passenger's side. The pan's depth is the same.

The same goes for the harmonic balancer. Some are weighted, and other applications require no additional weight.

Performance Engine Options

Chevrolet Performance offers limited options for 1985–1991 C4 upgrades. The ZZ6 base engine (part number 19433041) is priced at $9,200 and delivers 405 hp and 406 ft-lbs of torque, but it requires significant modification. While the engine includes a water pump, distributor, intake manifold, and oil pan, none of these components are compatible with the C4 platform or will fit under the hood of a C4. This greatly reduces the engine's overall value, as several parts must be replaced.

The Chevrolet Performance crate engine (part number 19435434) suits 1985–1986 C4s with cast-iron heads but needs oil-pan and pickup-tube replacement. Its Vortec Fast Burn heads require a new TPI manifold base, which is a critical but expensive component for accessing the engine's potential.

I recommend GM's ZZ4-ZZ6 short-block assembly (part number 19435619), which costs $4,200, for 1984–1991 C4s. Pick your camshaft, hydraulic roller lifters, and timing-chain components and install a new oil pump and oil-pump pickup tube. Top it off with Air Flow Research street or race cylinder heads in the $2,100 to $3,100 range and install your existing oil pan. You can achieve 500-plus hp without breaking the bank.

GM's ZZ4-ZZ6 short-block assembly (part number 19435619) requires the later one-piece rear main oil pan for 1984–1986 C4s. This engine combination's horsepower output is severely limited when coupled with a 1984 L83 Crossfire engine's intake-manifold assembly and throttle-body injectors.

Other suppliers offer 1985–1991 engine options that generate up to 500 hp and 500-plus ft-lbs of torque. ATK and BluePrint provide

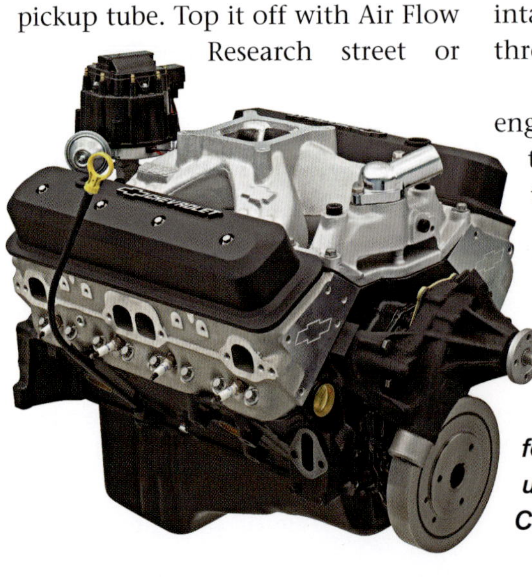

The Chevrolet Performance ZZ6 crate engine (part number 19434031), which produces 405 hp and 406 ft-lbs of torque, and the upgraded intake manifold and exhaust system will wake up your 1984–1991 C4. (Photo Courtesy Chevrolet Performance)

Another alternative for a crate engine is the ZZ4-ZZ6 short-block assembly (General Motors part number 19435619) for 1986–1991 C4s. The forged 1053 steel crankshaft and forged powdered-metal connecting rods with hypereutectic pistons are ready for the camshaft, intake, and exhaust system of your choice. (Photo Courtesy Chevrolet Performance)

Golen Engine Service provides excellent results and no-nonsense horsepower for your C4 Corvette. All of the attached parts are for your application. There are no takeoff parts. You pay for what you need and nothing else. Exhaust and intake system choices will affect the final horsepower numbers. (Photo Courtesy Golen Engines)

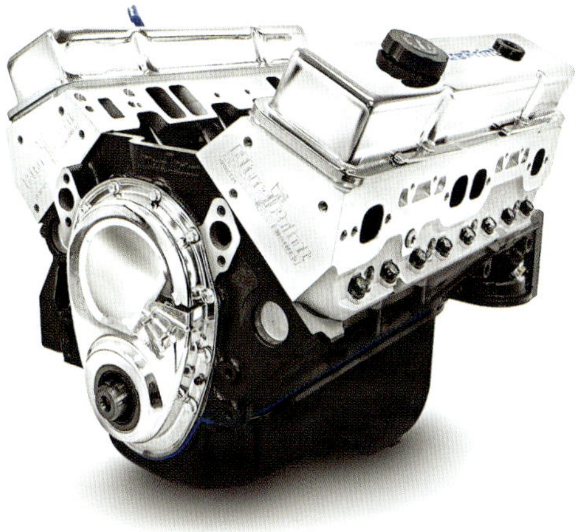

This all-new BluePrint long-block rotates a steel crankshaft with a 3.875-inch stroke and 6.0-inch connecting rods to achieve 396 ci. Forged pistons and BluePrint 64-cc aluminum cylinder heads squeeze the combustible mixture to 10.4:1. With 0.544-inch intake/0.555-inch exhaust lift and 230 intake/236 exhaust duration at 0.050 inch and a 110-degree lobe separation angle (LSA) hydraulic roller camshaft, it delivers 491 hp and 509 ft-lbs of torque. You get all of this with a 30 month/50,000-mile warranty. (Photo Courtesy Jason Bruce/BluePrint Engines)

This is the 396-ci LT1 engine by Golen Engine Service. It features a custom-grind hydraulic roller camshaft from Comp Cams (242/248 duration with a 0.580/0.580-inch lift and a 114-degree lobe separation angle (LSA) at 0.050 inch). The Comp Cams Ultra Pro Magnum rocker arms open the 195-cc Air Flow Research CNC-ported head's valves. Expect 560 hp and 500 ft-lbs of torque. (Photo Courtesy Golen Engines)

numerous 350- and 383-ci choices that approach 500 hp. All require oil-pan and pickup-tube modifications. These suppliers utilize aftermarket cylinder heads for achieving their advertised power figures. These suppliers may change oil pans and pickup tubes upon request.

BluePrint Engines manufactures its own block castings rather than reconditioning used blocks. While they are generally high quality, these blocks have certain peculiarities. Some standard bolt holes are omitted, requiring alternative mounting solutions for spark-plug wire retainers and other components. Their cylinder-head bolt holes are shallower than GM's equivalents. Verify fastener length to prevent bottoming out before achieving proper torque and potentially requiring washers for proper installation.

Custom crate engines provide the simplest installation with minimal preparation. Builders such as Smedling, Proformance Unlimited, Prestige Motorsports, and Shafiroff Race Engines offer dyno-tested, direct-fit solutions that are tailored to your specifications. These typically command premium prices and longer lead times. Be skeptical of suspiciously inexpensive custom builds with immediate availability. These anomalies often lead to disappointment.

Options for 1992–1996 LT1 and LT4 crate engines are scarce. Chevrolet Performance offers no replacement options. While some builders provide remanufactured and custom performance versions, the distinctive engine block remains in limited supply. Your local engine machine shop may be a source for a custom engine build. This saves on shipping costs. Check with local car clubs and other Corvette owners to hear their local experiences.

Golen Engine Service is the best LT1 performance short- or long-block custom engine builder. You can expect from 400 to 700 hp plus with its stroked 383- and 396-ci versions. Golen Engine Service has an excellent track record with no-nonsense horsepower. The 1992–1993 ECM handles up to 500 hp with minimal low-RPM performance tradeoffs. The 1994–1996 ECMs can handle the monster 700-hp Golen crate engine if that's where you want to go.

TECH TIP

Fuel-Injection Upgrades Required

Substantial modifications, such as intake manifold changes with aggressive camshafts and cylinder-head replacements, demand upgraded fuel-injection control systems. ■

Emissions and EPA Testing

For EPA approval, replacement engines must maintain the original configuration with intact emissions components. Performance engine builders typically designate their products for off-road use only and are not legal for highway operation. Consult local authorities regarding compliance requirements for engine replacements or modifications.

Factory ECM Limitations and Aftermarket Controller Options

Here is a common complaint after major engine upgrades or a crate engine installation: "My L98/LT1 engine runs worse than before."

This results from outdated factory computers struggling with modified engine requirements. The 1985–1989 ECM, although it is reliable, operates slowly by modern standards and was designed for stock camshafts with stable vacuum. Its batch-fire injection system sprays fuel to four cylinders simultaneously based on speed, throttle position, and temperature, regardless of whether intake valves are open. This strategy loads excessive unburned fuel at low RPM, which is less problematic at high speeds. When modifications demand more high-RPM fuel, the computer adds fuel across all RPM ranges, creating sluggish low-end response.

Regarding PROM/chip issues, diagnostic equipment manufacturers have abandoned 1984–1996 C4 engine control systems. Modern scanners are unavailable, and few tuners maintain equipment to modify fuel/ignition programs. In addition, the 1985–1993 programmable read-only memory (PROM) chips increasingly fail from age. Zip Corvette offers replacement chips with performance modifications, while PCM of North Carolina provides piggyback chips to enhance the fuel and ignition systems. Note that failing factory chips cannot be remedied with piggyback units alone. You need replacement stock and performance piggyback chips.

The 1990–1993 ECMs present unique challenges. Despite improved operating speed and idle-learn capabilities, they maintain minimal fuel injection control while suffering chronic reliability issues. Solder joint failures are common, but a few specialists are equipped to address these specific units. SIA Electronics in Tilden, Illinois, has provided the best repair results through board reflowing. Unfortunately, many repair services worsen ECM functionality, which is a lesson that I learned through multiple disappointing experiences.

The 1994–1996 PCMs, named for their multiple system control capabilities, introduced sequential fuel injection and remain reliable today. These units managed engine and transmission functions electronically. While the 1994–1995 PCMs implemented OBD-II standards, they required Corvette-specific scanning equipment, and 1996 units featured true OBD-II functionality with misfire detection. Owners maintaining Optispark ignition can effectively use these factory controllers. The 1994–1995 models can be tuned using Tunercat equipment, while 1996 calibrations work with both Tunercat and Jet Performance Products.

For serious horsepower gains with optimal drivability, aftermarket engine controllers are essential. However, important system implications exist for 1990–1996 C4s. The instrument cluster receives data from two sources. The digital displays require CCM information via serial data from the factory ECM/PCM. No conversion systems exist to maintain this functionality with aftermarket controllers, including LS factory ECMs.

While analog gauges will operate with original sensors, fuel-economy data disappears across all 1984–1996 applications. Fuel level indication remains functional on all models. The 1992–1996 acceleration slip regulation (ASR) traction control becomes nonfunctional as the system depends on serial data communication between factory ECM/PCM and electronic brake traction control module. Fortunately, the antilock brake functionality remains operational.

Select aftermarket engine/transmission controllers provide quick response times and sequential fuel injection, preferably with the capability for laptop or handheld tuning. Modern systems accommodate diverse sensors, injectors, and ignition setups. For power adders (nitrous oxide, supercharging, and turbocharging), they offer critical timing retard and fuel enrichment functions. Gone are rudimentary shifter-button nitrous-oxide activations. Comprehensive fuel and spark mapping enables seamless power delivery from idle to wide-open throttle.

Available EFI Upgrade Options

FiTech offers its TPI Retro-Fit EFI system (part number 38350). The system is based on FiTech's proven, self-learning EFI technology, which improves the performance and drivability of a stock or modified small-block engine paired with a 700-R4 or 4L60 transmission with a torque converter clutch (TCC) lockup.

The efficient and compact ECU is easily mounted and connected through a new wiring harness and terminated with factory-style connectors for the throttle-position, idle air control, coolant temperature, and knock sensors, the injectors, and the distributor. A new wideband oxygen sensor is supplied to monitor the air/fuel mixture, and there is a direct connection to the factory distributor. The injectors and sensors are easily calibrated to your specifications through a color touchscreen handheld controller.

The FiTech Ultimate Kit (part number 38351) provides two oxygen sensors, a three-bar manifold absolute pressure (MAP) sensor, and all of the attaching pieces for less than $1,000. This is made for your TPI and is not a universal kit with the same advanced self-learning technology as the 38350 kit. Two oxygen sensors take the kit to the next tuning and performance level, which makes it the leader in this category, considering the ECU's cost.

The versatile Holley ECUs can control all 1984–1996 engines. However, there is a caveat. Either the EFI Connection crank-camshaft sensor (LS conversion) or Lane Culver's Optispark shutter wheel is required for LT engine control. The HP and Terminator ECU offerings have four programmable inputs and outputs. All Holley ECUs allow data logging for road or drag-strip events. The "Quick Start" feature is included to get your fuel map close to what is

The FiTech Ultimate Kit 38351 provides two oxygen sensors, three-bar MAP sensors, and a coolant-temperature sensor for ultimate fuel control. This is made for a 1985–1991 tuned port injection engine and is not a universal kit. The advanced self-learning technology makes setup easy and allows fine-tuning. Dynamometer tuning is suggested for the highest possible power output and longest engine life. (Photo Courtesy FiTech Fuel Injection)

Engine Controller LT1/LT4 Option

The 1992–1996 LT1/LT4 ignition system's unique optical-sensor output is not compatible with most aftermarket engine controllers. One exception is the use of Lane Culver Automotive's Optispark shutter wheel that replaces the LT engine's OEM-style shutter wheel. The shutter-wheel design mimics an LS crank and cam sync position sensor. When the Culver Optispark trigger wheel is used, a cam synchronization pulse can be used for sequential fuel injection.

Lane Culver's custom Optispark shutter wheel is on the right. You can use the original Optispark distributor with a compatible aftermarket engine controller. We've used the Holley HP for this configuration with excellent results.

Calibration and Tuning Information

All engine management systems begin with a baseline calibration using engine specifications, with camshaft profile being particularly crucial. Self-learning systems adjust from the initial parameters based on selected components. However, even identical builds may require different fueling due to manufacturing variations. Professional wide-open-throttle tuning on a chassis or engine dynamometer remains strongly recommended for optimal results.

Professional tuners utilize exhaust gas temperature sensors on each header tube alongside dedicated oxygen sensors to verify aftermarket EFI readings. They ensure proper air-fuel ratios and safe ignition timing. Prioritizing maximum power over reliability is your decision and responsibility. Regularly inspect the spark plugs from both cylinder banks. Ideal plugs show slight tan coloration. Avoid white/blistered plugs (indicating a dangerous lean condition) and black-coated plugs (indicating fuel contamination of the engine oil).

The major concern with any aftermarket EFI system is the installer. Care must be taken in all aspects: wiring,

These crude terminals are a few of many that were found when diagnosing poor performance issues. Overheated terminals and wiring can be the result of poor crimp retention. The wire terminals that were fashioned from wire strands were a surprise. The bent alternator stud caused a poor connection. This would not only reduce overall performance but also create a fire hazard.

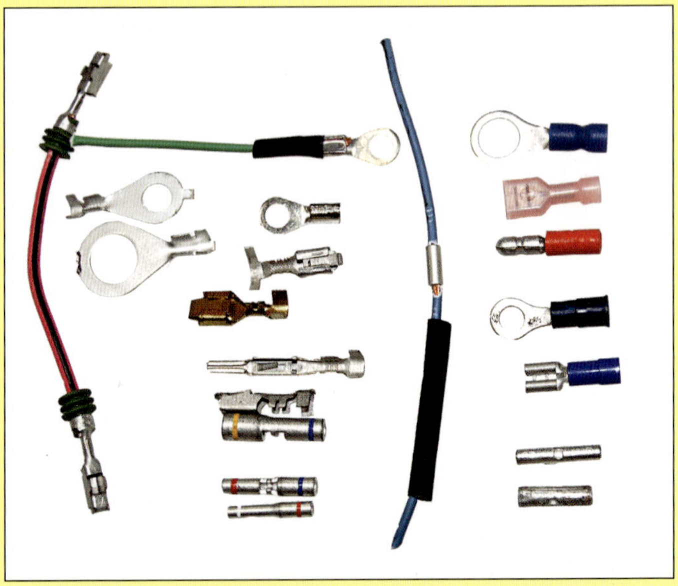

The generic terminals on the right are okay to use but aren't ideal. Crimp quality can be suspect, and there is no wire strain relief. The terminals on the left have two sets of retaining straps to grab the wire's insulation and prevent wire strand breakage. Non-insulated butt splices are recommended. They fit tightly to the wire before crimping and then heat-shrink is applied.

fuel-system plumbing, and tuning. No matter who you choose, read as much as possible and know what you're getting into before you start any of the modifications. Pay careful attention to the wiring requirements.

Proper Wiring and Terminal Installation Methods

For many years, I soldered wires for splices and to lengthen them. It was apparent that the solder rosin deteriorated the wiring over a long period of time. Rosin-core solder cleans the wire for the best possible adherence, but it leaves residue of the cleaning compound behind. Butt splices eliminate any cleaning residue and don't heat temper the wires. The one exception that I reserve solder for is high-amperage circuit terminal installation where it is difficult to get the ultimate crimp on the terminal.

Apply heat-shrink tubing to seal and aid in strain relief when a wire circuit is spliced or lengthened. I also use it on eyelets or open terminals for strain relief. OEM ground terminals have an added crimp section to secure the wire insulation. Strain relief can be a huge problem and cause wire strands to work back and forth until they break loose. Never cut off all of the wires at the same length. Cut them at different lengths to keep the butt splices separated and avoid a large knot in the harness. ■

Using the correct wire strippers and crimpers is important. Several W-style crimpers are required for proper terminal-to-wire retention. The blue-handled W-crimpers can be found on Amazon. The crimpers with "13" on the grip are from Wurth Industries. Matco made the other W-crimpers. The barrel, or butt, terminal crimper on the right is a Thomas and Betts version.

Here are more must-have C4 connector terminal tools to release terminals from their connectors. The medium tab remover (top) is part number 12094430. The others were found online. The yellow-handled remover is for Weatherpak bullet terminals. The C4s used round terminals in several places.

needed for the self-learning process.

The HP and Terminator handle all fuel and ignition control requirements on any 1984–1993 C4 engine. Staged programmable nitrous-oxide and boost controls with water/methanol injection are included. The Terminator ECU is required for 1994–1996 applications. One downside is the use of one oxygen sensor and the finicky handheld programmer. The use of a laptop is preferred and easier to navigate for tuning and setup.

If you have a project with forced induction (nitrous, supercharging, or turbocharging) and require electronic transmission control, the Dominator ECU is the best choice. It has staged, integrated nitrous-oxide injection with turbocharger boost control, water/methanol injection with two nozzles, speed inputs for precise fuel control during staged boost, and two oxygen sensors for ultimate fuel control. The Dominator handles "drive by wire" for your LS

The versatile Holley Terminator and HP engine control unit (ECU) can control a 1984–1991 L83, L98, or 1992–1996 C4 LT1/ LT4 engine when using the LS conversion crank-camshaft sensor from EFI Connections.

A Holley Dominator engine control unit (ECU) can be used for the ultimate C4 conversion: a turbocharged or supercharged LS engine swap with drive-by-wire throttle and plenty of racetrack controls. (Photo Courtesy Holley Performance Products)

engine swap. This is a powerful but expensive ECU.

Select aftermarket engine/transmission controllers provide quick response times and sequential fuel injection, preferably with laptop or handheld tuning capability. Modern systems accommodate diverse sensors, injectors, and ignition setups. For power adders (nitrous oxide/supercharging/turbocharging), they offer critical timing retard and fuel enrichment functions. Gone are rudimentary shifter-button nitrous-oxide activations. Comprehensive fuel and spark mapping enables seamless power delivery from idle to wide-open throttle.

A/C Control Switch

If you decide to retrofit to an aftermarket ECU, the A/C compressor will not function. Air compressor operation differs based on the control type. With electronic control panels (option C68, 1990–1996), the system functions except for compressor engagement, which is normally controlled via serial data from the factory computer. With manual controls (option C60), all of the original wiring remains functional. A switch must be wired into the compressor control circuit.

Our workaround is to place a simple on/off switch near the A/C panel to control the A/C compressor. Wire the switch power to the brown A/C system voltage wire. When the engine is shut down, the compressor will be shut down as well. There will be a wiring change at the A/C control relay and under the hood for the existing A/C system pressure switches.

CHAPTER 4

LS ENGINE AND TRANSMISSION RETROFIT

LS1, LS2, and LS3 engines fit like they belong under the hood of a 1985–1996 Corvette. The 1984 C4 engine bay will accept the LS engine, but it requires major hood modifications or switching to the 1985–1996 hood. (Photo Courtesy Andy Bolig)

Upgrading to an LS-series engine is the optimal C4 Corvette conversion. Having performed numerous installations, Throwback Automotive Inc. (formerly Petris Enterprises Inc.) now offers comprehensive conversion kits. While research is required, the benefits last for years. The L98 C4 owners typically gain 100 hp from a salvage-yard LS engine. With minor modifications, the same engine can exceed 400 hp. Additional benefits include improved fuel economy and emissions performance that is superior to any original C4 powerplant.

The LS engine conversion is proven. One customer has accumulated more than 75,000 miles on his 1990 LS1-powered convertible. This particular 1990 Corvette received the conversion on-stage at the Corvettes at Carlisle show. The entire pre-staged conversion took 9 hours total with a 3-person team. The most important factor in the quick turnaround was using a replacement LS-to-L98 integration harness that had been pre-prepped in the shop.

Once completed, we participated in the annual Corvettes at Carlisle parade. Then, we drove 700 miles home with only a minor incident concerning the A/C system wiring. After a bit of troubleshooting, we headed back with cold air blowing. Following the conversion, many miles have accrued in sunny Florida, which tests all facets of the procedure.

Gen V LT1

The 2014–present Gen V LT1 engines represent the future but remain in a beta retrofit stage (as of 2025). While the mounting is similar to LS series and requires redesigned adapter plates, the extended water-pump position presents challenges for accessory-drive integration. Throwback Automotive is currently developing and testing

This low-mileage 2004 LS1 takeout engine is ready for installation. The TCI flexplate has been bolted on and torqued to 74 ft-lbs with blue Loctite on the bolts. We're using Throwback Automotive's engine-mount adapter plates. Due to the C5 Corvette's winged oil pan, it was removed to create clearance for the transmission cooler line.

A 9/16-inch drill bit is used to remove extra rubber so that the bolts go in with ease. The amount of rubber that the drill bit has removed is on the bench. This excess rubber prevents the bolt from spinning or making angle changes.

component configurations for this application.

For engine management, you can use either a 2000-and-newer General Motors ECU or an aftermarket controller. Both require C4 electronics integration. The 1984–1989 Corvettes with option code C60 (non-electronic A/C) interface the most easily. The 1986–1996 C68 electronic A/C systems communicate via serial data between the ECM and A/C programmer, requiring a standalone compressor-control switch with LS conversions.

If you decide to use a complete engine-transmission takeout, transmission compatibility issues may be a concern. For example, a 2001–2006 4L65E transmission is required with a 2001 General Motors PCM (part number 12200411). Earlier 4L65E transmissions may not work. Holley Terminator X Max or Dominator ECUs can manage mixed components and support drive-by-wire throttle systems.

The same holds true when using the existing 1994–1996 C4 4L60E transmission with an LS conversion. The PCM will not be able to control the transmission. You can use the 2001 PCM and a PSI Conversion engine/transmission controller or use the Holley Terminator ECU for total system control. PSI Conversion also sells a standalone 4L65E controller.

Before proceeding, consult the book *LS Swaps: How to Swap GM LS Engines into Almost Anything* by Jefferson Bryant from CarTech.

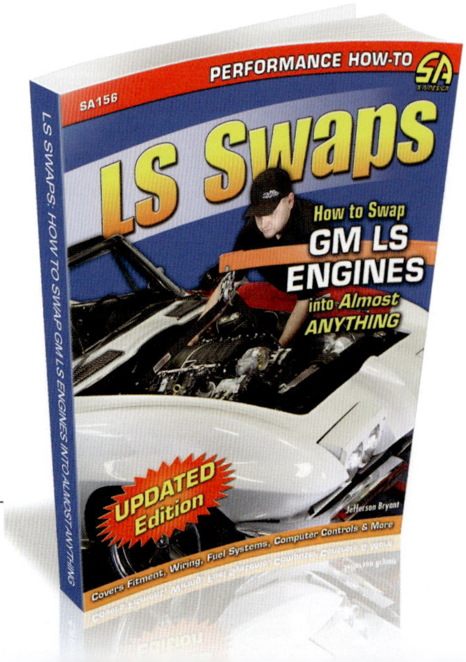

When selecting a transplant engine, note there are two LS crankshaft reluctor wheels: the early 24x black sensor and the late 58x gray sensor. Mismatching the sensor and reluctor causes high-RPM misfires and shutdown. Similarly, camshaft reluctors evolved from a single-depression design (marking the number-1 cylinder position) to a four-depression design with varying lengths (providing comprehensive cylinder position data).

Throwback Automotive Inc.'s triangulated proprietary-design engine-mount adapter plates

4L60 to 4L65E Adapter Plate (4-Bolt to 6-Bolt)

All C4 automatic transmissions use a four-bolt extension housing retention design, while other General Motors 4L65E applications employ six-bolt designs. This necessitates an adapter for using non-Corvette transmissions with the C4's unique rear torque beam. The engine and transmission will be moved forward 1.50 inches. This requires a universal pair of LS engine-mount adapters that allow the engine to slide back or forward. ■

The Advance Adapters four-bolt to six-bolt adapter (part number 51-0405) is 1.500 inches thick to allow a later 4L65E automatic transmission to bolt up to a Corvette extension housing. This requires either moving the engine forward or modifying the torque beam. (Photo Courtesy Advance Adapters)

(part number 0212332) bolt to the engine and are ready for OEM engine mounts. The engine-mount plates are thinner, sitting the engine lower in the chassis, and they are as strong as their universal counterparts. The plates have two top bolts and one lower bolt with studs for easy engine mount installation. When using the Throwback Automotive adapters, an LS engine can be directly bolted to an existing transmission.

We've had a difficult time installing motor-mount through bolts when setting the engine into place. The bolt holes fill up with rubber during the manufacturing process, so the mount holes need to be cleaned out. A TCI flexplate (part number 399753) with a torque converter pilot extension mates to the original C4 automatic transmission. An original 1997–2001 winged oil pan was used for adequate ground clearance. We were able to use the existing transmission-cooler lines.

Chassis and Transmission Considerations for LS Swaps

All C4 Corvettes use angle braces from the front suspension crossmember to the frame rails to stiffen the frame and keep the crossmember square. The 1984–1989 C4s have a smaller square tubing in this location that does not affect the LS oil pan. The 1990–1996 braces are beefier and will be too close to the oil pan. A simple notch will provide the required clearance without causing integrity concerns.

The automatic transmission coupling differs between the 1984–1993 700-R4/4L60 and the 1994–1996 4L60E electronic transmissions. The earlier 700-R4/4L60 allows a direct LS bolt-up with additional lower supports adapting to the LS's full-circle mounting face. This configuration requires a cable-driven throttle body to operate the transmission's throttle valve (TV) cable for proper pressure control. The 1994–1996 4L60E versions do not require a TV cable.

For manual-transmission compatibility, the General Motors bellhousing (part number 3899621) connects an LS engine to the 1984–1988 4+3 overdrive unit. The 4+3's durability depends on driving style, and the overdrive ECM requires bypassing for shift control. The ZF 6-speed requires a Quicktime RM-6039 adapter bellhousing and clutch conversion at significant cost.

The ultimate LS swap is paired with a T-56 or TR6060 6-speed transmission to provide superior torque capacity and shift quality compared to ZF units. This represents the most complex installation and requires custom mounting solutions to connect

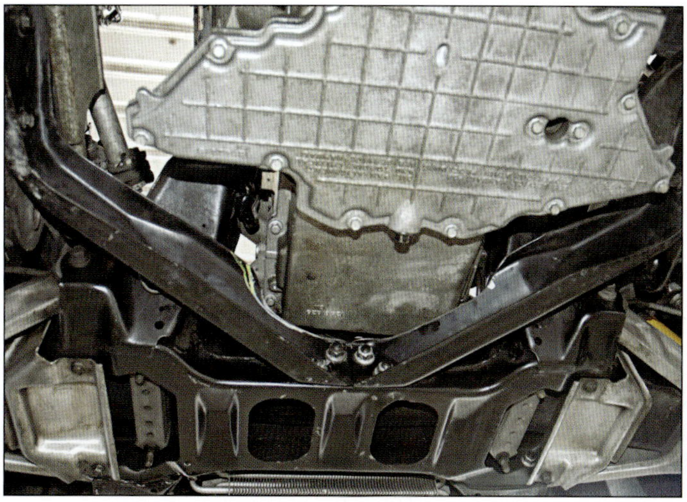
The notch is required on both sides. Set the engine in place and find the notch cutout requirements. The engine barely sits on the brace when using Throwback Automotive's LS-engine adapter plates.

This is my way to overcome the lack of torque-beam mounting surfaces for a T-56 6-speed conversion with an LS3. The entire piece is handworked to fit and takes many hours to ensure that the driveline angles are correct.

The T-56 installed in a 1991 C4 was a new Camaro replacement with through-bolt holes at the lower end. A plate was welded to the upper plate for a secure torque-beam mount.

The 700-R4, 4L60, and Corvette 4L605E transmissions use a bolt to retain the dipstick, which is important to have in place. We insert a 10-mm x 1.5 Heli-Coil in this position. There is no need to drill the hole for the Heli-Coil, which can be found at most major hardware stores or online.

We were able to use C5 shorty headers with the setup to make it an easy LS transition. With some creative trimming, we were able to use the L98's 700-R4 torque-converter cover.

the transmission extension housing with the C4's torque beam. Commercially available mounts from BRP Hot Rods (Muscle Rods) rely solely on the lower support without upper bracing.

My version has an upper support from the rear of the transmission case to avoid flexing. I've seen a few of these that relied on the lower transmission-mount surface and the upper being loose, allowing it to flex and rotate. The torque beam connects the engine/transmission as an assembly with the differential. They are suspended as an assembly on the differential cover via mounts to the unibody frame.

Few 1984–1996 C4 accessory components can be easily reused. The LS engine's wider profile, when compared to L98/LT1 engines, positions the power-steering pump and water-pump outlets perilously close to the front suspension crossmember. Kwik Performance's alternator/power-steering accessory support kit is an option that provides minimal clearance to the crossmember.

This is the Throwback Automotive LS power steering/alternator accessory drive kit. It includes a new power-steering pump and pulley, reservoir, supply hose, support plates, and top-quality washer-head fasteners. This kit provides the most clearance that is available for the power-steering pump pulley.

The kit comes assembled as shown with both plates, the idler pulley, and the required spacers in place. Thin nuts retain the pieces until you're ready to install the assembly onto your LS engine. The supply hose is not placed onto the power-steering fitting until after the assembly is in place and torqued down. The reservoir is pulled up off the support for bolt access.

Kwik Performance assembled this A/C accessory-drive kit. It features a C5 Corvette belt tensioner that requires a Sanden SD-7-series A/C compressor. (Photo Courtesy Kwik Performance)

Throwback Automotive's new design nets the most power-steering pump pulley clearance. The Throwback Automotive alternator/power-steering accessory support kit requires a General Motors CS-130-series alternator from a 2000–2002 Camaro. These are available in 100- to 240-amp versions, and all require proper alternator output wire lead sizing to attain the alternator's maximum power available. Four-gauge wire is required for 100 amps, and up to 1/0 gauge is needed for the 240-amp alternator.

The C4's counterclockwise-rotation power-steering pump was replaced with a clockwise-rotation version. You can be resourceful and overhaul the existing pump. The pump-rotor housing can be installed 180 degrees from its original position to convert it to clockwise rotation. The existing steel pump supply elbow is removed, and a short 90-degree fitting (after verifying orientation) is installed into the pump. The power-steering pump's 90-degree fluid suppy fitting is available at Kwik Performance.

Kwik Performance has a ready-to-go A/C accessory-drive kit that uses a Sanden compressor. All of the necessary installation components are included, with an idler and belt tensioner. The aftermarket air-conditioning accessory-drive system consists of a C5 Corvette belt tensioner. The Corvette harmonic balancer kit is recommended, and it allows the most available balancer-to-crossmember clearance.

Throwback Automotive's version uses the Kwik Performance A/C compressor kit. The A/C compressor and all attaching pieces are mounted onto the support assembly. The supplied Sanden seven-series compressor is compatible with all C4 A/C systems after a R-134a retrofit. The Throwback Automotive–designed A/C main hose assembly mounts to the rear of the compressor with a mounting block for quick installation.

The LS C5 Corvette water-pump heater inlet and outlet tubes are very close to the C4 suspension crossmember. Our solution was to remove the press-in heater-hose fittings, which are national pipe thread (NPT) tapped, and to install 90-degree heater-hose fittings. Eliminating the heater hoses and plugging the water

This is Throwback Automotive's ready-to-go A/C accessory-drive kit. Simply remove the thin nuts and mount the assembly to your engine. Shimming may be required after a test run. Check the belt position on the idler. Shim installation instructions are included in the kit.

The suction and discharge hoses connect directly to the existing A/C compressor, evaporator, and condenser. The tube assembly is supported at the front to prevent tube cracking under high-RPM use.

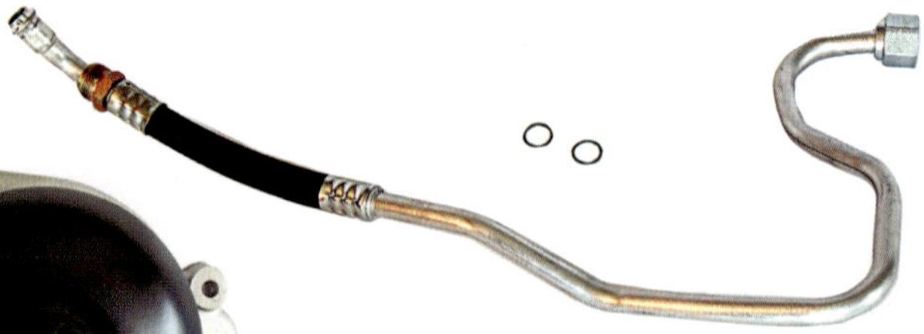

The A/C evaporator-to-accumulator line assembly fits snugly near the frame rail and lays across the top of the upper control arm. The tubes get busy in the area under the A/C compressor. Make sure that they do not rub on the pulley.

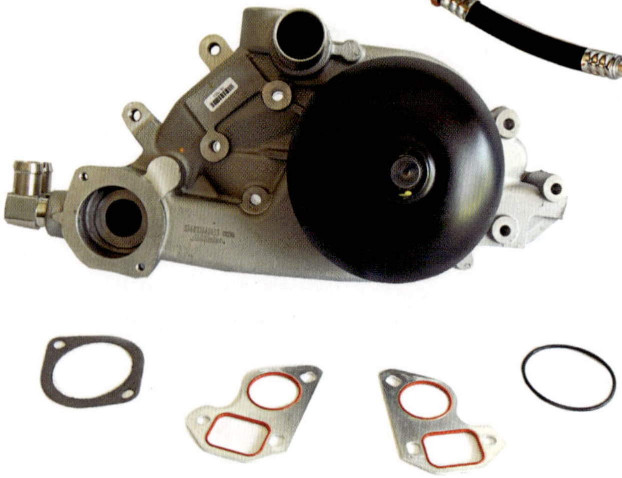

Another Throwback LS component that is ready to be installed is the water pump, which has the heater-hose fittings installed. The latest version has tight-fit push-in aluminum fittings to avoid electrolysis and provide the most upper control-arm shaft clearance that is available.

pump is possible but is not preferred. General Motors utilized the 3/4-inch outside-diameter water-pump heater hose as the cooling system fill point for the C5 Corvette. This ensures proper coolant fill.

A C4 LS A/C main hose handles refrigerant going from the accumulator to the A/C compressor and the high-pressure discharge to condenser. Sanden A/C compressors have various styles of ports for hose connection. You can use a single O-ring port or a block-type fitting. Suppliers, such as Cold Hose, have all of the required pieces to make hose assemblies, and they are very helpful with suggesting solutions.

The LS engine's wider stance requires rerouting the A/C evaporator to the accumulator line to avoid A/C compressor interference. This can be accomplished with a long hose (routing it under the A/C compressor). Otherwise, a custom tube can be designed with the hose at the accumulator end. The hose must be used with a tube to prevent the tube from cracking. This is another area where Cold Hose can help out.

All of the LS conversion A/C hose and tube concerns were considered, and suitable pieces were designed by myself at Throwback Automotive Inc. A complete main hose assembly with a support tab for factory-assembled fitment is available. The evaporator-to-accumulator tube was designed to go down to the frame rail, and a section of hose was used to connect the accumulator. The 1994–1996 C4s have metric A/C

TECH TIP

A/C Anomaly

The 1988 C4 condenser used integrated block fittings instead of threaded connections. This difficult-to-find component can be replaced with a 1989 condenser and hose assembly configuration. The Throwback Automotive A/C main hose is viable with a 1989 condenser installed. ■

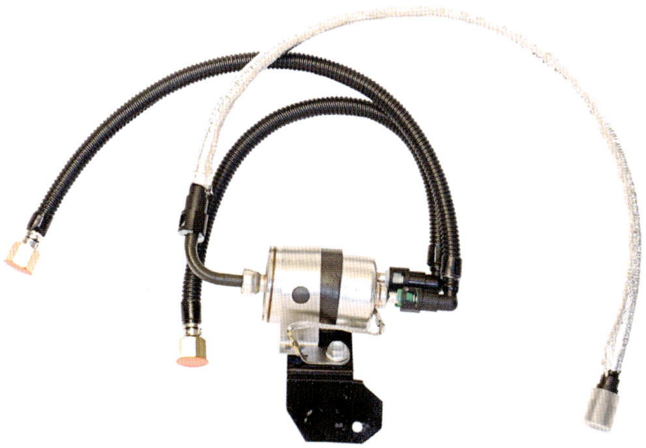

This is the Throwback LS conversion fuel system. All of the tubing is ready for installation with the fuel-filter adapter mount bracket in place. All of the attaching hardware is included. (Photo Courtesy Throwback Automotive)

fittings to address this, and I recommend using the A/C main hose and tube assembly with a 1990–1993 A/C accumulator.

The Throwback Automotive C5 Corvette fuel filter assembly supplies the required 60- to 62-psi fuel pressure, and it filters enough fuel for 500-plus naturally aspirated horsepower. Abrasion and heat-barrier-protected flex-fuel lines are provided. The flex-fuel lines are zip-tied to the fuel-filter bracket in the correct orientation and are trained to keep their circular shape during installation. Do not cut the zip tie until the tubes are connected. New O-rings and instructions are supplied for a complete installation kit.

The 1992–1996 fuel filter shield has been removed to show how the setup works. Once the fuel lines are connected, the zip tie can be cut. The supplied fuel-filter bracket was designed to hold the fuel filter and fuel-frame lines in place, and the existing frame-rail fuel-filter screw hole is used to retain the bracket.

The OEM fuel rail needs to be rotated 180 degrees for the fuel filter-to-fuel rail connection. Corvette, Camaro, and Firebird LS intake manifolds allow for fuel-rail rotation. Be sure to install the fuel-rail crash-barrier tabs at the rear of the intake. The supplied fuel line is routed to avoid kinking and heat damage after installation.

The fuel rail is rotated 180 degrees with the fuel line routed up from the fuel filter between the evaporator case and the inner fender liner. When the fuel line has been properly routed, it will not be close to the surge tank bleed or recovery tank hoses.

While 1985–1996 C4 in-tank pumps can provide the additional pressure that is needed, a new pump is recommended no matter what the horsepower goals are. The 1984 C4 pump is only designed for 10 to 12 psi and cannot manage LS pressure or volume requirements.

The 1984–1993 automatic transmission applications require a TV cable for the correct shift points and to avoid internal component

This Throwback Automotive throttle, throttle-valve (TV), and cruise-control cable bracket is bolted to a 2000 Corvette LS intake manifold using its cables and modified throttle body with the TV lever installed.

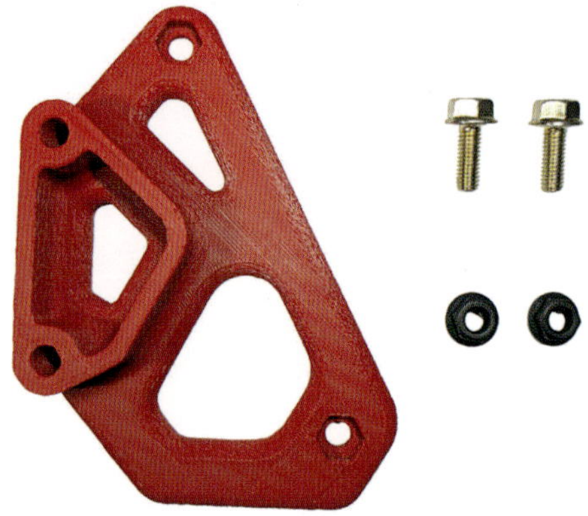

This Throwback Automotive LS conversion drive-by-wire adapter has the stepped area welded to the adapter plate. The stepped area mimics the OEM accelerator-pedal pivot bracket and fits into the provided firewall pad recess.

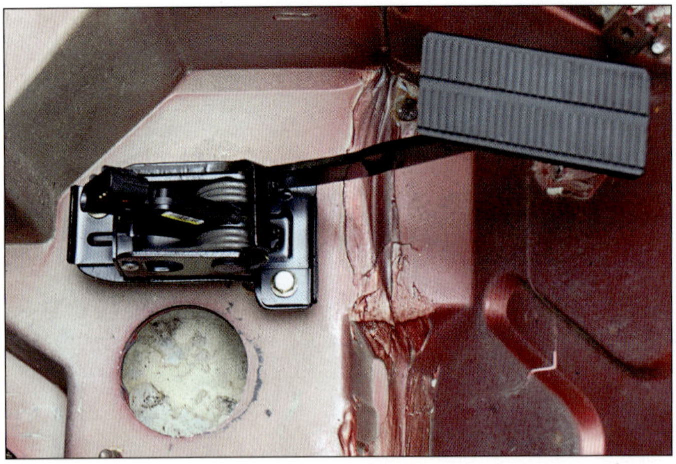

Once the OEM pedal is removed, install the drive-by-wire adapter and bolt the Throwback Automotive drive-by-wire pedal assembly to the adapter. Throwback Automotive modifies a new drive-by-wire accelerator pedal's lever to fit the tunnel properly with a modified pedal pad for OEM pedal feel.

failure. The Throwback Automotive–designed throttle cable bracket supports the proprietary throttle, TV, and cruise control cables. A mechanical throttle body is required and can be supplied or modified by Throwback Automotive for TV and cruise-control cable usage.

For 1984–1996 manual transmission and 1994–1996 automatic-transmission throttle control, drive-by-wire offers greater flexibility and easier installation despite requiring accelerator-pedal wiring. Verify ECU compatibility with your chosen throttle system.

Throwback Automotive configured an adapter for drive-by-wire pedal assembly (GM part number 25835421) to bolt to the firewall using existing firewall studs. No original firewall pad modifications are required. An in-house fixture is used to modify the drive-by-wire pedal assembly for the correct accelerator-pedal location. The accelerator pad is also modified to mimic the C4 accelerator pad.

The radiator hose configuration presents challenges when integrating components from different systems. After struggling to find appropriate premade hoses, I transitioned to custom solutions by using aluminum tubing with silicone elbows. Speedway Motors and Pegasus Auto Racing Supplies have an extensive supply of silicone hoses and elbows available. Speedway Motors also has straight or radius tubing connectors available.

Gates Power Grip SB heat-shrink band clamps are used to secure the silicone elbows to the aluminum tubes. These are excellent to use because they get tighter as heat builds and coolant leaks are eliminated as the hose becomes part of the tubing. The heat-shrink bands can be used at the radiator and engine side. Race applications usually work well with standard hose clamps. Cutting and shrinking the band clamps under race conditions takes too much time.

Making the Connections: LS Wire Harness and Module

There are multiple approaches for the conversion. Interconnect an aftermarket universal harness with original wiring or use a custom interface harness. After performing numerous engine swaps over the span of 40-plus years, I prefer custom harnesses that fit precisely without excess wiring that requires

This Throwback Automotive set of radiator hoses for 1990–1996 C4 LS conversions are ready to install. The hoses have heat-shrink band clamps carefully placed that cover the end of the silicone hose at the aluminum tubing for a professional look.

We used step-down silicone hoses and aluminum tubing to make the LS-to-L98 radiator transition in multiple configurations. Silicone holds up well to coolant for many years, but it does not like oil or grease. If you have oil leaks, keep it off the hoses.

The silicone and aluminum-tube upper radiator hose has been fitted onto a 1990 C4 LS swap. The aluminum coolant tubing helps cool the engine. It sheds heat as coolant flows through it.

concealment. However, this is the most expensive option.

While online resources offer valuable information, factory service manuals provide essential information, identifying circuitry. Limited information, particularly 1984–1989 factory service manuals, are not as beneficial as the 1990–1995 factory service manuals, which include improved connector documentation with alphanumeric designations and function descriptions. The 1996 manuals featured the most comprehensive layouts. Identifying wire functions from connector views often requires tracing wires through the harness. Note that despite color-coding with stripe tracers, wire colors frequently repeat across different circuits due to the limited palette of colors.

Always use year-specific factory service manuals because significant harness variations exist even within a generation. For example, the 1985 wiper-control wiring was in the C-100 bulkhead, but it is in the center firewall connectors for 1989. In addition, complexity comes from harness variations among transmission types and A/C options (RPO C60/C68).

Patient novices can complete this work by methodically identifying wires with a multimeter (ohms testing) and tagging each connection. Proper harness interfacing requires specialized crimping tools. A single crimper rarely suffices due to varying terminal designs. Using a proper crimping technique remains critical for reliability. Some installers expose harness sections, locate necessary wires for aftermarket ECU connections, and splice accordingly, which leaves unused wires in place. While functionally adequate, this approach sacrifices aesthetics. Next, identify which harness connectors will integrate with the LS-swap harness or aftermarket controller.

There are going to be some functions that are altered or inoperable due to serial data challenges. None of the C4 ECM/PCM/CCM components' serial data streams work with later General Motors ECMs/PCMS or aftermarket ECMs.

The stacked C-100 main connector has a 1/4-inch hex-head screw between the upper and lower connectors. It is difficult to access or feel the screw head. It also takes quite a bit of rotation for the screw to come out. Take your time with this. The plastic tabs can be broken if you get frustrated and bend them back too far.

The connector requires disconnection between the engine-main and forward-lamp harnesses close to the firewall bulkhead connector. Once disconnected, the engine-main harness can be separated from the forward-lamp harness.

Remove this harness from the center of the firewall behind the passenger-side valve cover no matter what year C4 you're working with. Later models have 7-mm screws with a plate. Earlier models have a large, single rubber grommet.

When using LS controllers, all C4 Corvettes lose fuel mileage and distance information. Work continues with technical specialists to develop an emulator that allows data stream integration. Analog engine gauges remain functional through adapter components that utilize the original gauge sensors.

Regarding vehicle speed sensors (VSS), the 1984–1989 C4 instrument clusters received low-voltage magnetic analog VSS signals, buffering them for speedometer operation, and then forwarding them to the ECM. Integration requires splicing the VSS output wires to the LS controller. Factory LS computers use this input for idle control and cooling fan operation. If using VSS input with the factory ECU/PCM, programming adjustments are necessary to prevent inadvertent speed limiter activation. Most aftermarket ECUs do not use the VSS, which affects cooling fan operation.

In 1990–1996 C4s, the VSS analog signal fed both the ECM/PCM (for buffering) and the FX3 selective ride control module. The ECM/PCM converts this to a Hall Effect (square wave) signal for the CCM (speedometer), cruise control, and radio (speed-compensated volume). The LS ECMs accept the two-wire analog VSS input and provide square wave output. For proper system operation, connect the original VSS wiring to the LS ECM/PCM and then route the ECM's square wave output to the VSS dark green/white wire at the passenger-side under-dash connector.

The 1992–1996 acceleration slip regulation (ASR) system interfaces minimally with engine controls. It monitors RPM increases relative to throttle position, first retarding timing via the ECM/PCM and then mechanically reducing the throttle to control wheelspin. ASR will no longer be functional after C4 ECM/PCM replacement. Most LS-conversion owners prefer direct throttle control over electronic intervention. The antilock braking system (ABS) remains functional, provided the engine RPM data wiring is completed to the module.

The 1984–1996 C4 engine harness integrates with dashboard, forward lamp, and A/C harnesses. Dashboard connections provide gauge operation, while the forward lamp harness includes cooling fan control, evaporative emissions solenoids (1984–1990), and the air injector reaction (AIR) pump (1992–1996). The A/C engine control harness provides data for cooling fan operation and compressor engagement.

The underhood harnesses should be removed, starting behind the battery at the C-100 bulkhead connector, which consists of the engine main and forward lamp harness connector. The connector is nasty, full of anti-corrosion grease, and requires cover removal after separating the upper and lower halves. Mineral spirits or kerosene work well to remove the grease.

You do not have to remove the forward lamp harness from the engine compartment. I don't recommend it unless repairs are required. The forward lamp harness is quite difficult to remove and reinstall across the underside of the front bumper.

There is a center firewall A/C control harness bulkhead connector with various connector methods. This harness is part of the main engine harness and should be removed. Disconnect the inner harness connectors and remove the harness and wiring as an assembly. The A/C system's vacuum supply and the 1984–1987 C4's heater-control valve lines must be disconnected from under the dash for removal of the harness.

There are multiple connectors to disconnect under the passenger-side dash concerning the A/C and engine interface passing through the firewall. The fuel-injector power, ECM ignition (12 volt), and VSS connect to the main engine harness here. The service engine soon (SES) light control, fuel-pump control, and grounds also pass through these connectors, as do the wires for air conditioning, windshield-washer pump, and wiper-delay control. To find out which wiper/washer wire does what, look at the windshield wiper-washer page in the factory service manual (not the engine controls section).

The 1984–1989 main engine harness is routed under the A/C blower motor. It must be disconnected before engine harness removal. A red, high-amperage, 12-gauge wire supplies 12-volt battery power to the A/C high blower relay. Check the connector for melting due to overheating. The wire terminal connectors are often misshapen, which can cause overheating.

This is what you'll find under the passenger-side dashboard. The connectors are marked with General Motors factory service manual connector designations to locate wires to be utilized in the LS swap harness. They must be identified and marked for interfacing with the LS harness.

This 1984–1989 harness connector is routed under the A/C blower motor. Note the black nylon tube next to the three-wire T56 connector. This is the A/C control system vacuum and must be retained for correct A/C system operation. The black ground wire is the A/C blower-motor ground.

We use a Waytek-supplied Littelfuse fuse/relay panel (part number 45982) to handle an LS engine swap's harness power requirements. The relay handles the original LS wire harness configuration that powers the fuel-injector and ignition-coil fuses. While the fuse portion of the panel powers the fuel injectors, ignition coils, MAF, and ECU ignition power circuits, part number 45982 has all of the pieces required except the terminals and wire seals. Waytek has the 280 female terminals available in various wire gauges for complete coverage. A W-crimp wire terminal crimper is required to properly install the terminals on the wiring. It is available from Waytek for a reasonable price.

General Motors and most aftermarket ECU suppliers make sure that the ignition-coil ground wires are bolted to the back of the cylinder heads. This can be difficult to access for wire terminal installation, so it is highly recommended to heed the warning that the grounds must be bolted to the back of the cylinder heads. Moving the wiper motor out of the way helps on the driver's side, but the passenger's side is difficult to access. This ground wire eye terminal has two metal tabs for wire strain relief, which over time keeps the wire strands from breaking away from the terminal.

It is always a good practice to place ground wires in different locations to avoid crosstalk and allow one ground circuit to seek a ground from another. I split them up and place a few on the driver's and passenger's side of the engine, and some end up on the frame. Always have at least a 4-gauge cable connected from the engine to the frame.

Now that you've examined what's involved in an LS swap, carefully prioritize your component selection:

LS Swap Summary/Cost Factor Index	
Cost	Item
$	The 1984–1993 automatic-transmission C4s with original transmissions provide the most economical option. These use cable-operated throttle bodies without engine-transmission controller compatibility concerns. The 1984 cars require major hood modification or replacement.
$$	The 1984–1988 4+3 overdrive manual-transmission C4s require affordable bellhousing swaps and hydraulic clutch upgrades. No controller compatibility issues exist. The 1984–1987 models need cable throttle bodies, while 1988 models without TV cables can use drive-by-wire if desired.
$$$	The 1989–1996 ZF 6-speed and 1994–1996 automatic C4s demand greater investment. ZF conversions require expensive bellhousings and clutch assemblies, while 1994–1996 automatics require aftermarket controllers, preventing the use of donor-engine ECUs.
$$$$	New LS/LT crate engines paired with T-56/TR6060 manual transmissions or high-performance 4L65E automatic transmissions represent the premium tier. As always, maximum performance commands maximum investment.

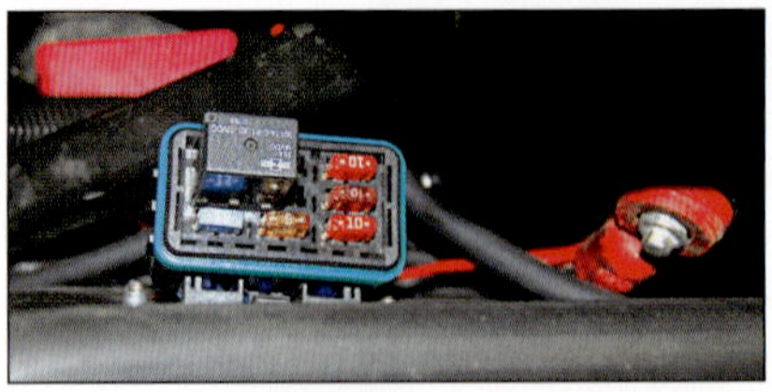

This simple Littelfuse 18-circuit fuse/relay panel handles all of the LS-engine swap harness power requirements. The fuses are for the fuel injectors, ignition coils, and electronic control unit (ECU) ignition power. The 5-amp fuse is for mass-airflow (MAF) sensor power.

The engine harness and positive battery cable cross over the rear of the engine. It is best that the wire harness and positive battery cable are retained to avoid pinching them between the engine and transmission during assembly.

An original 1990–1996 C4 ECM/PCM support can be modified to retain any ECU. This area will work for all C4 applications 1984–1996 after a plastic support has been fabricated to avoid inadvertent voltage loading. The majority of aftermarket and later General Motors ECUs are weatherproof, so there's no need to keep the ECU under the dash.

The ground wire can be difficult to access for wire terminal installation. Having the wiper motor out of the way helps on the driver's side. The passenger's side can be accessed with some difficulty.

More ground wires for the LS engine swap are placed on the driver's side of the engine. Note the black heat-shrink tubing on the wiring and terminals. This provides strain relief, keeps the wire and terminal tight, and keeps some of the typical moisture and debris off the terminal wire crimp.

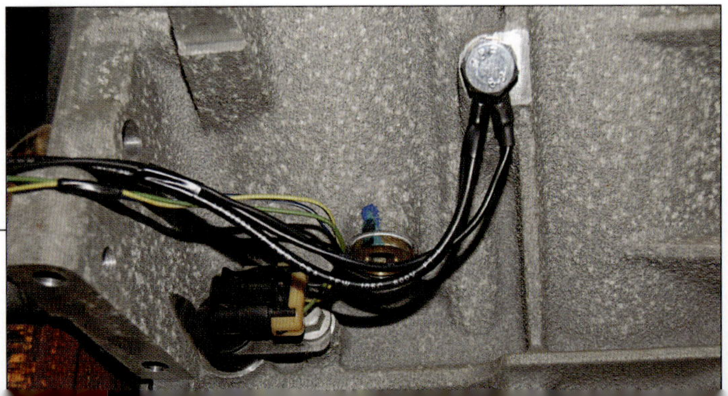

CHAPTER 5

Nitrous Oxide, Turbocharging, and Supercharging

A nitrous oxide (N_2O) system is simple to install, the least expensive option to increase power, and a way to make huge power gains. Supercharging is instant gratification with a smooth idle if you retain the original General Motors camshaft. Turbocharging can be a bit slower to react but makes you planted in your seat under full throttle. Both supercharging and turbocharging cost considerably more than N_2O. Internal engine damage can be extensive if installation and tuning is performed improperly.

N_2O Systems

Adding an N_2O system provides the most cost-effective power enhancement, and today's systems feature sophisticated multistage applications. For those seeking intermittent performance boosts and are willing to manage bottle changes, this is the most economical option. N_2O circumvents the L98 TPI intake restrictions by expanding intake air directly into the cylinders to provide the quickest and most affordable major power enhancement for TPI engines. The LT1/LT4 engines, with their superior airflow, respond even more favorably to nitrous.

N_2O provides substantial power enhancement potential with minimal impact on engine longevity when properly installed and tuned. However, an improper setup can cause catastrophic damage. Fundamentally, activating the system triggers a rapid oxygen increase, elevating cylinder pressure (not compression ratio) and demanding additional fuel, resulting in immediate horsepower gains. Before installation, thoroughly research how N_2O affects the intake charge and engine tuning requirements.

N_2O kits start at 50 hp and scale upward based on budget. Higher power levels necessitate corresponding internal engine reinforcements to withstand the increased pressure on rotating components. In my experience, regularly exceeding 150-hp shots warrants strengthened internals. Systems come in two varieties. Wet kits incorporate supplementary fuel delivery, and dry kits rely on existing fuel injectors and programming for additional fuel.

Dry N_2O kits have power limitations due to fuel-delivery constraints. They require either increased fuel pressure or ECM/PCM programming adjustments, and aftermarket ECUs provide the most reliable solution. For budget-conscious installations, evaluate the dry-versus-wet system cost differences. For 1985–1991 C4s, dry systems perform the best with fuel-management units that increase pressure, while 1994–1996 PCMs offer improved performance through programming. When upgrading to aftermarket engine controllers, wet N_2O systems become the logical choice.

A great way to learn the ins and outs of N_2O installation is to read CarTech's *How to Install and Tune Nitrous Oxide Systems* by Bob McClurg.

Holley's NOS-brand N_2O wet kit has the correct plate to introduce fuel and N_2O with accuracy into a tuned port injection (TPI) L98, LT1, or LT4 engine. Start at 75 hp and increase to what your engine's rotating components can handle. (Photo Courtesy Holley Performance Products)

Installing N_2O on your 1984 Corvette will require some ingenuity. There are no single throttle-body plates to feed the intake under the throttle bodies. A machine shop can make a sandwich plate that is captured by the existing throttle body. It can be used wet or dry, and it takes two sandwich plates and a lot of plumbing. Another option is to place nozzles in the center of the intake manifold. I suggest a dry system or find a shower head–type fuel nozzle that can disperse the fuel equally to make it a wet system.

There is absolutely a dry-system fueling concern, which makes the wet system more agreeable. A 1984 C4 dry system requires boosting fuel pressure, which will throw off the entire fueling circuit. Poor low-speed throttle performance is expected. A wet system is fuel tunable with the proper jetting. I use nylon bolts and tethers for the intake manifold top plate in the event of a backfire.

All 1985–1996 Corvettes respond favorably to wet N_2O kits, which offer easier tuning at a minimal cost. Although they require additional fuel plumbing, these systems allow jet changes for precise tuning. Installation involves sandwiching the N_2O plate between the throttle body and the intake plenum to provide the most discreet integration. Supply lines can route alongside the intake-manifold base with control solenoids mounted inconspicuously on the firewall. Activation options include simple switches or sophisticated throttle-position-based programming. These systems typically deliver at least an additional 100 hp when the bottle pressure remains adequate.

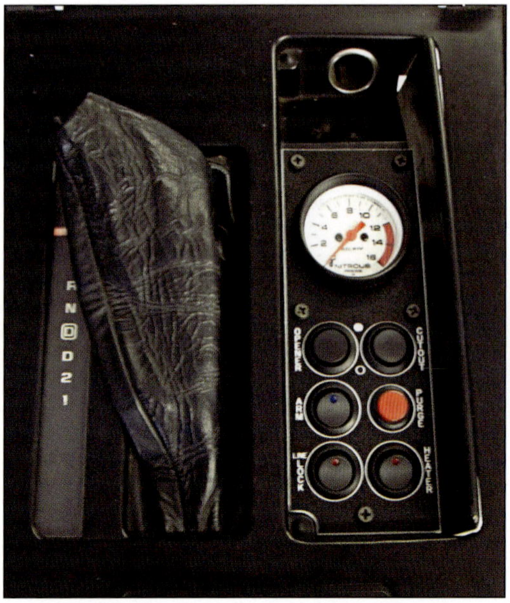

This hidden C4 panel in the console features an N_2O switch assembly that is available from eBay seller "blothruv6." Two versions are available: one for C4 Corvettes from 1984 to 1989 and one for C4 Corvettes from 1990 to 1996. The gauge is not included. The fabricator will configure up to six control switches per your request. An activation switch can be mounted on the shifter knob or controlled through an aftermarket fuel-control system.

Advanced port-injected N_2O systems provide virtually unlimited power potential for serious racing applications. These setups integrate dedicated fuel/N_2O injectors with sophisticated engine controllers that start at 300-plus hp gains. Controllers stage nitrous delivery strategically for optimal traction management. Such applications demand purpose-built engine internals, so the cost considerations are secondary to performance. Users must monitor the bottle level and temperature constantly for maximum effectiveness. Specialized hardware is needed for serious drag racing applications.

The bottle placement presents significant challenges in C4 Corvettes. A standard 5-pound bottle is 19 inches long (including the valve) by 6 inches in diameter, which is difficult to conceal within the limited interior space. The proper orientation (valve-end elevated) for maximum extraction further complicates positioning in coupes and convertibles.

Always install the N_2O bottle's high-pressure blow-off tube. Make sure that it exits the passenger compartment and will not blow back into the passenger compartment. This important tube connects the N_2O bottle's pressure-relief valve to an outside area in the case of an overheated bottle or leaking valve, which can lead to N_2O entering the passenger compartment.

Bottles may require heating for optimal performance. A temperature of 84°F to 97°F must be maintained to keep N_2O in a liquid state. To prevent N_2O loss between uses, close the main valve. This necessitates either manual operation or electric valve actuators that must be remembered before engagement. Nothing disappoints like a failure to launch when competition awaits. You can find switch panels available with an arm, bottle openers, heater control, purge, etc. for 1990–1996 C4s on eBay. The 1984–1989 C4s require the same switches, but you need to come up with on your own and make a plate for the switches that you need.

Turbocharging

Turbocharging is an attractive solution, but it has a premium cost when compared to other power adders.

A turbocharger harnesses exhaust energy to drive a compressor wheel that pressurizes intake air to create efficient power gains. While early systems suffered noticeable lag during spool-up at lower RPM, modern designs with optimized turbine blades accelerate more quickly. With sufficient investment, contemporary systems virtually eliminate lag.

This represents the most technically demanding conversion, and it requires fabrication and welding expertise. Configuring exhaust routing, turbocharger placement, intercooler integration, and intake systems demands meticulous planning and comprehensive tool access. Personal welding ability or professional fabrication assistance is essential. Unlike other modifications, no dedicated C4 Corvette do-it-yourself turbocharger kits have been developed since the model's introduction.

The engine's internals are another consideration. Increased boost demands progressively stronger and more expensive components to manage additional pressure. This complex undertaking requires extensive commitment. However, a properly designed, engineered, and tuned installation creates a truly distinctive C4. I recommend doing thorough research, starting with CarTech's turbocharging book, *Turbo: Real World High-Performance Turbocharger Systems* by Jay Miller, and comprehensive planning before purchasing any components.

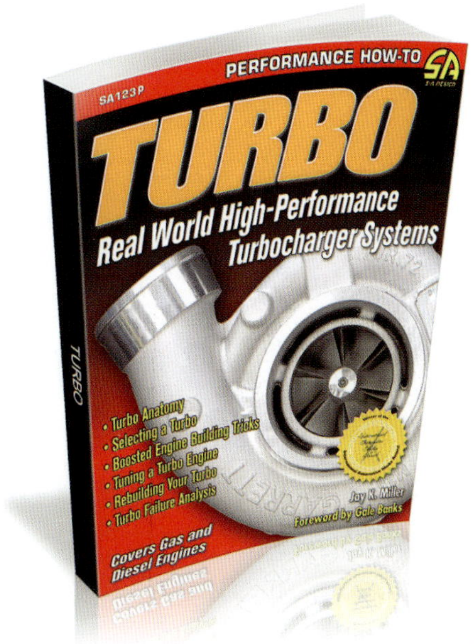

Reeves Callaway took the C4 to the next level when it designed and built its turbocharged C4 Corvettes. General Motors was impressed enough to have regular production option (RPO) B2K available to C4 owners. This was no small feat. The C4 Callaway Corvettes were built, warrantied by General Motors, and passed emissions standards of the era. The B2K option started at $18,000, and near the end of its run in 1991, it was $27,000. It's a bargain when you consider the thought, analysis, and commitment to the transformation.

The engineering was top notch with twin turbos and intercoolers fed by National Advisory Committee for Aeronautics (NACA) ducts in the hood. All of this beautiful work, except for the NACA ducts, was stuffed under the stock-appearing hood. The transition, as boost was applied, was smooth and potent, pushing you back into the seat. At speed, the exhaust note was clean and not overpowering.

Electronically controlled additional fuel injectors added fuel as boost pressure rose. The serpentine-belt tensioner was retrofitted as a scavenge pump for turbo's oil return. It was true engineering for the long haul. All of the Callaway cars are built for the highway—not for sitting in a garage. It was always impressive to see a Callaway twin-turbo car drive a thousand miles and then compete at a local track without wavering.

Driving a C4 Corvette is a great way to enjoy 400 hp and 575 ft-lbs of torque. This Callaway gets 20 miles per gallon.

This Calloway Corvette uses additional fuel injectors to spray fuel onto the throttle body blades to continually cleaned them under acceleration. The air inlet is a thing of beauty and is sculpted for maximum flow in the constrained area.

This is one of those scenarios where buying a complete car may make the most sense. The typical auction prices are $25,000 to $40,000 for low-mileage examples, but they may need maintenance performed up front. Scratch-building a

The twin turbos and intercoolers make under-hood chores tougher. The intercooler design was well thought out and can easily be removed for spark plug changes or valve-cover gasket changes.

turbocharged C4 is going to exceed $25,000 no matter how nice the car is before you start. Callaway has a strict policy concerning supplying proprietary parts. You must have a vehicle identification number (VIN) and proof of ownership to avoid clones. There are some cloned bumpers and exterior pieces available, but under the hood is where it counts. The Callaway turbocharging system is unmistakable.

Supercharging

Supercharger kits that were available during the 1985–1996 Corvette production era provided weekend installation for mechanically-inclined owners. These systems used boost-sensitive ignition timing controls connected to vacuum/pressure lines for wide-open-throttle adjustment. Fuel management units (FMUs) with supplementary pumps increased fuel pressure proportionally with boost to reach 100 psi. The 1985–1991 factory ECMs required FMUs for satisfactory low-RPM performance. Among 1992–1996 models, 30-lbs/hour fuel injectors were used early on, and throttle performance suffered. FMUs replaced the 30-lbs/hour injectors for enhanced drivability, while 1994–1996 PCMs supported 30-lbs/hr injectors with proper programming to eliminate FMU dependency. Batch-fired versus sequential fuel injectors was covered in previous chapters.

Supercharging's primary disadvantage involves heat generation during air compression, which raises the intake air temperatures. Systems incorporate intercoolers (essentially heat exchangers that are mounted ahead of the radiator) to cool the pressurized air. This solution has merit with a few concerns. Adding an intercooler (an air-to-air radiator) in front of the A/C compressor and radiator creates friction, slowing and limiting the airflow through all of the components. When your C4 is sitting in traffic, flow through the intercooler is limited, and heat builds. It takes a few miles to stabilize this heat and cool the supercharger's incoming airflow.

In 1987, Gregg Carroll at Carroll Supercharging, now blowerworks.net, began developing supercharged C4 Corvettes using water/methanol injection from reservoirs to cool the intake charge and add power. Gaseous intercooling applied the much-needed water/methanol cooling liquid under all supercharged events. If you're sitting in gridlock traffic, gaseous intercooling is ready immediately upon acceleration. Don't leave the gridlock throttle to the floor. Let the engine temperatures stabilize no matter what intercooling system you use.

Detonation-induced (ping or spark knock) piston damage is why some form of intercooling is required. The 1987-and-newer Corvette's hypereutectic lighter-weight pistons, which have reduced ring friction that is beneficial for naturally aspirated applications, are a liability under boost. Factory cast pistons should be replaced with forged alternatives before supercharger installation. Forged pistons will not succumb as easily to spark knock. Prolonged spark knock damages the crankshaft rod and main bearings.

Race-trim supercharger systems that exceed 12 pounds of boost require mechanical intercooling. Using both intercooling methods is the best plan to maximize horsepower and prevent engine damage as boost pressures rise. One major downside to mechanical intercooling is the required real estate of components. There are many connecting parts, and the engine compartment gets tight. Tight engine compartments are to be expected with true racing engine setups, and they are usually designed for the quickest access with removal panels.

Water/methanol injection requires maintenance. Infrequent use can create clogged spray ports, especially if you aren't following the recommended fluid mix requirements. Alarms must be in place to inform you when fluid level or pressure is down.

Lubrication has two avenues to follow. Use pressurized engine oil or have an oil reservoir in the supercharger housing to recirculate the precious liquid. The onboard lubrication system prevents engine oil contamination in the event of a compressor bearing failure. There is no way to cool the recirculating onboard oil, which is concerning because it endures severe service under boost conditions. The use of pressurized engine oil requires more labor to install as well as a source and return system to be plumbed. If the blower bearing fails, the engine oil is contaminated and requires further inspection. Any time engine oil is contaminated, it requires oil-pan removal for a complete cleaning.

Look into the BlowerWorks "white papers" regarding the development, installation, and use of superchargers on 1985–1996 C4s. The company has specialized in producing C4 Corvette supercharging kits from its inception and can help you build a reliable road warrior.

Supercharging C4s: Tips and Pitfalls

I was among the first Vortech supercharger installers and I performed an installation on a magazine editor's nearly-new 1992 Corvette. Days later, despite following the preliminary instructions adequately, the vehicle returned on a flatbed. An investigation revealed that the harmonic balancer hub and balancer were dangling from the shredded serpentine belt. The underlying issue was that General Motors eliminated the crankshaft key from LT1 balancer hubs. It was deemed unnecessary because ignition timing adjustments weren't required.

Today, the ATI Super Damper (part number 917274) is available, which is a better choice if your budget allows. The hub and balancer installation was covered in chapter 2, which also covers installing a crank trigger on your LT1. Enhanced harmonic cancellation and a keyed hub are important.

ProCharger supplies complete supercharging kits for 1985–1996 C4s. Expect a minimum on-demand horsepower gain of 50 to 75 percent. Performance gains are limited to how far you want to stretch your wallet. Internal engine components will also require upgrading. ProCharger advocates the use of an intercooled intake air system for the best possible performance.

A fuel management unit (FMU) changes your mundane, 250-hp, smooth-idling cruiser into a 350-hp-plus bruiser while maintaining excellent low-speed drivability. An FMU senses manifold vacuum as it drops and regulates fuel pressure to 100 psi when in full boost. The fuel-rail inlet (or supply line) must be connected to the FMU, and the "out" (or boosted) pressure line connects to the fuel rail. Then, a 5/32-inch vacuum hose is connected to the manifold vacuum, sensing the switch to boost pressure.

The 350-ci 5.7L engines with centrifugal superchargers require a minimum 20 to 22 hp to attain 5 pounds of boost. Twelve pounds of boost on the same 350-ci engine may require 50 to 60 hp to spin it. System heat affects the supercharger's boost output and the horsepower that is required to create it. This is why turbocharging is the better option for overall performance. However, the cost versus the reward makes the supercharger a good option for the do-it-yourself C4 owner.

Forced-induction systems provide excellent horsepower gains while preserving smooth-idle, low-end torque, and drivability. However, they create packaging challenges, require additional maintenance, and demand thermal management awareness. The highest-risk situation is during extended idling in traffic with temperatures exceeding 210°F, followed by sudden, full-throttle acceleration. This combination often leads to detonation-induced piston damage, particularly

The crankshaft keyway was machined, an early-style key was installed in the crankshaft, and the balancer hub was secured with red Loctite on the bolt, which was torqued to 70 ft-lbs. This resolved the issue permanently. Subsequently, all our installations included keyway machining.

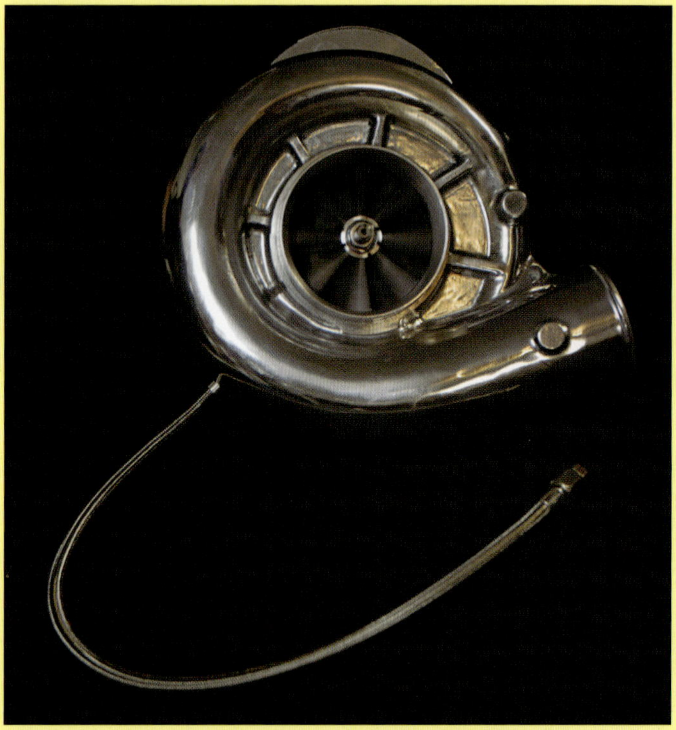

The compressor wheel of this early Vortech supercharger forces air out of the fan blades and into the outer circular housing. The steel braided line is an oil-supply line to provide lubrication and cooling for the spinning bearing at speeds of up to 50,000 rpm.

ring-land failure on stock L98/LT1 cast pistons. Discipline is crucial. Allow engine temperatures to stabilize below 200°F before applying full power. ■

This 1985 Corvette features an engine swap and major power upgrade: a 1993 LT1 Corvette engine with a Vortech supercharger. The Vortech supercharger was a complete kit with an oil-feed system. There is no extra room for anything at the front of the engine.

A timing pointer was added after checking the top dead center (TDC) position. We felt that it was necessary for tuning purposes after the Holley HP engine control unit (ECU) was added to control the engine fuel load and spark timing.

The early Vortech kit required removal of the supercharger for belt replacement. A BlowerWorks serpentine belt retrofit was installed on this 1992 LT engine. The retrofit applies to all 1992–1996 models. The oil-fed supercharger was replaced with an onboard-sump oiling system.

Fuel management units (FMUs) allow fuel-pressure adjustments with shims to raise fuel pressure to typically 100 psi at 8–10 pounds of boost. Clamp the vacuum-boost hose to the FMU and the vacuum source to keep the hose in place at maximum boost.

CHAPTER 6

Fuel System

All C4 ECM/PCMs manage fuel-pump priming duration and use programmed fuel maps to determine the fuel-injector pulse width. Throttle position, manifold absolute pressure (MAP), mass airflow (MAF), and temperature sensors all contribute to fuel-delivery calculations.

During start and warmup engine cycles, open-loop fuel strategy is used. Open-loop strategy does not adjust fuel delivery via oxygen-sensor input. Once the catalytic converters reach an operating temperature (600°F to 650°F) and a 180°F coolant temperature is achieved, the oxygen-sensor input closed-loop fuel strategy takes over. At wide-open throttle (WOT), depending on throttle activation speed, fuel strategy reverts to open loop. Closed-loop fuel control remains under slow throttle-speed ramp up. Once you achieve a steady throttle state, closed-loop fuel control takes over up to WOT. This information can help immensely when diagnosing fuel-system performance issues.

Open- and closed-loop fuel strategies occur in cells or blocks that are in an engine tuning map. The cells are in a volumetric efficiency (VE) table with RPM on one axis and MAP and/or MAF on the other. Open-loop operation uses the VE table to determine fuel requirements. If the engine doesn't perform well at start-up or WOT, ECM/PCM programming is the concern if fuel requirements are met. This is where having a scanner and the factory service manual comes into play and the fuel integrator or fuel trim can be viewed. If the engine has reduced power at WOT and during the scan the fuel trims in closed-loop are maxed out when adding fuel, there is a fuel delivery problem.

Closed-loop uses air-fuel ratios of 14.7 (14 parts air to 1 part fuel), which is the perfect stoichiometric air-to-fuel ratio. The cells, or blocks, strive to maintain the programmed air-to-fuel ratio while in closed-loop operation. For 1984–1991 C4s, fuel adjustment is shown through the fuel integrator, where a value of 160 indicates adding fuel and a value of 96 indicates reducing fuel. For 1992–1996 C4s, fuel adjustments are represented by fuel trim values that are positive (adding fuel) or negative (removing fuel) percentages.

If the scanner oxygen-sensor reading is below 0.850 at WOT, this is when engine damage can occur. If adjusting fuel pressure does not

When fuel-pressure testing takes place, testers should have long hoses to allow the pressure to be viewed under throttle. If you have a scanner, it should be connected to check the oxygen-sensor voltage. You do not have to check oxygen sensor wide-open throttle (WOT) readings in the higher gears (fourth gear or overdrive). Second gear is sufficient and most likely will keep you out of trouble.

This high-load spring and diaphragm control the fuel pressure. You can add 1/2-inch flat washers between the cover and use a large spring to boost pressure. Typically, the goal is 50 psi with no engine vacuum applied to the cover. The injector spray pattern was crisper, so we added more fuel to the pound-per-hour equation. The downside is possibly removing the cover multiple times to obtain the desired fuel pressure.

The Lingenfelter Super Ram intake manifold on this 1985 C4 383-ci engine has an adjustable fuel pressure regulator. This is one of the few benefits of the Super Ram (when it comes to access).

This BBK adjustable fuel-pressure regulator cover kit allows simple adjustment of 1985–1991 tuned port injection (TPI) fuel pressure. Fuel pressure must be relieved before replacing the fuel-pressure regulator cover. Transfer the disc from the original cover to the adjustable fuel-pressure regulator cover. Install the new cap. Turn the center 8-mm screw clockwise to increase the fuel pressure. (Photo Courtesy BBK)

have an effect on the oxygen-sensor readings, fuel-injector and/or flow restrictions may be the concern. Programmable read-only memory (PROM) chip programming is another area of concern. Maintaining the required consistent fuel pressure is key. Inadequate pressure compromises performance and increases the risk of engine damage.

Insufficient pressure creates lean conditions. Typically, power drops before potential catastrophic piston failure. While simplified, this explanation acknowledges that throttle position, manifold pressure, mass airflow, and temperature sensors all contribute to fuel-delivery calculations. Fuel system performance critically affects maximum power output.

Excessive fuel pressure causes increased consumption and a sluggish throttle response. At WOT, the injector pulse width remains unchanged while delivering more fuel with increased fuel pressure and reduced maximum power while depositing soot on oxygen sensors. This contamination distorts sensor readings and potentially triggers additional fuel delivery during closed-loop operation to worsen the overfueling cycle. While midrange performance might briefly feel enhanced, peak power diminishes due to insufficient combustion temperatures. Severely excessive fuel pressure creates lazy throttle response throughout the power band.

Regarding pressure fundamentals, fuel systems use restrictions to build pressure with excess returned via bleed-off circuits. Increasing restriction raises pressure, but flow dynamics complicate this relationship. With additional pump capacity, pressure can increase while maintaining the same restriction. Conversely,

Fuel System Safety

Exercise extreme care when testing pressure or modifying fuel systems. Residual pressure remains after pump shutdown and can reach 20-plus psi on hot days. Always remove the fuel cap before servicing to relieve tank pressure. Fuel spraying at 45 psi creates severe fire hazards. Pressure bleeds gradually and requires minutes to deplete even after pump deactivation. Any fuel line leakage requires immediate repair. ■

Fuel-Pressure Regulator Access

The 1985–1991 L98 TPI engine's fuel-pressure regulator access is restricted. It requires a bit of finesse to access the screws around the fuel regulator cover. It's not impossible, and removing the distributor cap will help you gain more access. I use a short T15 anti-tamper Torx bit with a short wrench to break the screws loose and then ease them out. ■

if flow diminishes under increased demand, pressure drops accordingly. Therefore, pumps must provide excess capacity to maintain pressure during peak demand. Given these relationships, accurate fuel-pressure testing becomes essential when diagnosing performance issues.

Fuel-injector flow rate rises exponentially as fuel pressure rises. Using an adjustable fuel-pressure regulator allows you to add fuel for performance upgrades. A scanner set on oxygen-sensor readings with an assistant allows you to check oxygen-sensor voltage while under WOT. With a target of 0.920 to 0.950 maximum oxygen-sensor voltage, higher readings indicate that it is too rich. A chassis dynamometer is recommended for the best possible tune. On the dynamometer, the engine makes more power at 0.920 than 0.940, which makes the dynamometer valuable when seeking the maximum performance.

Fuel Filters

The first priority is to verify that the fuel filters are clean and unrestricted. Always replace the fuel filter for new projects and during maintenance. Although the General Motors manual does not specify an interval (a fact that is often cited by resistant owners), this reflects GM's inability to account for varying fuel quality from different sources.

The 1984 Corvette fuel-pressure testing presents unique challenges without factory test ports. Accurate readings require tapping into the line before the injectors. One method involves disconnecting the output side of the under-car fuel filter and installing a tee fitting between filter output and the throttle-body supply line.

For 1985–1996 C4 fuel filter replacement, locate and remove the fuel-pump fuse in the main fuse panel. Start the engine, run it for a few seconds, and turn it off. Do this a few times. This procedure will keep free-flowing fuel out of your armpits. With 1985–1991 models, replace the fuel filter. For 1992–1996 models, disconnect the hoses at the fuel rail. Follow the fuel-rail braided hoses to the A/C evaporator case. Remove the 10-mm nut and clamp to lower the lines as an assembly. Remove the fuel filter from the fuel lines and drop the fuel filter and lines together for filter exchange.

Three O-rings are required for 1992–1996 models: one for each side of the fuel filter and one for the return line. The O-rings do not come with the fuel filter. The fuel return line O-ring has a 5.1-mm inside diameter, an 8.3-mm outside diameter, and is 1.6-mm thick. The supply line has a 5.7-mm inside diameter, a 9.5-mm outside diameter, and is 1.9-mm thick. The fluorocarbon-based fluoroelastomer (FKM) material is available from McMaster Carr or theoringstore.com. The same O-rings are required for the 1985–1991 C4s.

For the 1992–1996 C4s, the plastic fuel-line release tools are pushed onto the fuel line to push the retaining springs back. Then, the line can be pulled off the tube. The tool works best if the flex-fuel braided hose is pushed toward the fuel line before pushing the release tool toward the hose.

Accessing the 1992–1996 fuel filter can be an issue. If you have a convertible, the X-frame makes it even tighter. The lower fuel return line was removed first, and the fuel filter and line assembly can now be removed to replace the fuel filter.

Fuel-Pressure Requirements

The 1984 Corvette L83 engines operate at 10 to 13 psi with their shower-head injection system. This design relies on engine vacuum to draw the air-fuel mixture into the cylinders after it is mixed in the intake manifold. The minimal pump demands contribute to long-term reliability, although the system still requires a minimum constant pressure of 10 psi for proper operation and suffers performance degradation with pressure loss.

The 1985–1996 Corvette L98, LT1, and LT4 engines require 36- to 42-psi fuel pressure. The vacuum-referenced regulator system decreases pressure (36 to 39 psi) during high-vacuum conditions (idle/light load) and increases pressure (42 to 46 psi) during low-vacuum conditions (high load). This effectively provides adaptive injector flow rates according to engine demand.

There is a pressure-test port on the fuel rail that requires a 90-degree fitting. When you finish your testing, have a cloth available to gather the fuel that will leak out. Slowly loosen the fitting to let the pressure drop before fully removing the connecting hose.

Fuel Tanks, Pumps, and Senders

Regarding fuel tanks, pumps, and senders, water contamination invariably causes corrosion damage. The critical C4 filler-boot drain hose frequently clogs and allows water accumulation that trickles into the tank that can degrade performance and prevent starting. Over time, plastic bladders deteriorate and allow moisture to collect between the bladder and steel shell, which promotes corrosion and eventual leakage. Suspected contamination warrants immediate tank inspection. C4 fuel tanks are susceptible to "middle-age bulge" when the liners succumb to the ravages of fuel blends, causing liner growth. Fuel capacity is limited. The fuel-sender float arms eventually hang up on the bulge and create inaccurate fuel-gauge readings. The bulge eventually protrudes enough to stop the fuel sender float arm from rising or falling.

Access to the C4 fuel pump/fuel level sender for pump replacement is excellent. Remove the fuel-pump fuse and perform the fuel pressure relief procedure. After removing the fuel-filler door, remove the fuel-filler boot. Remove the return, supply, and vent hoses. Be careful when removing the hoses. It is a big deal if the hose requires replacement. If the 10-mm sender retaining screws are tight when they are removed, work them in and out a few times to knock off corrosion and avoid breaking them.

There is a plastic trough at the bottom of the fuel tank. These troughs break off from the plastic pins that they are secured to, resulting in poor acceleration or loss of fuel flow during hard cornering. They worsen as fuel levels drop. Grit, metal, and organic pieces accumulate here, which is bad for the fuel-pump impellers. They stop the impeller or break off vanes and limit the amount of available fuel pressure. If you install a new pump and the supplier finds debris while investigating why it stopped working, the warranty will be void.

Complete fuel tank replacement kits are available without the OEM plastic safety bladder, which raises potential safety concerns, given the tank's proximity to occupants. However, 28-plus-year-old plastic bladders likely offer minimal crash protection advantage over modern steel tanks. Major suppliers, such as Corvette Central, Mid America, and Zip Products, offer comprehensive kits, including the tank, sending unit (minus pump), sender seal, mounting straps, filler boot, and hardware.

If it comes to fuel tank replacement, it is not as friendly. Fuel tank replacement requires removal of the rear bumper cover and support. Remove the two tank tethers under

The LT1 and LT4 fuel pressure regulators are much easier to access, as shown on this LT1 fuel rail. This direct-fit regulator requires return-line removal, and two Torx-bit screws are removed for replacement on the fuel rail. Always replace the O-rings.

The entire fuel pump/fuel-level sender can be removed after the fuel door has been removed for pump replacement. If you drop a screw when removing the assembly, it can be a time-intensive process to retrieve it. A fallen screw may be in the area below, in the spare tire carrier, or in other areas that are difficult to access.

This cutaway C4 fuel tank, which is lying on its rear side, shows the bladder liner growing. The white tray to the right is where the fuel-pump pickup sits and denotes how close the fuel-level float arm is.

This plastic tray at the bottom of the fuel tank is used to set the fuel-pump pickup screen into. It prevents fuel starvation under high-G loading. All grit and debris must be removed before replacing the fuel pump.

the tank that attach to the rear anti-roll bar mounts. These keep the tank with the body if a crash occurs. The bumper cover is not terrible to remove, but it requires patience, as most of the studs will be corroded, requiring a back-and-forth nut-removal procedure. Coating the studs with rust penetrant helps avoid stud breakage. After the cover has been removed, remove the eight 18-mm, hex-head bolts from the rear bumper crash guard/tank support (there are four on each side of the frame rails).

Alternatively, universal fuel cells offer numerous configurations and are mandatory at certain racing levels. True fuel cells incorporate bladders, foam baffling,

If necessary, drain the fuel tank and have an assistant or two help to lower the tank. Don't forget that the tank tethers under the tank. The entire assembly is dropped down for tank removal from the support.

and rollover-protection valves to control fuel movement and prevent explosions during accidents. These feature replaceable bladders that require periodic service to maintain safety. Fuel cells accommodate virtually any pump (or multiple pumps), pickup assembly, and fuel-level sender to ensure optimal delivery under all conditions. The C4 factory fuel gauges require a 0-ohm empty level/90-ohm full level resistance fuel sender.

Molten Metal Racing sells made-to-order C4 fuel cells. These feature a vital cell protection cage (in narrow or standard width) and have aluminum or steel construction. A tow hook, fuel-level sender, and Hydramat can be added for additional low-fuel starvation protection. Standard foam baffling will keep the engine fed on a level track. (Photo Courtesy Molten Metal Racing)

Molten Metal Racing can configure the perfect fuel cell for serious C4 performance cornering. It can provide fill from the stock location with AN connections for high-horsepower fuel-system requirements. Track time increases with 2 additional gallons of fuel capacity over the C4's original fuel tank. The early-style bumpers require modifications. (Photo Courtesy Molten Metal Racing)

This Aeromotive 15-gallon fuel cell (part number 18660) is the start for a do-it-yourself fuel cell. A significant amount of labor was required to make this ready to use. (Photo Courtesy Jackson Lueg/ Aeromotive)

Vapor Recovery Regarding Tank Pressure

While some pressurization is normal, caps shouldn't forcefully release when opened. Federal regulations mandate onboard vapor-recovery systems to capture and subsequently burn off fuel vapors during steady-state operation. Many 1984-1991 C4s develop corroded vapor-recovery steel lines that cause excessive tank pressure and persistent fuel odors, particularly in enclosed spaces. This is considered to be an emissions system component and does not reduce performance in any way. I always make sure that they are functional, that there is no fuel odor, and that only a small amount of fuel is consumed by the engine.

When we perform engine swaps, the vacuum-control valve on top of the vapor canister is connected to the manifold vacuum. The original evaporative 5/16-inch vacuum line is tee'd into the engine's PCV main hose. The vacuum-control valve empties the charcoal canister when using an aftermarket engine control ECU without electronic fuel-vapor control. The ECU can handle the

The vacuum control valve on top of the vapor canister can be connected to the manifold vacuum. Check the vapor canister's filter at the bottom. If charcoal begins spilling out, it's time for replacement.

This 1991 C4 shows that ethanol-enriched fuel languished for many years and melted the rubber sleeve around the pump. The fuel-pump pickup sock (filter) was full of rust debris from the sending unit.

extra fuel without causing any drivability issues.

Conversely, negative pressure (vacuum) when opening the cap signals potential problems. Incorrect caps combined with powerful pumps can collapse tanks through excessive suction. It typically causes fuel starvation before a complete implosion. Proper atmospheric venting remains essential for system operation. Aftermarket ECUs lacking vapor recovery support may require original caps but risk pressure buildup. The accompanying photos demonstrate alternative vapor management with aftermarket controllers.

Building a Performance Fuel System

The 1985–1996 Corvette fuel pump, which is rated at 225 to 255 liters per hour (lph), safely supports 350 hp. Our testing confirms a capability of 800 hp (naturally aspirated) using quality 340-lph pumps with the original 3/8-inch (outside-diameter) fuel lines. Approaching 1,000 hp requires 450- to 525-lph pumps coupled with upgraded 1/2-inch (outside-diameter) fuel lines to maximize flow capacity. The definitive test is maintaining consistent fuel pressure during wide-open-throttle operation.

The fuel sender is an integral part of the fuel pump. Rust or corrosion destroys fuel senders because the corroded flange extends into the tank area and continually drops pieces of metallic debris into the tank. The worst thing that you can do is scrub the corrosion away with a wire brush. The wire brush removes the rust and rust-inhibitor coating, so the rust will continue to grow and fall into the tank. This will shorten the life of the fuel pump. Either replace the complete sender assembly or painstakingly clean the surfaces and carefully apply an interior fuel-tank coating to the scrubbed surfaces.

The fuel pump and sender require a pass-through voltage and ground connection, which can be a point of much aggravation. Use a replaceable wire lead assembly to connect the fuel-pump sender to a bulkhead connector. If the terminals are compromised, possibly from multiple removal and installation episodes, they will lose connection. I've seen numerous blackened terminals at the fuel-pump-sender bulkhead connector that caused a no-start issue from having no fuel pressure. A minimum of 16-gauge wire should be used for 340-lph replacement fuel pumps.

If you're fueling big horsepower numbers, a replacement pass-through connector is the best policy. Run 12- to 14-gauge wires through the connector for a high-output fuel pump installation. The wires are sealed in place to prevent fuel from leaking out. Be sure to use acetal, nylon, polytetrafluoroethylene (PTFE), or polyurethane insulated wire for in-tank fuel use. It will withstand gasoline, ethanol, and methanol.

Eliminating the 1988–1996 fuel-pressure pulsator that connects the fuel pump to the fuel-output tube is recommended. The Aeromotive 340-lph fuel pump (part number 11569) can handle more than 600 hp (naturally aspirated). It includes all of the attaching pieces. High-quality

This pass-through connector had its fuel-pump wires soldered to the pass-through-connector male terminals. Soldering is recommended for all applications that are less than 500 hp with new, 16-gauge, fuel-compatible wire insulation.

An Aeromotive 340-lph fuel pump is installed in the 1992 C4 fuel sender/pump assembly. The fuel filter, or sock, is removed for the photo. Never leave the pre-filter off. There is a screen that will catch rocks but not smaller debris that can break off pump vanes.

Located at the rear of the L98 and LT1 engines, Aptiv 1.5-mm wire terminals (rated at 24.0 amps) are used to connect the fuel pump and oil-pressure switch. The fuel pump and oil-pressure switch is under a constant 8- to 10-amp load while the engine is running. These terminals are often damaged from overheating.

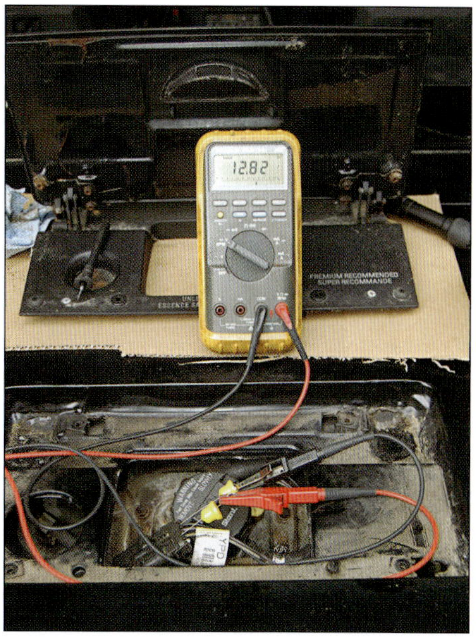

If fuel-pump voltage is below 11.6 under full load with the engine running, check the wiring and terminals for poor fitment or corrosion. Low fuel-pump voltage can cause low fuel pressure and pump damage.

pumps have screens to keep out the big stuff. Always replace the fuel-pump prefilter or sock. A Precision part number L0148, ACDelco G1, or GM 25091503 sending unit to fuel-tank seal is required when installing the fuel pump unit back into the tank.

Increasing the flow requirements elevates the importance of fuel-line routing. Each bend creates restriction, and the tight bends cause significant flow reduction. Upgrading from 3/8- to 1/2-inch lines represents major work that requires fuel tank and differential removal for proper installation. While some use rubber or braided hose to simplify routing, these compromise longevity and heat dissipation. Higher-flow systems necessitate upgraded fuel filters to prevent flow bottlenecks. At this point, you're at race-car status with all custom-built supporting components.

An often-overlooked consideration is that large-capacity pumps (450 to 525 lph) create substantial excess capacity and heat during low-demand operation to potentially shorten pump service life. Companies such as Aeromotive address this with fuel-pump controllers that monitor demand and modulate voltage accordingly.

The C4 fuel-pump diagnostics challenge newcomers due to its unusual control strategy. During starting, the ECM/PCM supplies

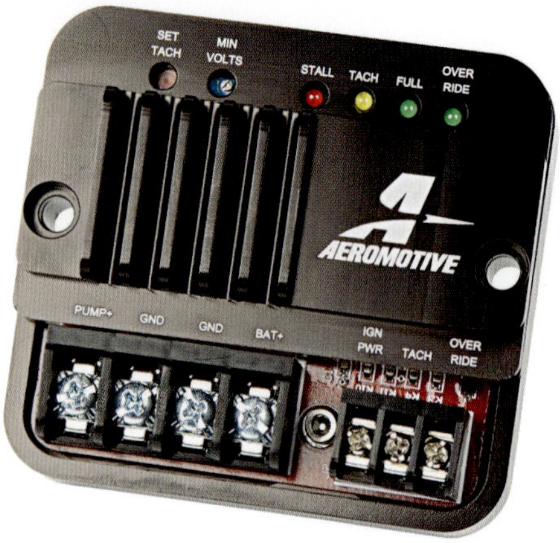

This Aeromotive fuel pump speed controller (FPSC) (part number 16306) monitors engine RPM, matching the duty cycle of the pump to minimize fuel heating and vapor-lock problems. At low demand, the FPSC slows down the fuel pump, reducing the chance of suction-side cavitation and vapor lock. When demand increases, the FPSC returns the fuel pump to a 100-percent duty cycle for maximum flow. (Photo Courtesy Jackson Lueg at Aeromotive)

12 volts through a 20-gauge dark green/white wire to the pump relay for initial priming (2 to 5 seconds). Once running, an oil-pressure switch assumes control and closes contacts to power the pump directly. Therefore, the fuel-pump relay functions only for system priming, not continuous operation. With the relay failure, extended cranking allows oil pressure (above 5 psi) to engage the pump through the pressure switch. If you experience a no-start issue with no fuel pressure, check the wiring and connections at the fuel-pump/oil-pressure sensor connector before replacing the fuel pump.

Fuel-pump wiring presents multiple reliability concerns regarding terminal connections. For maximum longevity, thoroughly inspect the electrical supply and ground quality throughout the extensive 14- to 15-foot wiring run to the pump. Terminal distortion from repeated disconnections creates additional failure points. Modern engine systems, including the LS, incorporate complete ECU control of the pump from startup through operation. It's an improvement worth implementing during LS conversions.

Fuel-Pump Voltage Concerns

Checking fuel-pump voltage at the end of the line is paramount for fuel-pump longevity. Mac Tools and other professional tool suppliers sell thin pins that slide beside the wire into the terminals to avoid wire or wire-seal damage. Typical battery voltage is 14.30 to 14.60 at 1,200 rpm. A 1.5-volt drop is acceptable, considering the length of the required wiring and terminals to get to this point. As voltage drops, so does the fuel pump's efficiency. If the voltage is below 11.6, check the wiring and terminals for poor fitment or corrosion.

Upgrade

Aftermarket innovators, such as Throwback Automotive, developed enhanced fuel-pump power delivery systems. Their kit employs an alternator-sourced 10-gauge direct supply wire that operates through a dedicated relay. This arrangement allows the OEM oil-pressure switch to control the relay with minimal current load. An improved 12-gauge-pump ground circuit optimizes fuel-pump performance. This

The Throwback Automotive fuel-pump direct power kit begins at the top of the fuel tank. Remove the fuel-filler door and boot. Disconnect the existing fuel-sender connectors and connect the supplied in-line harness. When the key is on direct battery, power is supplied to the fuel pump and there's no voltage loss from multiple connections.

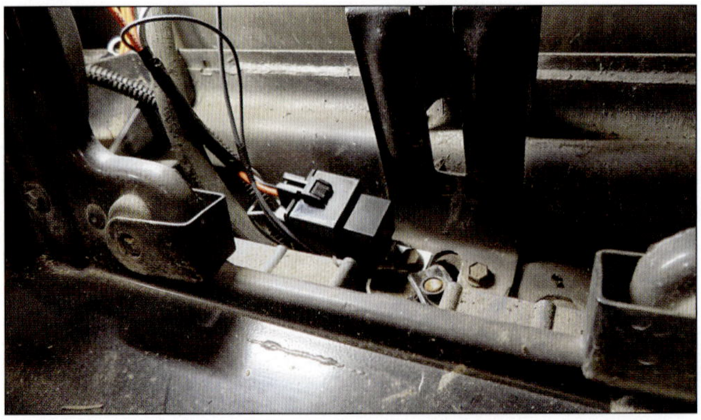

Remove the license plate and drop the fuel-pump relay down for placement on the 10-mm hex spare-tire mount screw. The screw is removed. Then, the relay tab and ground wires are held with the existing screw. The engine is still protected by the low/no oil pressure safety feature. A 20-gauge fuse is provided for circuit safety.

Remove the driver's side lower panel that covers the battery. For 1985–1992, add the orange 10-gauge wire to the battery junction stud. For 1993–1996, add the orange wire to the fuse relay panel power lead stud. The 10-gauge orange wire must be routed under the driver-side lower valance panel over to the fuel pump. Avoid pinch points and the hot exhaust.

system does not circumvent the oil-pressure/fuel-pump switch control. The engine will shut down with oil-pressure loss.

Fuel-Injector Design and Early Challenges

General Motors used two opposing low-impedance fuel-injector composition strategies: pintle and seat-and-ball seating. Bosch and Lucas pintle-style injectors were used from 1985–1988. The injector was placed deep into the cylinder head for the optimal air-fuel mixture, which was ultimately its demise. Labor-intensive TPI intake-manifold fuel-injector access raised warranty cost concerns when injectors failed. Another concern was the injectors causing coking (major carbon deposits) on the intake valves, which caused hard-start concerns.

The coking formed a "walnut" around the intake-valve stem, per Chevrolet technical service bulletins, which caused hard-start complaints as fuel soaked into the growth. The procedure to remove the walnut was labor intensive and required the intake manifold to be removed to break up the walnut. Pintle wear was also a concern and caused minor fuel leakage, especially with contaminated fuel.

GM's in-house Rochester fuel division supplied Multec injectors for 1988–1996 C4s with a unique ball and seat for fuel control. Stories abound concerning fuel-injector coil electrical windings bathed in fuel. The concept works as long as clean, unadulterated fuel is present. To avoid earlier issues with coking, Multecs were shortened, which positioned the nozzle higher in the cylinder head. Some say that it affects performance negatively. The ball-and-seat idea was excellent. A myriad of closure positions kept the injectors drip-free for years.

Common Failures and Cleaning Myths

Fuel-injector cleaning presented a problem: harsh chemicals diminished the internal fuel injectors' coil winding insulation, which shorted them to ground. A shorted-to-ground fuel injector shuts down an entire bank of 1989–1993 C4 cylinders. If the engine starts, it sounds very strange and has zero power. If two injectors are shorted to ground on opposing banks, the engine will not start at all. It's another reason to dislike bank-to-bank fuel-injection strategy.

There was confusion at the dealership level. Many pushed fuel-injector cleaning with standalone fuel-injector machines that use caustic injector chemicals to bathe the injectors. This is a short-term solution. In the long term, the fuel injectors failed from insulator damage. Chevron's Techroline fuel additive is the recommended safe fuel-injector cleaner for all 1989–1996 C4s with Multec fuel injectors.

Well-informed performance and repair shops perform a fuel-injector ohm test when a no-start or poor-performing C4 is involved. The target ohm reading is 12.9 to 14.0. Lower numbers indicate compromised injector windings. C4s stored for long periods of time are susceptible to winding failure. Check the injector ohm reading before attempting to start the engine. If one high-ohm-reading injector is found, replace all of the fuel injectors.

Diagnosing, Sizing, and Upgrading Fuel Injectors

Diagnosing for fuel-injector leakage requires a fuel-pressure tester. Fuel pressure should stay steady after engine shutdown for 5 to 10 minutes and slowly bleed off. If pressure bleeds off as soon as the key is off, leaking injectors or a failing fuel-pump check valve are possible. Leaking fuel injectors can be identified by black smoke from the exhaust and an extended start time. Malfunctioning fuel-pump check valves increase start times as fuel pressure builds, especially after brief shutdown periods, and no black smoke is observed.

The LT1 and LT4 engines allow visual fuel-injector leak testing. Injector rail removal is simple. Disconnect the ignition-coil primary power supply. With the fuel-injector rail sitting up, out of the intake, turn the key to "run" and observe any leakage from the injector tips. Any fuel is no good. They should stay dry. Cycle the key a few times as you observe the injectors.

The L98 TPI engines are on

another level. Removing the injector rail for a visual inspection requires many hours of detailed labor. Remove the fuel door and filler boot. With an assistant, clamp the fuel-supply hose at the fuel sender with hose pinch-off pliers while you observe a fuel-pressure gauge. The clamp must be applied as soon as the assistant shuts down the engine. If the fuel pressure drops off quickly, perform the same procedure with the fuel-pump return hose. Finally, both hoses must be pinched off for verification. At that point, continued fuel leakage warrants fuel-rail removal for inspection.

Fuel injectors are often overlooked and subjected to threats from contaminated fuel and dormancy. The average C4 fuel injector should be replaced due to age and regardless of mileage. Stagnant fuel in dormant fuel injectors turns to varnish that can be difficult to remove. External fuel-injector cleaning will not bring them back to a healthy spray pattern. Worn and water-contaminated fuel injectors typically have damaged pintles and/or ball sealing surfaces, which leads to minor or major fuel leakage.

Correct injector sizing is paramount for overall performance. The OEM fuel-injector flow rate is controversial. Some say that it is 22 lbs/hr, and others say that it is 24 lbs/hr. A flow rate that is off by 2 lbs/hr is not a concern, but one that is off by 6 lbs/hr or more is an issue. Choosing the correct injector requires a fair assessment of engine horsepower to use a brake specific fuel consumption (BSFC) calculator. This value varies with engine load and RPM. Lower numbers indicate greater efficiency. Generally, naturally aspirated engines operate around 0.50, supercharged engines operate at 0.55 to 0.60, and turbocharged applications operate from 0.60 to 0.65. Alternative fuels demand substantially more, as E85 and methanol require 0.63 to 1.0-plus BSFC, particularly with forced induction.

Formulas and Maintenance

The BSFC formula is:

(500 hp x 0.5 BSFC) 250 ÷
(8 injectors x 0.75 injector duty cycle) 6
= 41.66 lbs/hr.

This prime example adds 100 supercharged hp to our LT1:

(450 hp x 0.60 BSFC) 270 ÷
(8 injectors X 0.75 injector duty cycle) 6
= 45.00 lbs/hr is required.

A 1985–1993 fuel management unit (FMU) is required for aggressive low-speed throttle response and full-power at WOT. The 1994–1996 PCM programming handles the additional fuel load. The fuel-injector duty cycle should never be at 100 percent because injector windings overheat and failure is imminent. A 70- to 75-percent duty cycle is recommended with an 80-percent maximum for injector longevity, which allows for some wiggle room when tuning.

A Bosch, or Lucas-style, fuel injector (left) has a longer cone that sprays fuel deeper into the intake manifold and closer to the cylinder head and intake valve. The Multec injector (right) has a higher spray position that keeps carbon buildup off the cone and stays cleaner.

Fuel-injector cleaning, rebuilding, and flow-matching services are available. Fuel Injector Connection provides all of these services for new and rebuilt injectors. The people there will guide you through the selection process and whether you need Multec OEM replacements or 50 lbs/hr Bosch injectors for a 600-hp application.

Quick Check

Hard starting can occur if the connectors for the fuel system, coolant-temperature sensor, or intake air-temperature sensor have failed or are disconnected. This adds copious amounts of fuel for minus 40°F ambient temperatures. In rare instances, a ruptured fuel-pressure regulator diaphragm sprays pressurized fuel into the intake manifold. If the engine starts, it will bellow black smoke.

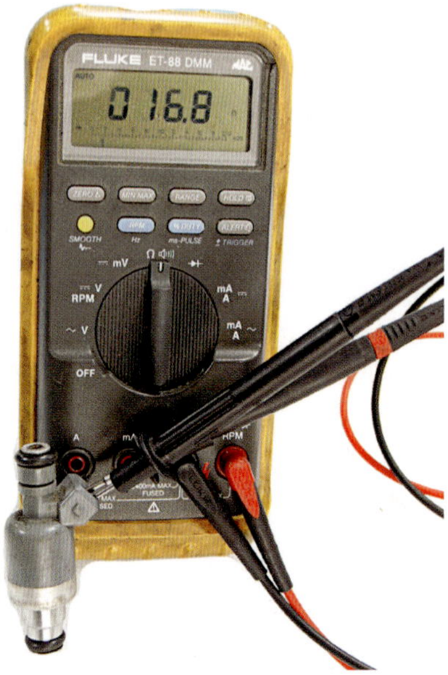

Poor performance or no starting for a 1989–1993 C4 can be attributed to internally shorted fuel injectors. This injector's 16.8-ohm reading is perfect. This gray or black plastic-bodied Multec injector is most susceptible to harsh fuel injector cleaners. Consider an ohm check when changing spark plugs.

EXHAUST SYSTEM

Exhaust system performance encompasses the distance from each cylinder's exhaust port to the tip of the exhaust pipe. Correct exhaust-tube sizing is as important as the tubing bend radius. Blending each exhaust bank's outlet flow aids the overall flow. Exhaust system engineering can increase power or take it away.

These 1985–1991 C4 L98 exhaust manifolds flow well for up to 350 hp after grinding the weld beads and matching the gaskets. The ports have plenty of material to match up to the gaskets. The trick is for the exhaust-manifold ports to match the cylinder-head ports. At the bare minimum, the exhaust ports should be larger than the cylinder-head ports.

Exhaust Manifolds

The 1984–1996 Corvettes employ center-dump exhaust manifolds, which is a design that dates back to 1955. The 1984 L83 Crossfire versions use welded 409 stainless-steel tubing with minimal flow considerations. The 1985–1991 L98 models feature slightly larger tubing with improved welds, which is suitable for their low-RPM/high-torque design parameters. For L98 performance enhancements, using 5/8-inch long-tube headers without the corresponding intake modifications will yield minimal gains and will not justify their cost. A more economical approach involves port matching and weld cleaning the stock manifolds with a rotary (Dremel) tool to improve flow characteristics.

If you upgrade 1985–1991 L98 intake systems with high-flow components, including Mini Ram or Accel Super Ram manifolds, complement them with long, equal-length tube headers for optimal results. This combination supports long-duration camshafts and supercharging applications. Turbocharged setups require custom exhaust manifolds designed to withstand the extreme heat and pressure.

The 1992–1996 LT1/LT4 manifolds utilize cast iron for heat retention, which is essential due to their proximity to the catalytic converters. These are the best-flowing factory C4 manifolds that feature unique center-outlet blend chambers for cylinders 4 through 6 and 3 through 5, plus well-defined D-shaped ports that minimize flow restriction. Budget-conscious builders benefit from these capable designs, which can be further ported to match the cylinder-head openings. General Motors incorporated reinforcements to maintain alignment during thermal cycling. These 1992–1996 cast-iron pieces can replace their 1984–1991 L98 tubular counterparts. Their primary drawback involves potential stud extraction difficulties during disassembly.

The outlet end of these 1985–1991 tubular manifolds requires grinding to smooth the welds. When the port is matched and all excess weld slag is removed, they are pretty good, stealthy pieces. Put the covers back on the manifolds and go have some fun.

Stainless Works has a similar set of headers and front pipes with mini catalytic converters for the 1992–1996 C4. It also has a version of the rear pipes with an X-pipe included. The idea is to have headers that fit in the tunnel and are level with the oil pan.

Emissions Systems

The air injection reaction (AIR) emissions control system, which is often misunderstood and disliked by performance builders, injects non-combustible air into the exhaust for approximately 2 minutes at start-up to reduce cold-start emissions. For 1984–1991 C4s, this system directs air into the catalytic converter via a 1/2-inch tube that connects the converter to the front-mounted control valve to accelerate converter light-off. This federally-mandated system should remain intact and unaltered. All AIR systems incorporate check valves that are positioned near exhaust sources to prevent dangerous backflow.

An electric AIR pump was used for model years 1992–1996. The pump was ECM/PCM controlled and typically ran for the first 2 minutes after start-up with no horsepower loss.

All C4s legally require catalytic converters for public road use under federal and state regulations. While some jurisdictions offer age-based exemptions, others strictly prohibit any modifications, particularly emissions-control components.

The 1984–1991 C4 system utilized a single centrally located monolithic converter with 3-inch connections. This placement delayed reaching the required 450°F to 650°F catalyst operating temperature. The 1986–1991 models added pre-catalytic converters at the manifolds while retaining the central unit. The 1992–1996 design positioned larger converters close to the manifolds to improve flow characteristics and accommodate performance modifications up to 500 hp.

The 1992–1996 catalytic converters were large, monolithic, free-flowing units close to the exhaust manifold for quick warmup and operation. The 1992–1993 C4s had two upstream oxygen sensors close to the catalytic converters. The 1994 models had an additional downstream oxygen sensor to monitor the passenger-side catalytic converter's performance. The 1995–1996 C4s had it all with two upstream and two downstream oxygen sensors. Omitting catalytic converters illuminated the service-engine-soon light on 1995–1996 C4s. Off-road race PCM programming eliminates the sensor coding issue.

Catalytic converters typically deteriorate gradually and progressively restrict power. Primary causes include excess fuel and retarded ignition timing, which eventually fracture

Here, an Air Injector Reaction (AIR) check valve was removed from the exhaust system and a vacuum/fuel pump pressure tester is connected. Exhaust back pressure of less than 4 psi is acceptable. Anything higher means that your catalytic converter is clogged and slowing you down. An oxygen sensor can be removed to check for excessive back pressure.

the honeycomb structure and clog the outlet. Modern high-flow designs minimize performance restrictions. Always verify your state's specific regulations regarding C4 exhaust and emissions compliance.

Shorty versus Long-Tube Headers

Shorty headers flow adequately for 1985–1991 L98 styles with increased-inner-diameter runners and a ported intake manifold. To date, there are no 1984–1991 C4-specific shorty headers available. The 1992–1996 Hooker headers (part number 2061HKR) are a good fit and will connect directly to the existing exhaust system. Beware of universal tight fit or block-hugger shorty headers that mimic the C4 Corvette's center-outlet design. The header tubes or flanges are close to the oil-pan rail.

Beware on Block Hugger shorty headers. The tubes or flange may hit the knock sensor and be close to the oil-pan rail. This is a set of official 1992–1996 shorty headers in place.

This set of American Racing headers clears the straight spark plugs well. The number-2 cylinder tube is routed up and away from the 1985–1991 C4's fuel lines. My suggestion is to save the box, be careful during installation, and check for fitment before making modifications.

A set of Hooker Super Competition coated headers is installed on this 1985 C4. They fit very well with the best ground clearance of all of the headers that I've used. The sleeves at each bolt hole allow the use of factory accessory braces and exhaust-manifold bolts. Some minor accessory brace trimming is required.

When selecting long-tube headers, prioritize fitment and function, particularly ground clearance and proximity to fuel lines, especially on 1985 to 1991 models. Beware of headers routing tubes against fuel

Long-tube headers can be installed much more easily from the bottom. Remove the negative battery cable to avoid accidental arcing (sparks) when the header passes by the starter. Remove the coolant-temperature sensors and spark plugs to avoid breakage. Have a couple of header bolts handy and put at least one into the header flange from the bottom.

The wrapped American Racing headers had no space for the shortest small-block Chevy oil filter that was available. A remote oil filter was mounted on the frame rail. The -10 stainless-steel hoses were used to plumb the Canton 22-592 oil filter adapter with 1/2-inch NPT thread ports to the Canton 22-260 remote-mount filter that uses a Wix 51060R 5-inch-tall filter with an anti-drainback valve.

lines or requiring shorty spark plugs due to clearance issues. The tube sizing should match the engine specifications: $1\frac{5}{8}$-inch primaries suit up to 350-ci/450-hp applications, 1¾-inch primaries for 383 ci/450-plus-hp applications, and $1\frac{7}{8}$-inch primaries for maximum-output engines. Proper oxygen-sensor placement is critical. Position the sensors after the collector merger but before the front pipe connection. Check the supplier's return policy and pay close attention to it. Avoid scratching the header tubes. If you scratch them, you own them.

The stainless-steel headers are covered top to bottom with a Design Engineering titanium exhaust wrap. We also used Stage 8 locking fasteners per the customer's request.

Coatings and Coverings

Header manufacturers recommend starting the engine for the first time with uncoated headers. Tuning is important. Retarded ignition timing and a rich fuel mixture will burn the best coating off in minutes. Header coating damage can be avoided by using an infrared heat imaging tool to monitor header-tube heat as the engine runs. If the header tube's heat builds to more than 900°F, shut down the engine and let it cool. I prefer uncoated headers for a few reasons, mainly concerning fitment. If a header tube is close to a heat-sensitive area, a modification can be made for clearance. Once the fitment is perfected, they go to a ceramic coater.

Exhaust wrapping is controversial. The 304 stainless steel is durable even with the possibility of condensation being trapped between the wrap and header tubes. Uncoated steel or 409 stainless-steel header tubes are a concern. Chances are good that there is considerable corrosion occurring under the wrap. Race engine builders are not concerned with corrosion, but reduced heat matters. They replace the headers and wrapping as required.

For system connections, slip-fit or ball-style collector joints are preferred over three-bolt flanges. Slip-type collectors aren't ideal for enthusiasts who frequently disconnect the exhaust for track events. Ball-style connectors offer easier removal and reinstallation for weekend track use. Traditional three-bolt flanges tend to come into contact with road surfaces and suffer damage over time.

Equal-length header tubes offer optimal performance but command premium prices. Budget online options have diminished due to emissions regulations and liability concerns regarding tampering. Legitimate street-legal headers must be certified and include provisions for the AIR system. The C4 exhaust-component market continues to shrink as EPA requirements evolve and market demand shifts elsewhere. Before you purchase header tubes, thoroughly research availability and confirm stock status and anticipated delivery timeframes for backordered components.

Header Gasket and Fastener Choices

In my early hot-rodding experience, headers inevitably meant constant maintenance with perpetual gasket replacement and fastener tightening. The progression from initial ticking sounds to complete gasket failure seemed inevitable, despite numerous combinations. The breakthrough came with carbon-graphite composition gaskets, which have demonstrated exceptional durability. They have maintained seal integrity beyond 300,000 miles in numerous applications.

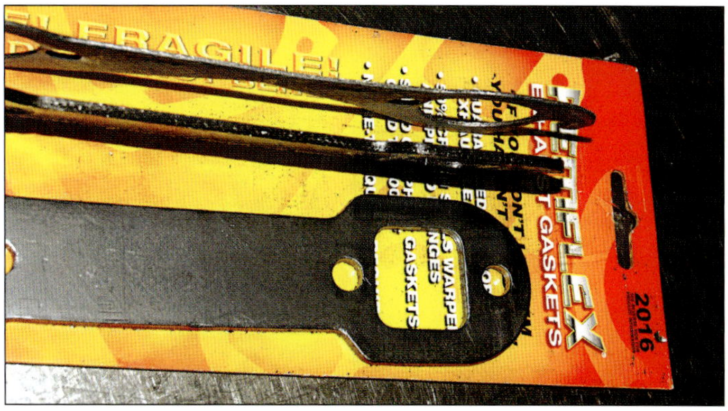

Header gaskets made from aluminum, copper, and multilayer steel (MLS) work best with thicker header flanges and ultra-smooth, flat surfaces. These 0.125-inch-thick Remflex header gaskets are my favorite. Install them, tighten them one time, and go for 100,000 miles-plus with no header leaks. They are super tough when it comes to heat, but they will break easily if they are bent or twisted.

Header flange thickness significantly impacts gasket longevity. Thin 5/16-inch flanges flex under thermal cycling and compromise the seals. Opt for 3/8-inch or thicker flanges for long-term reliability. Before installation, verify bolt clearances and make any necessary adjustments for proper tool access. There should be 1/2 inch of the bolt threads exposed with the header gasket in place on the header flange. Excess-length bolts can bottom out. Apply anti-seize compound to all of the threads, especially for stainless bolts, to prevent galling.

The supplied fasteners in header kits are often substandard. While their products may be a work of art, the fasteners could be junk. A recent set of high-end stainless-steel headers had massive hex-head, incorrect-length, non-stainless-steel bolts included. Retain all headers with stainless-steel bolts to prevent corrosion on the bolt heads.

For exhaust sizing, 2.5-inch-diameter pipe adequately supports up to 450 hp, while 3-inch systems handle approximately 750 hp with minimal restriction. True dual-exhaust configurations further increase flow capacity. Various premanufactured 2.5-inch-diameter pipe systems accommodate both shorty and long-tube headers in these diameters. The 3-inch and larger-diameter systems require custom fabrication with significant under-car packaging challenges.

H-Pipe or X-Pipe Exhaust Cutouts

The X-pipe or H-pipe crossovers optimize flow and sound quality in dual-exhaust systems. However, 1984–1991 catalytic converters and 1992–1996 resonators already incorporate crossover functionality and make additional X-pipes redundant. For aftermarket dual-converter systems, an X-pipe is beneficial to smooth the exhaust pulses and enhance muffler tone. Between designs, X-configurations generally deliver superior flow characteristics when compared to H-patterns.

For either quiet cruising or an aggressive sound, exhaust cutouts provide versatility at the touch of a button or cable. While later Corvettes incorporated electronically-controlled muffler bypasses, C4s can be retrofitted with similar functionality. I've installed numerous electric cutouts on C4s,

The position of the X-pipe should be at the hottest point of the exhaust system. As exhaust exits in pulses, it begins to roll and creates a minor restriction and heat builds. The X-pipe uses pulses from opposing sides to smooth the flow and help eliminate the bottleneck of exhaust gases.

This is an extreme plan for electric exhaust cutouts. A cut-off wheel in a high-speed grinder was used to carefully remove the bottom of the compartment. Then, it was glued back in at the same depth as the driver's side.

These Spelab exhaust cutouts provide adequate ground clearance. The wiring was routed into the passenger's compartment to connect the control switch or use the supplied remote control to open and close the cutouts. The remote allows operational checks from under the car.

although mounting space remains limited while maintaining ground clearance. One 1986 owner reported noticeable power increases with open exhaust during Daytona track sessions. For reliable operation, activate the cutouts regularly to prevent the opening mechanism from binding.

Muffler Drone

Muffler selection remains highly subjective. One person's perfect sound represents another's annoyance. The 1985–1996 C4s notoriously suffer from aftermarket exhaust drone, which is a pressure-related resonance that creates skull-compressing cabin pressure rather than excessive volume. This phenomenon primarily affects coupes rather than convertibles and is likely due to the hatchback configuration's tendency to amplify and trap certain frequencies. Before investing in exhaust components, thoroughly research drone characteristics through forums and reviews. Whenever possible, experience other C4 systems firsthand at shows or during test rides for the most accurate evaluation.

The 1984 Corvettes had a terrible exhaust drone right off the assembly line. However, they are less obnoxious with no mufflers or straight-through, fiberglass-packed mufflers. With catalytic converters, these straight pipes aren't really that bad on 1985–1996 C4 coupes, either.

In the coupe exhaust drone category, one supplier stands above the rest: Corsa. The mufflers fit well, look great, and require little manipulation to get them in place. The muffler hangers are designed to work with the existing C4 hardware and supports.

These exhaust band clamps stretch as they tighten and conform to the pipes, which works well for header-to-front-pipe connections. A few pieces of supplied aluminum padding seal where the clamps meet the steel center block for sealing. They do not crush the outer pipe when tightening, which allows for easy removal if required.

These strap clamps form the outer pipe to the collector. The downside is that they make front pipe removal from the header collector difficult. I prefer to use these strap clamps throughout the rest of the exhaust system. They come in coated steel and stainless steel. They are pricier than the old-school saddle clamps that severely distorted the pipes and often came loose.

If you carefully cut a 1/8-inch slot in the outer pipe in two places to relieve pressure, the rigid outer pipes will clamp down on the inner pipe and eliminate movement. You can also apply a light coating of anti-seize to the inside of the pipe to make removal easier in the future.

Preventing Spark-Plug Wire Damage

Exhaust-header heat and spark-plug wires can be difficult to tame because the header tubes are often close to the spark plugs. Spark-plug boots become overheated and crack, which allows spark leakage to the closest exhaust-header tube. If possible, set up your spark-plug wires on the engine stand. If done correctly, they may be able to stay on the engine until it's time to rebuild the engine again.

The LT1 and LT4 spark-plug wires were protected by spiral wrap. The high-density polyethylene (HDPE) spiral wrap is rated for 280°F of continuous exposure, while Teflon can handle more than 450°F but is pricey. Using the Design Engineering or Heatshield Products reflective insulated tube is a better choice for header applications.

This is the best way to route street or race-engine spark-plug wires. Placing the plug wires over the header tubes continually bakes the life out of them. Under the header tube is a cooler location, although you must repair oil leaks as soon as possible to keep the wires in good condition.

Custom wire pins for the four-wire spark-plug wire retainers were made to hold these Moroso plug wires on the L98 tuned port injection (TPI) engine. This prevents them from burning on the rear header tubes. Note that cylinder number-7's spark-plug wire crosses over the number-5 spark-plug wire to prevent crossfire.

In the final step, the spark-plug wires have spiral protective wrap placed over them at the header tube area.

Spark-plug heat shield boots are the best policy for race applications. Header-tube heat can exceed 1,200°F at full speed on the racetrack.

Heat Management: Radiator and Cooling Fan

Engine heat management rivals oil pressure and flow in importance, as it affects horsepower, often in unexpected ways. After 30 years of providing nationwide technical advice to Corvette owners, coolant temperature consistently dominates discussions and underlies countless performance issues across all operating conditions. Although convention once favored maximum cooling regardless of application, modern understanding reveals a more nuanced approach.

The introduction of the 1984 C4 coincided with federal emissions standards that mandated elevated operating temperatures, which made it the warmest-running Corvette engine to that point. While owners typically disliked seeing 210 to 230°F gauge readings, these higher temperatures ironically extended engine longevity. Benefits included cleaner, less acidic oil, as moisture evaporated more completely; reducing fuel dilution past the piston rings; and dramatically extending exhaust-system component life. The latter significantly impacted specialty exhaust-shop business models.

The downside of operating temperatures that are more than 220°F is a reduced margin for error if cooling components fail, requiring immediate driver response to temperature fluctuations. Supporting the higher-temperature approach, NASCAR engines operate at 280 to 300°F and with coolant pressure in the 26- to 33-psi range for optimized horsepower and efficiency. The C4 systems maintain 15 to 17 psi to prevent coolant boiling until approximately 265 to 270°F.

Trash, leaves, and grit are common at the bottom of the radiator and A/C condenser housing. The space between the radiator and A/C condenser is often more than half full of this mixture. Ignoring it will diminish horsepower gains and destroy an otherwise decent engine.

Heat Soak

C4s frequently experience high heat-soak conditions during idle and low-speed congestion, particularly in urban environments. This phenomenon parallels NASCAR's vulnerability during extended red-flag periods, where stationary heat-soak can cook oil in galleries and result in catastrophic component damage.

NASCAR engines use cold air moving through the cowl induction at the windshield base to create their power formula: hot combustion chambers + cold intake air = maximum output.

Conversely, C4s draw heated air from road surfaces, which is particularly problematic in traffic situations where radiators ingest hot exhaust air from preceding vehicles while simultaneously collecting ambient debris.

Conversely, drag racers pursue maximum heat reduction between runs to cool the intake charge temperatures. Purpose-built drag engines feature minimal or zero coolant capacity, with blocks often filled with epoxy or concrete for cylinder reinforcement. These engines operate just long enough for a quarter-mile or eighth-mile pass before external cooling. Street/strip competitors typically raise their hoods and sometimes apply ice directly to intake manifolds between runs. The pattern emerges when cold intake air combined with controlled combustion temperatures yields optimal power.

The 1984 C4 featured a unique forward-tilting radiator design. All radiator cores measured $14\frac{7}{8}$ inches tall by $23\frac{5}{8}$ inches wide through 1989. Although, 1985–1989 models reversed the top angle rearward. Option B4P (1986–1989) added a front-mounted pusher fan ahead of the A/C condenser, reportedly accompanied by a thicker core with enlarged tubes.

Coolant sensors must remain submerged for accurate readings. Exposed probes report falsely lower temperatures. To address warranty concerns, General Motors added coolant-level sensors beginning in 1986. The 1986–1989 radiator-mounted sensors frequently triggered warning lights that owners often dismissed after observing seemingly minor level drops.

However, during operation, dynamic coolant movement revealed substantially lower actual levels. Some "experts" suggested sensor extensions to prevent warning activation, which is a dangerous practice that masks genuine issues. Temperature-gauge fluctuations (cooling during acceleration, heating at idle) provide additional evidence of inadequate coolant levels.

TECH TIP

Coolant-System Filling

Proper coolant-system filling for the 1984–1989 C4 requires specific procedures. Some elevate the front of their C4 during filling, which helps. An effective hot-fill technique involves positioning the coolant container, radiator cap, and funnel within easy reach. Start the engine and monitor the temperature. At 160°F, disconnect the A/C cooling-fan pressure switch that is located on the 5/16-inch aluminum line near the under-hood A/C evaporator box.

This activates the cooling fan and prevents overflow when the thermostat opens. When the thermostat opens, which is indicated by sudden level drop, completely refill the radiator. Raise the RPM to 1,500 while topping off the coolant and secure the cap. RPM drops that exceed 200 rpm cause significant overflow. Enlist assistance for throttle control during the filling/capping process. ■

Major Cooling System Improvement

From 1990 onward, a firewall-mounted surge tank was positioned well above the engine to enable complete system filling and render the retained coolant-recovery system largely redundant. The most significant advancement appeared in 1992–1996 LT1/LT4 engines: reverse-flow cooling that prioritized the cylinder heads before block circulation, reducing detonation potential. This allowed 11.1:1 compression ratios that matched 1970 levels and delivered unprecedented base-engine performance. The design eliminated coolant routing through the intake manifold and prevented gasket failures. The B4P option disappeared and was replaced by standard larger radiators and dual cooling fans that substantially improved thermal management.

The ZR1 (LT5) featured an external oil cooler positioned between the A/C condenser and radiator. These external systems typically outperform coolant-to-oil exchangers by eliminating additional cooling-system heat load. Most incorporate thermostatic control to prevent oil circulation until optimal temperatures are reached to reduce condensation-related engine oil contamination.

Adapting a 1990–1996 radiator module to a 1984 C4 requires hood modifications or replacement, significantly increasing upgrade costs. However, installing a 1990-and-up radiator module into a 1985–1989 C4 is a simple drop-in with no hood modifications required. The conversion for 1984–1989 C4s necessitates 1990–1996 air-cleaner assemblies, although this presents an opportunity for improved intake airflow with enhanced cooling capacity from the larger core and dual fans.

For maximum street performance, a 160°F thermostat offers advantages by reducing the intake air temperatures that pass through the manifolds and heads. Achieving optimal results requires continuous fan operation to maintain minimal engine temperatures. However, this approach (rarely adopted by most owners) causes fouled plugs, sluggish throttle response, and accelerated wear during normal driving. For

The 1992–1996 LT1 and LT4 engines have a specific thermostat. A disc on the bottom goes down as the thermostat opens to close off the water-pump bypass port. Coolant then travels through the cylinder heads and the block to the radiator. An incorrect thermostat does not close the bypass port and recirculates coolant through the engine (not the radiator) and can result in severe engine overheating.

The L83 and L98 General Motors Print-O-Seal thermostat with a rubberized sealing ring (part number 10105135) prevents recurring coolant seepage. The 1992–1996 thermostat requires a rubber seal that surrounds the thermostat. The 1984–1991 small-block Chevy thermostat may not have an air bleed, but you can make your own with a 1/8-inch drill bit. Drill a hole in the outer circumference of the thermostat to allow the air to purge.

It's common to see a cracked housing after thermostat replacement due to debris left in the L83 or L98 thermostat recess from cleaning the gasket surface. Another reason for a cracked housing is if the thermostat was not seated in the recess. This requires the replacement of a unique and difficult-to-find water outlet.

balanced performance, I prefer 180°F thermostats that maintain approximately 200°F operating temperatures.

A critical consideration is to properly pair thermostat and fan activation temperatures to prevent control conflicts. When fan activation closely follows thermostat opening, constant cycling occurs. If fans activate at 185°F with an 180°F thermostat, they'll run continuously. Our shop programs fan activation at 200 to 205°F with 180°F thermostats and 195°F deactivation to maintain thermostat-open conditions and prevent frequent cycling.

Cooling System Performance Maintenance: Prevention is Key

The traditional green ethylene-glycol coolant in 1984–1995 C4s offered 2- to 3-year/30,000-mile protection intervals. The 1996 models introduced extended-life Dex-Cool with 5-year/150,000-mile protection, although reports of congealed coolant caused many owners to avoid it during service. My observations showed minimal gelling, primarily around the filler necks. Likely causes of gelling include air exposure from insufficient levels and depleted corrosion inhibitors, which are issues largely prevented through regular service intervals.

Use Acustrip 1550 coolant test strips to check the pH level. Strive for a pH range between 8.0 and 10.5 (8.5 to 10.0 is preferred). A pH level that is low (acidic) or too high (alkaline) leads to corrosion of an engine's internals along with the radiator, water pump, and heater core. Those who drive year-round should check the coolant level for freeze protection.

Once corrosion inhibitors deplete, cast iron rapidly deteriorates and circulates particles throughout the system. Severe cases develop internal rust sleeves in the rubber coolant hoses that "crunch" when squeezing the hoses. Standard cleaners are ineffective against advanced corrosion. Acidic products, such as Rusticide, produce better results but require multiple treatments, followed by baking-soda neutralization and secondary flushing. Extensive corrosion typically necessitates complete component replacement.

Even professional caustic cleaning services cannot fully restore severely corroded blocks. Extensive manual scrubbing is necessary after chemical treatment. At this stage, block replacement is typically more economical than restoration. While commercial flush machines that connect to heater hoses adequately service well-maintained systems, they cannot guarantee complete exchange in neglected systems. Without knowledge of internal engine conditions, traditional complete drain and refill procedures provide greater assurance.

TECH TIP

Coolant System Failure Points

Properly functioning reservoir tanks show "hot" levels (nearly full) at operating temperature and drop to minimum levels when cold. Static levels indicate air leakage, which promotes accelerated corrosion. Common failure points include the radiator cap, which is responsible for pressure maintenance, expansion management, and pressure relief; loose clamps; or damaged hoses. Temperature-gauge oscillations, particularly during engine-speed changes, provide additional evidence of inadequate coolant levels. ■

This is the beginning of a cooling-system nightmare. I can't stress enough the importance of draining the entire 4 gallons of coolant and flushing the entire system at two- to three-year intervals.

This digital multimeter is set to the millivolt DC scale with the negative probe on the engine ground. Do not allow the positive probe to touch the radiator filler neck. It should only touch the coolant. Conduct this test with the key on and engine off and then conduct the test with the engine running and all electrical accessories on. Voltage below 300.0 millivolts from idle to 2,000 rpm is acceptable. Higher voltage confirms that electrolysis is filling the coolant with scale and contaminants. A telltale sign is black-coated cooling-system internals.

A steady stream of coolant coming from the engine block and radiator steam tubes is visible. Check the recovery, radiator, and engine bleed tube/hose assembly for free flow. Air bleed or steam tubes from the radiator to the surge tank are often clogged and cause difficult coolant refills.

If the coolant reservoir system leaks at any connection point, the transfer of liquid will not occur. As the engine heats up, expanding coolant is pushed into the reservoir. During cool-down, coolant is drawn back into the radiator, preventing oxygen intrusion. Tight clamps maintain the correct seal on all required plumbing.

The 1984–1991 models have a knock sensor on the passenger's side of the engine. The driver's side has a 9/16-inch hex-head plug. The 1992–1996 models have two sensors and require shield removal to access them. Use a 21-mm universal socket for removal. A screwdriver is sometimes required to push through the sediment to get them to drain. Torque the knock sensors to 20 ft-lbs. Over-torquing damages their internals.

Radiators

By 75,000 miles, most C4 radiators require removal for core cleaning. Our process often involves an hour of careful tapping against wooden blocks to dislodge accumulated debris. While compressed air provides assistance, manual agitation is necessary to mobilize embedded particles. Preventative awareness, such as avoiding landscaping activities near roadways, can minimize accumulation.

Factory C4 aluminum radiators incorporate plastic tanks, which is their primary vulnerability. Thermal cycling, particularly the instant temperature spike from ambient to 180°F-plus when thermostats open, eventually causes cracking and leakage at the upper radiator-hose connection area. Aftermarket units with aluminum tanks offer superior durability. These replacements utilize either stamped side tanks (lighter and dimensionally precise but thinner) or welded assemblies (heavier with potential distortion from fabrication heat).

The 1990–1996 Dewitt radiator uses the same tube sizes and can be fitted with its 11.00-inch dual electric cooling fan package. A Black Ice two-part epoxy coating is available on all C4 radiators.

Dewitt's 16-inch, 2,360-cfm Spal Automotive fan for 1984–1989 model years is designed to mount to the stock plastic radiator shroud/surround assembly and is retained by the stock cooling fan's four retaining bolts. An included Direct Fit adapter plate allows it to easily replace the stock fan assembly. (Photo Courtesy Dewitt)

Undeniably, increased horsepower generates proportionally higher engine temperatures. Aftermarket radiators address this reality for high-performance applications. Traditional multi-row copper cores, while theoretically superior, often underperformed, as their increased thickness restricted airflow and offset theoretical capacity gains. Revolutionary progress came with 1-inch aluminum tubes that replaced traditional 1/2-inch designs and simultaneously improved flow-volume and heat-transfer surface area. Modern options span from 1/2-inch to 1½-inch tube designs across various manufacturers. For serious cooling, avoid traditional 1/2-inch copper tube radiators entirely.

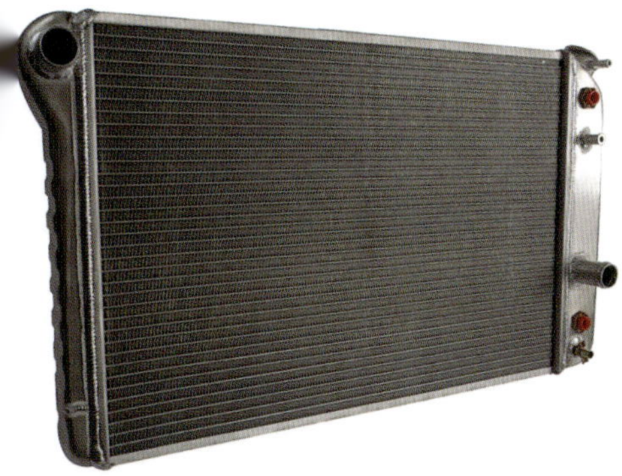

Dewitt's 1984–1989 direct-fit radiator is available with one row of 1.500-inch tubes or two rows of 1.00-inch tubes with press-formed tanks. An LS-swap radiator is available with two rows of 1.00-inch tubes. Natural aluminum or black finishes are available. (Photo Courtesy Dewitt)

The lower radiator cushions require modifications to fit most aftermarket radiators into the lower radiator housing. The left-side cushion was cut and ground with a small-diameter grinder. Rubber grinds relatively easy and will be smooth when you finish cutting. Sneak up on the fit. Try the cushion on the bottom of the radiator a few times instead of removing large amounts of material.

This "Big Mouth Performance Air Dam" from Auto Accessories of America was installed for maximum air induction to cool a Florida-based 500-hp 383-ci engine with A/C. The center divider bar was removed to prevent airflow disturbance. Be mindful of parking stop bumpers. The aluminum panel is not as forgiving as the original plastic piece.

The option code KC4 auxiliary plate-style coolant-to-engine-oil cooler for model years 1984–1991 is shown. It is perfect for road-race applications with less than 500 hp. It can be found on eBay and at Corvette swap meets. The compact design is good for a 20°F to 40°F oil-temperature reduction. It typically costs less than an air-to-oil cooler.

Engine Oil Coolers and Plumbing

Engine oil coolers can add more load to the cooling system or remove heat. OEM factory-provided oil coolers use engine coolant to lower the coolant temperature, which also raises it to some degree. External air-to-oil coolers removes engine-oil heat and can lower coolant temperatures. Air-to-engine oil coolers require thermostats to prevent overcooling and are usually found in race applications. Engine oil coolers are important for continuous high-RPM engine use.

The 1984–1991 option code KC4 coolant-to-engine oil cooler was a plate-type cooler sandwiched between the oil filter and engine block. They're perfect for road-race applications with less than 500 hp. They can be found on eBay and at Corvette swap meets. The compact design is good for a 20°F to 40°F oil temperature reduction.

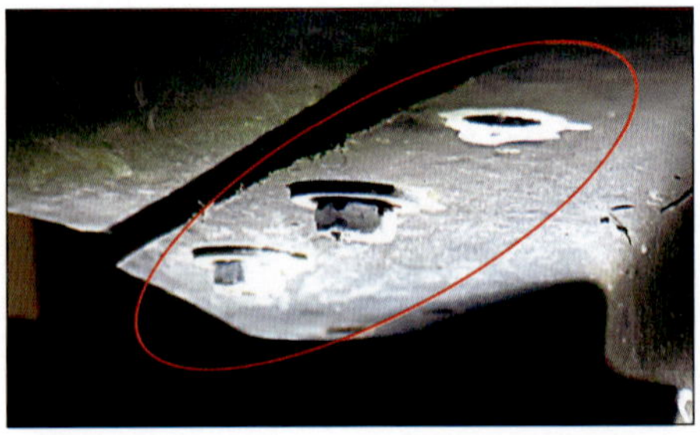

The 1990–1996 radiator upper housing has three difficult-to-remove screws on each side. They are accessed from below the frame rail in a tight location and removed with a wrench. Remove the cooling-system surge tank on the right side and air pump on 1992–1996 LT1 C4s. Reversing the fold-over or U-nuts from the upper to lower radiator housing will simplify future screw removal and installation. The 7-mm hex heads can then be accessed from the underside in the radiator module opening.

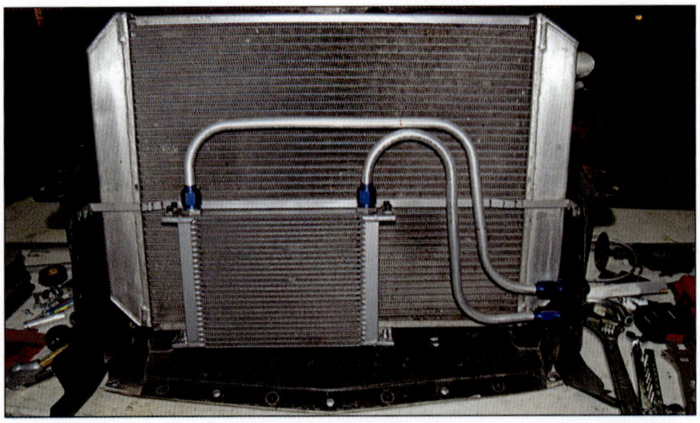

The Mocal OC5257-10 oil cooler and the required plumbing are installed in a 1993 C4. The use of -10 AN (0.625-inch) tubing sheds heat, whereas a stainless-steel hose doesn't. A 0.500 x 0.120 flat bar was configured for the top mount, and screws retain the cooler through the module at the bottom.

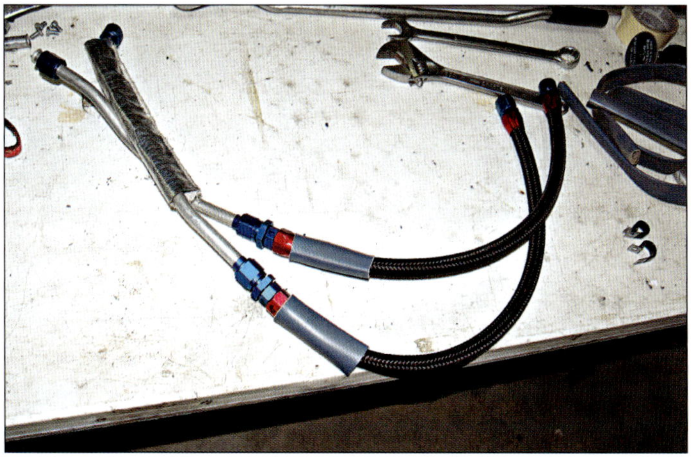

A piece of -10 AN aluminum tubing (0.625-inch outside diameter with a 0.035-inch wall) was configured from the oil-filter adapter to the oil cooler 90-degree fittings. The 5052 aluminum alloy tubing is preferred for its resistance to internal and external corrosion properties. A -10 AN hose and hose fittings with heat shielding keep heat off the cooler lines. Always use the hose end manufacturer's recommended hose. Mixing and matching fittings and hoses can lead to problems.

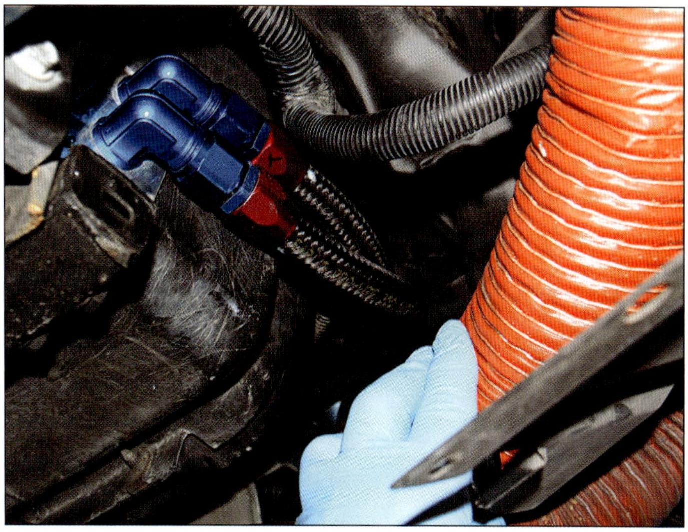

The two -10 AN (0.625-inch) lines using an in-house-configured bulkhead plate with 90-degree fittings are connected. Don't overtighten the fittings. AN wrenches are recommended, and you should only use enough pressure to seat the tube on the fitting. The 3-inch orange brake-duct hose from lower front spoiler intake ducts keeps the brakes cool on hot summer track days.

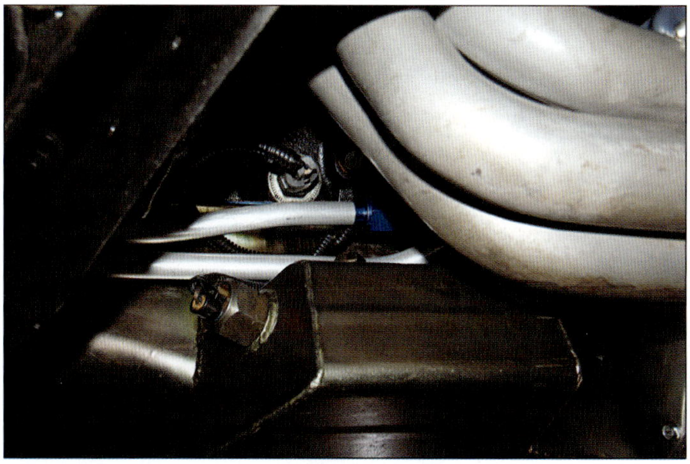

Nestled in the darkness are the oil-cooler lines connected to the Moroso oil-filter sandwich adapter (part number 23692). I chose the Moroso adapter because of its thin profile to allow the longest possible oil filter.

They're typically less costly than an air-to-oil cooler.

Aftermarket finned oil coolers are available in a multitude of configurations and sizes. They require custom installation, where the aluminum tubes must be bent and fit for oil transfer from the cooler to the engine. This can be tough for the beginner. Once the tubing is bent, there is no going back. Purchase less-expensive soft-wall tubing to practice on until you get the hang of it. You'll need a 37-degree tubing flare tool. Close flare to bends have to be well thought out. You'll find out too late if there was not enough room for the flaring tool after making a bend. It's better to make the bent leg at least 0.500 inch longer than necessary and then cut off the extra before making the flare.

Water Flow Enhancement

All C4 water pumps feature aluminum housings with stamped-steel impellers that adequately support up to 450 hp. Higher-output applications benefit from brass-impeller or electric alternatives. Flow improvements primarily benefit idle and low-RPM operation. Factory pumps provide sufficient flow above 2,500 rpm. A critical specification is that the 1984–1991 applications require reverse-rotation (counterclockwise when viewed from front) pumps with 0.750-inch-diameter shafts.

The 1992–1996 LT pump features a direct camshaft drive with ball bearings, utilizing dual chambers with separate inlet/outlet ports that direct flow through the heads before the block. Electric alternatives provide consistent flow regardless of engine speed, which is ideal for low-RPM operation with an

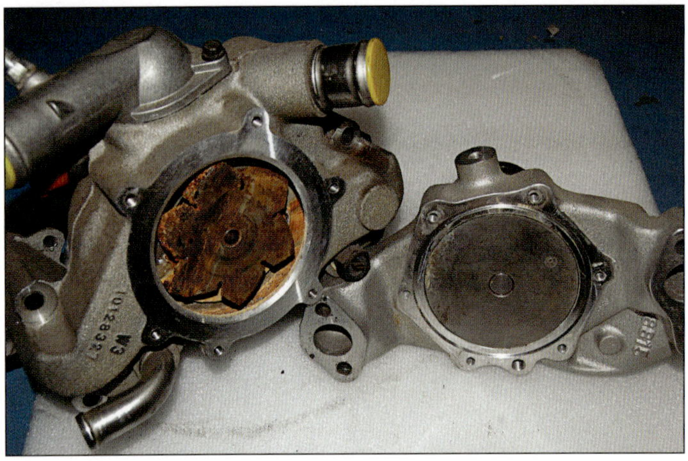

Notice the stamped impeller of the rusty OEM LT1 pump (left), and the full-circle stainless-steel impeller on the Edelbrock reverse-rotation L98 water pump (part number 8815). The tight-fitting Edelbrock impeller increases water flow especially at low RPM, which is the most important.

This Meziere all-billet, reverse-rotation, belt-driven pump's (part number WPR401) true beauty can be seen in the performance chart and on the temperature gauge. It's 5- to 7-gpm higher than any competitor, and the off-idle flow will keep the engine cool when the cooling demand is at its greatest. Expect a 10-hp gain over stock water pumps at wide-open throttle. All pumps are now produced with bypass and heater ports. Electric 1984–1991 pumps are available. (Photo Courtesy Meziere Enterprises)

Meziere has an electric LT1 version for 1992–1996 Corvettes. This heavy-duty motor pumps 55 gallons free flow per minute and has a 2,400-plus-hour life expectancy. It features all stainless-steel hardware, and the entire unit weighs 4.6 pounds. Meziere pumps are made in the USA with two-year, unlimited-mileage warranties. (Photo Courtesy Meziere Enterprises)

effectively neutral efficiency impact. The mechanical drag reduction is balanced against increased electrical load.

Cooling Fan Operation

The 1984–1996 C4 Corvette cooling-fan operation remains contentious, and widespread misconceptions drive unnecessary modifications. Many owners aim for early/continuous fan operation despite significant drawbacks. Electric cooling fans lack continuous-duty ratings and cause premature failure. Increased electrical load strains alternators when combined with A/C, lighting, and other accessories. Proper wiring remains critical. I've witnessed dangerous modifications that bypass relays with direct battery connections through unfused cabin toggle switches. Such arrangements create fire hazards, as a single wire nick creates 800-plus-amp short circuits. Always utilize proper relays to control high-amperage loads with low-amperage switching.

Many C4 Corvette owners have no idea of when or what engine parameters the ECM/PCM uses to control the fan(s). Are your fans operating as intended? The following table provides the answers.

This original 1984–1991 B4P boost cooling fan helps when you're in gridlock. Mounted in the radiator air intake, the boost fan is controlled by a standalone coolant-temperature sensor and dedicated relay.

C4 Corvette Fan Operation	
Year(s)	Details
1984	• Fan on: 238°F • Fan off: 201°F • On-off standalone switch control in the passenger-side cylinder head • No ECM or VSS control of cooling fan • Fan on: A/C refrigerant pressure switch above 238 psi
1985–1989	• 1985–1986 fan on: 234°F via ECM control • 1987–1989 fan on: 226°F via ECM control • Fan on: A/C refrigerant pressure switch above 233 psi • Fan off: vehicle speed above 35 mph • 1986 fan off: speeds above 40 mph, coolant temperature below 234°F, and A/C refrigerant pressure below 233 psi
1990–1994	• 1990–1993 primary fan on: 226°F • 1994 primary fan on: 219°F • Primary fan on: A/C refrigerant pressure above 240 psi • 1990–1993 secondary fan on: 235°F • 1994 secondary fan on: 228°F, also activated when primary fan is on for more than 2 seconds. Secondary fan on: refrigerant pressure above 240 psi • Both fans off: 45 mph, A/C pressure below 248 psi, and coolant temperature below 226°F
1995–1996	• Primary and secondary fans on: 226°F at half of full rotational speed (low speed) • Primary and secondary fans on: 235°F at full rotational speed (high speed) • Primary and secondary fans drop to low speed when coolant temperature drops 5°F • Primary and secondary fans on: full rotational speed, A/C refrigerant 248 psi or above • Primary and secondary fans off: 45 mph, A/C pressure below 248 psi, and coolant temperature below 226°F

The B4P boost cooling fan significantly helps during gridlock conditions. It is mounted in the radiator air intake and operates independently via a standalone temperature sensor and dedicated relay, activating at 235°F to 238°F and deactivating at 225°F. Our shop often modified these to operate simultaneously with the main puller fan for accelerated cooling.

How to Circumvent ECM Control of Cooling Fans

Cooling-fan control can be modified. This covers the least-costly and simplest ways to circumvent their control. Sometimes saving money creates more labor and does not provide the best possible solution.

1984

Reduce operating temperatures by replacing the original 238°F fan switch (located between the number-1 and number-3 cylinders in the driver's-side head) with aftermarket alternatives that offer 170°F to 210°F activation temperatures. This direct replacement controls the factory relay system at lower thresholds.

1985–1993

The optimal control modification involves PROM chip reprogramming to customize fan activation temperatures. For 1985–1989 B4P-equipped models, an alternative is to replace the original boost fan switch (relatively accessible compared to non-B4P and later models) with lower-temperature alternatives that require additional wiring between the replacement switch and relay.

For 1985–1989 B4P options or 1985–1994 models, remove the 5/16-inch plug between the number-1 and number-3 cylinders to install the low-temperature switch. Route a new wire to the appropriate relay location: the battery area/inner fender (1985–1989) or the driver-side radiator module upper cover (1990–1996).

The 1985–1989 non-B4P and 1990–1994 C4s require removing a 5/16-inch square internal plug between the number-1 and number-3 cylinders. These plugs, which are challenging when new, become extremely difficult after decades of heat cycling.

1995–1996

Fan override modifications are generally discouraged due to complex three-relay control systems managing dual-speed operation. If proceeding, remove the 5/16-inch square plug between the number-1 and number-3 cylinders and install a low-temperature switch. Disconnect and isolate the relay with pink/dark-blue/black/white wires. Locate the relay with the pink/light-blue/dark-green/red wires and splice the dark-green wire to the new switch. Optionally, splice an additional wire from the new switch to the dark-blue wire on the pink/dark-blue/red/white relay for simultaneous fan operation.

The 1994–1995 override modifications trigger quad driver failure codes 36 and 78. Code 36 appears during scanning without illuminating the SES light. The 1996 models permanently illuminate the SES light with code 78 without performance degradation.

Cooling System Troubleshooting

Prioritize inspecting the cooling system for radiator debris. This is capable of causing both immediate and gradual overheating conditions. Problems may appear suddenly or develop incrementally. Typically, debris-related issues primarily manifest at idle/low speeds and improve with increased velocity unless obstructions cover extensive core areas.

Elevated temperatures during idle and highway operation suggest circulation restrictions due to internal radiator clogging, partial thermostat sticking, or water-pump impeller deterioration.

Continuous overheating indicates thermostats that are stuck

TECH TIP: Removing Stubborn Engine Plugs

A proven technique for stubborn plug removal involves draining coolant below the cylinder heads. There will not be enough heat absorbed if coolant is not drained. A specific 5/16-inch square male socket is required for plug removal. Do not attempt plug removal with a 1/4-inch extension. The tool must fit tight into the recess. ■

Coolant must be drained at least 2 to 3 inches below the plug's port. Focus the acetylene torch on the cylinder head around the plug and not on the plug. The plug gets softer and is easier to round out if too much heat is applied.

Do not hold the torch in one spot for a long period. Keep circling and apply candle wax to the threads around the plug. The capillary effect draws the wax between the threads and plug to aid in plug removal. This may take several tries and requires patience.

Stubborn plugs will come out without damage if you apply the wax and be patient. A 5/16 square male pin socket is required. A 1/4-inch drive will not work because it's too loose.

COOLING FAN SWITCH INSTALLATION (1985–1994)

The 1985–1996 Corvette low-temperature cooling fan control switch is installed in this location (the driver-side cylinder head between the number-1 and number-3 cylinders).

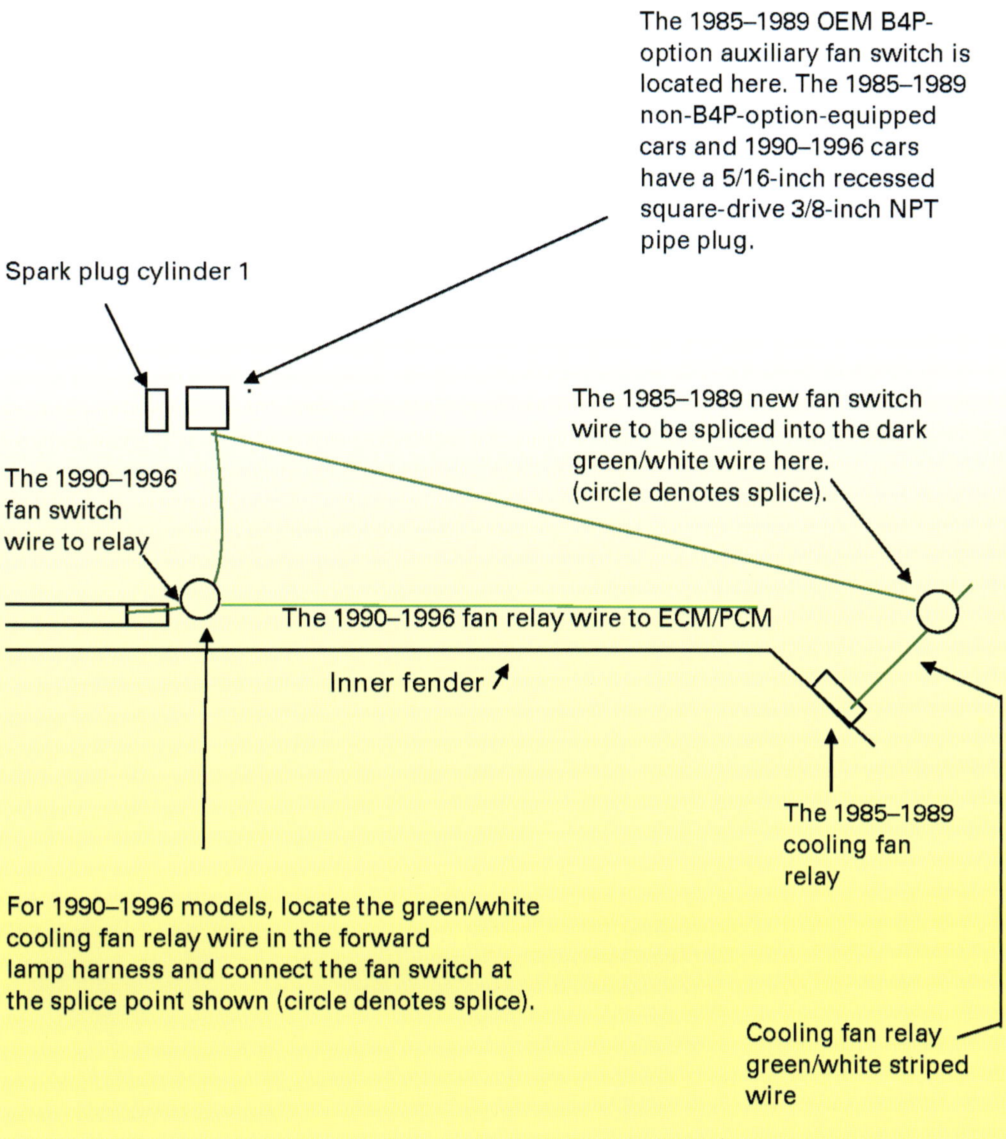

closed. Idle-only overheating suggests a cooling-fan failure, which additionally compromises A/C operation, particularly in 1992–1996 models, where it prevents compressor engagement. Prolonged overheating can cause head-gasket failure or cracked heads.

Post-service overheating typically results from trapped air pockets during filling, especially with LT1/LT4 engines. Allow the engine to completely cool before reinitiating the filling process. Check for steady coolant flow at the surge-tank filler neck lower steam hose.

Excessive coolant concentration raises operating temperatures. While a 40/60 coolant/water ratio can reduce temperatures, ensure sufficient freeze protection for your climate with at least a 10-percent safety margin.

Automatic Transmission Upgrades: 700-R4, MD8, and 4L60

The 1984–1993 C4 Corvette 700-R4, MD8, and 4L60 mechanical-shift transmissions evolved through numerous iterations before the 1994–1996 electronically-shifted 4L60E was created. An early significant upgrade replaced the 27-spline input shaft with a stronger 30-spline design, although some early-production 1984 models retained the smaller shaft.

All 4L60E transmissions use 30-spline, 298-mm input shafts. Modern aftermarket components offer a capacity of 700 ft-lbs for these applications. Input-shaft support improvements continued with increased pump-body bushing width in 1990. Sun Shell failures (connecting the reverse clutch drum to the planetary sun gear) commonly caused the loss of the reverse, second, and fourth gears and produced grinding noises. Current aftermarket shells handle up to 900 ft-lbs of torque.

A significant 1987 improvement introduced the auxiliary valve body that controlled forward and reverse engagement. This assembly incorporated accumulator and abuse valves to protect against high-RPM gear engagement and facilitated quicker shifts when rocking out of mud and snow. The forward sprag (one-way clutch) assembly underwent multiple revisions, as did the third/fourth clutch friction plates that spawned numerous aftermarket solutions. All Corvette applications featured the largest-volume second/fourth band servo, which made these transmissions particularly desirable as donor units.

Pump/stator shaft designs evolved from 7-vane to 10-vane and ultimately 13-vane rotors. Planetary-gear assemblies progressed from 4-pinion to 6-pinion configurations, and oil weirs were added to protect pinion roller bearings to address the common 1984–1986 bearing failure issue. Later funnel-style filter seals significantly complicated removal, where seal-extraction tools potentially scarred pump bores and introduced air paths into the fluid system.

The transmission case design is a significant departure from other applications. It eliminates transmission mount provisions due to the torque-arm support system. General Motors configured two versions: one as shown and another with two reinforcement ribs where all other General Motors car-line mount holes normally appear to create a unique C4-specific case.

Bowler Performance Transmissions can remanufacture 1984–1993 C4 700-R4 transmissions to handle the torque that you request. It can provide all of the items shown in the photo to complete the package. It also has 4L65E options available to handle almost any torque you require with a four- to six-bolt extension housing adapter. (Photo Courtesy Bowler Performance)

ATI Performance products have a different twist. It will rebuild 1984–1991 700-R4 and 1994–1996 4L60E transmissions and provide dynamometer testing at an additional cost if requested. It also has various levels of rebuild kits and hard parts for the do-it-yourselfer. (Photo Courtesy ATI Performance Products)

Modern upgrades enable even early 700-R4 units to handle torque loads of 400-plus ft-lbs. Remember that torque, not horsepower, primarily determines transmission durability. Sticky tires maximize the torque transfer to rotating components and accelerate wear. Engine dyno sheets typically show torque values exceeding horsepower figures. RPM considerations significantly impact converter and pump reliability, which makes proper torque converter selection critical for matching engine torque curves.

Stock 1984–1986 700-R4s remain suitable for factory-level applications. When your budget permits, utilize 1987-and-newer units for the earlier Corvettes, particularly when facing substantial rebuild costs. When torque exceeds 300 ft-lbs, an upgrade to later-model transmissions is necessary.

The 700-R4/4L60E shift kits are available from numerous suppliers, such as ATI, B&M, Transgo, Superior, and Sonnax, with many kit levels. If possible, read the installation instructions first. You may not want to get that deep into your transmission's internals. The main concern is following the instructions explicitly.

Numerous crate transmission suppliers offer application-specific units. Confirm the torque capacity and RPM limitations before you make a purchase. Basic 4L60E rebuilds that are capable of 450 ft-lbs typically start at $2,000. For custom builds, provide comprehensive vehicle data and get a consult before making additional driveline changes. Critical specifications include camshaft profiles and rear gear ratios, which significantly impact torque-converter selection. For serious racers, lower first-gear ratio options exist, which are ideal for time-constrained projects or those who are uncomfortable with transmission work.

High-end builds that handle 900-plus ft-lbs of torque can reach $8,000 or more. This is appropriate for dedicated drag applications versus the 400 ft-lbs Saturday night/strip warrior setups. Specialized transmission builders often deliver superior value through expertise rather than parts compromise. Their accumulated knowledge represents a significant investment in experience and allows optimized component selection while maintaining reputation-dependent quality.

The 1984–1993 throttle valve (TV) cable is the most critical external component that affects transmission longevity, shift quality, and timing. If it has been disconnected or damaged, use only light throttle until it is repaired. Disconnected cables cause catastrophically low line pressure that guarantees clutch failure during moderate-to-heavy throttle application. The 1994–1996 4L60E eliminates this vulnerability by electronically controlling the line pressure through the PCM.

TV cable operation proportionally increases the line pressure based on the throttle position and maximizes the clutch holding force. Critical calibration requires perfect throttle-to-valve correlation. Installing modified throttle bodies with shorter lever arms reduces cable travel and prevents full valve actuation at WOT, which creates dangerous low-pressure conditions. Compensatory adjustments often create excessive line pressure at low throttle positions and cause unnecessarily harsh shifts.

Dyno operators commonly reduce TV cable tension on 1984–1993 C4s to maintain a direct 1:1 third-gear during testing. However, this frequently resulted in delayed 3-4 clutch pack failure weeks later due to sustained low-pressure operation under high load.

To adjust the 1984–1991 throttle valve (TV) cable, push the cable-release button with a screwdriver, push the cable back toward the firewall, release the lock button, and put the accelerator to the floor. The cable's internal ratchet allows the cable to lengthen and put maximum pressure on the TV valve at wide-open throttle. The 1992–1993 TV cable adjustment is more involved due to the acceleration-slip regulator (ASR). The accelerator cable rotates the ASR drum, and another cable activates the throttle body. The TV and cruise-control cables rotate on the drum. The adjustment procedure is similar with a ratcheting mechanism. There is a balance to apply maximum TV cable pressure and allow full throttle-body opening at the wide-open throttle (WOT) position. An elevated idle speed indicates improper adjustment.

Throttle valve (TV) cable operation is shown. At wide-open throttle (WOT), this valve should bottom out against the aluminum housing. If you see the valve out like it is in this photo, low line pressure is occurring which will damage the clutch plates. If shift points are late or early, the valve-body springs or governor springs require tuning. The cable should not be backed off to allow shifts to occur sooner.

TV Cable Testing and Adjustment

The throttle-body TV cable lever concerns were discussed earlier. If the throttle-body lever is too short and the TV cable is adjusted properly, the throttle valve is already actuated, which raises the line pressure and causes late and violent shift points from the abbreviated cable travel. If the cable is backed off (moved forward), expect better shift timing, as WOT clutch damage can result from low line pressure. Longer-than-required throttle-body shift levers result in delayed abrupt shifts, and backing off the TV cable results in poor shift timing. This is why the length of the lever is so important. When determining the lever's length, use the measurement from the original throttle body's TV lever cable connection point to the throttle-shaft centerline.

Rebuild, Upgrade, or Service

When is it time to rebuild, upgrade, or service your automatic transmission? Transmissions with firm, prompt shifts (less than one second) likely respond well to timing or shift-point adjustments. Soft shifts with extended lag may benefit from shift kits that increase line pressure and reduce shift intervals. However, flaring (RPM increases between shifts) typically indicates clutch slippage and requires a complete rebuild. Slipping during shifts generates extreme heat that permanently damages friction materials. No additive remedies this condition.

Occasionally, increased line pressure temporarily masks slippage, but underlying damage persists. Evidence includes burned fluid that often contains metallic particles. If you pursue a rebuild, reference comprehensive guides, such as CarTech's *GM Automatic Overdrive Transmission Builder's and Swapper's Guide* by Cliff Ruggles. Expect specialized tool requirements (some can be substituted for budget considerations) and numerous spring assemblies that require careful handling. A successful rebuild demands a clean and organized workspace.

Early in my apprenticeship, I nearly lost my position for leaving a thrust washer on my bench. Any leftover component raises questions about what might be missing from the assembly. Seemingly minor errors, such as mispositioned plates or pistons, create extensive complications. This is a critical rule: if the transmission doesn't rotate freely after assembly, do not install it. Catastrophic failure will follow.

Automatic transmissions feature remarkable engineering. Friction materials transfer enormous loads, while torque converters move multi-ton vehicles through a fluid coupling alone. This hydraulic action generates substantial heat and requires dedicated cooling systems. Operating conditions drastically affect fluid longevity. Gentle driving may extend service intervals to 100,000 miles, while aggressive operation quickly degrades fluid to a brown, overheated condition that requires frequent replacement.

Maintenance is Key

Fluid service philosophies divide people into opposing camps. One is to avoid changing high-mileage, never-serviced fluid. This "never change" argument suggests that accumulated varnish becomes functional. Clean fluid potentially mobilizes deposits and creates blockages. The reality is that if never-changed fluid accompanies shifting problems, replacement won't save the transmission. Failure is imminent. In contrast, regular maintenance eliminates these concerns entirely. My practice is 75,000-mile intervals for standard vehicles and annual changes for performance applications.

Another maintenance debate contrasts complete fluid exchange versus simple filter replacement with partial drainage. Exchange machines extract fluid through cooler lines while it is simultaneously replaced to provide total fluid renewal. When properly performed, even moderately darkened fluid returns to bright red condition. Filter replacement becomes necessary during second service intervals. If it's required before 75,000 miles or due to filter-media contamination, a transmission overhaul is likely needed.

Filter changes typically remove 8 to 9 quarts after extended draining (an overnight draining time is the minimum). The total system capacity exceeds 12 quarts, even thorough pan draining replaces only two-thirds of fluid. Quick services replace barely 40 percent. Brown fluid, burnt odor, metal particles, or friction material fragments indicate that a rebuild is necessary (not a need for maintenance).

Fluid Choices and Costs

What transmission fluid should you use? Mineral or synthetic? Synthetic fluids provide superior protection for street applications, with specialized products like RedLine for performance use. High operating temperatures quickly degrade conventional mineral-based fluids. If you go the crate-transmission route, consult builder recommendations for specific Dexron designations (II, III, VI) to optimize shift quality and longevity. First-time servicers should default to General Motors specifications unless otherwise directed.

While Dexron VI technically supersedes earlier formulations, specialized builds may require specific alternatives.

Shift Kits

Shift kit installation is manageable do-it-yourself work. Elevate the vehicle, remove the transmission pan, and prepare for significant fluid release. Expect fluid to run down your arms during the process. Remove the filter by pulling downward and wiggle it to break its seal and release additional fluid. Loosen the valve-body bolts and allow the fluid to drain. If possible, come back the next day and drop the valve body. Anticipate ongoing seepage from the torque converter drainage. Normal pan deposits include dark-gray metallic paste, but actual metallic shavings indicate an imminent rebuild.

While service manuals show factory configurations, previous modifications may have altered check-ball placement or quantity. Unknown modification history may require multiple attempts to restore proper operation. Note that check balls create witness marks on plates and provide reinstallation reference. When reusing spacer plates, inspect check-ball contact areas for wear or distortion. Replacement is typically necessary. Most kits require specific spacer plate holes to be enlarged and often provide appropriate drill bits. Follow the size specifications precisely and chamfer holes after drilling to eliminate sharp edges.

The arrow denotes where the case check balls are located. The torque converter clutch fluid supply filter screen has been removed and will be replaced during valve body upgrades. The hole to the left with the marker indication is the fourth clutch-fluid exhaust hole. Make sure that this is clear when the pan gasket is installed.

Extract the filter-to-pump seal using a large flat-blade screwdriver while protecting the pump body surface. Early 700-R4 transmissions will have the O-ring seal. Always use the new ribbed-style seal when replacing the filter. Lubricate the filter pickup tube with transmission fluid before installation.

Clean the valve body with mineral spirits or a safe petroleum-based solvent. Identify the valves and springs to be replaced. The throttle valve is removed for inspection, and a large spring replacement often comes with the valve-body upgrade kit.

Valve Bodies

Valve bodies are complex assemblies that control flow, pressure, and timing through numerous springs, plugs, and valves. Prepare a clean, spacious, and contamination-free workspace. If metal particles are found in pan sediment and the valves are stuck, significant internal failure is expected. Valves sometimes

The weight of the punch being dropped on a sticking valve loosens it in its bore. Once the valve begins moving, the punch can be used to work them in and out. Avoid hitting the valve lands with the punch—if you do, you'll have to start over.

Install the pins that retain the valvetrain plugs from the top side. If you need to make spring changes for shift firmness or timing, the springs can be changed without dropping the valve body.

stick from wear and scoring, which means that the valve body needs to be replaced. Torque-converter failures can cause immense amounts of debris in the pan, resulting in sticking valves. In this case, a complete transmission overhaul is required.

From time to time, valves have minimal wear and light scoring that can be polished to restore function. If the valves are sticking from a previous failure and no metal is found in the pan, there will be a tedious process of removing the valves one by one and polishing them until they drop on their own weight into position. Sticking valves will cause hard or soft shifting and delayed shifting as well as overall poor shift performance.

Accumulators-Servos

Accumulators buffer clutch engagement. Without them, shifts become violent. Optimal performance requires positive shifts that occurs rapidly without component damage. Automatic transmissions simultaneously disengage one clutch pack while engaging another, and dual holding mechanisms are required for loaded output-shaft rotation. Accumulators regulate the engagement and release phases, which critically affect shift feel and longevity. Extensive engineering has optimized C4 shift characteristics. Always follow kit-specific accumulator spring recommendations. Substitutions risk unpredictable results.

Accumulator seals evolved to one-piece rectangular rubber designs with the 1987 auxiliary valve body. Square scarf-cut Teflon seals indicate outdated pistons that require replacement. Inspect the bores for damage and replace the housings as needed. Verify the accumulator assembly configuration, as shift kits often coordinate accumulator spring packages with valve-body spring changes. Similarly, all spacer-plate drilling modifications must be completed according to specifications for proper system operation.

Never reuse original gaskets regardless of kit provisions. Gaskets are marked with orientation indicators: "V" for valve-body side, and "C" for case side. Pre-soak the spacer plate gaskets in transmission fluid to improve valve body-to-transmission case torque loading. Petroleum jelly effectively secures the check balls in position during reassembly.

While aftermarket deep pans increase fluid capacity, C4 ground clearance limitations make them vulnerable points. Factory pans offer superior ground clearance and avoid a major leakage risk if impacted. Their rigid flanges with embossed bolt holes provide excellent sealing characteristics. Regardless of pan type, premium gaskets are critical. ACDelco part number 8654799 justifies its higher cost over kit-supplied alternatives. Torque the pan bolts to 120 in-lbs in multiple passes. Avoid using impact tools that risk distortion.

If your 700-R4 has the thinner, square, scarf-cut Teflon seals on the accumulator pistons, the pistons themselves will need to be replaced. Check the accumulator piston bores for gouges. Install the shift kit with the recommended accumulator piston and springs.

This Sonnax S74480C servo-release check valve is installed into the case to prevent soft 2-3 shift engagement and 3-2 downshift hunting. Its major contribution is extended 3-4 clutch-plate life. Drilling the check valve's orifice depends on the application. This check valve should always be installed with any shift kit installation.

This internal snap ring retains the 1984–1993 C4 700-R4 main pressure-regulator valve. The valve is spring loaded and can be accessed during valve-body service once the filter is removed.

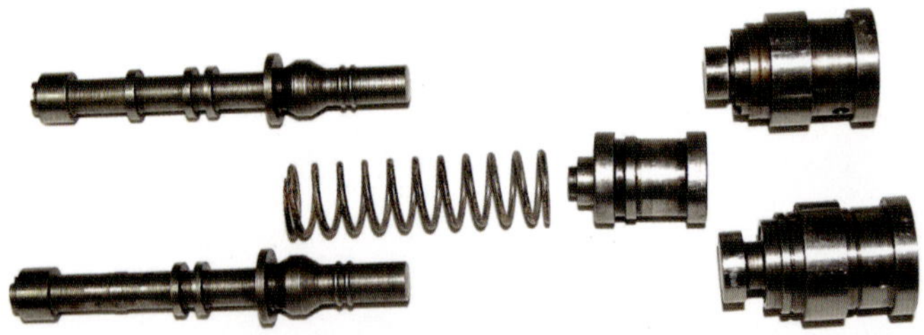

This is what you'll find after the snap ring is removed. The long valve controls the main system pressure. The lower valve has been modified. The land between the two lands and the bottom of the valve was ground off. This stabilizes pressure and is a must-do when installing shift kits. Sonnax also has O-ringed valves available (part number 700-R4-LB1) with a high-pressure spring.

It is important to make sure that the replacement spacer plate gaskets don't cover any of the holes in the spacer plate and that they match the shape of the valve-body passages. Note the "C" and the triangle. The "C" gasket goes between the case and spacer plate, and the triangle goes between the plate and valve body. Vaseline works well to hold the check balls in place on the plate and valve body during assembly.

The second-gear servos are hidden behind this cover in the process of removal. Once the snap ring is removed, the cover will pop out. Pull down on the O-ring and cut through it. Pull out the cut O-ring, and the cover will come off easily. Dropping the exhaust system at the front is helpful to access the servo.

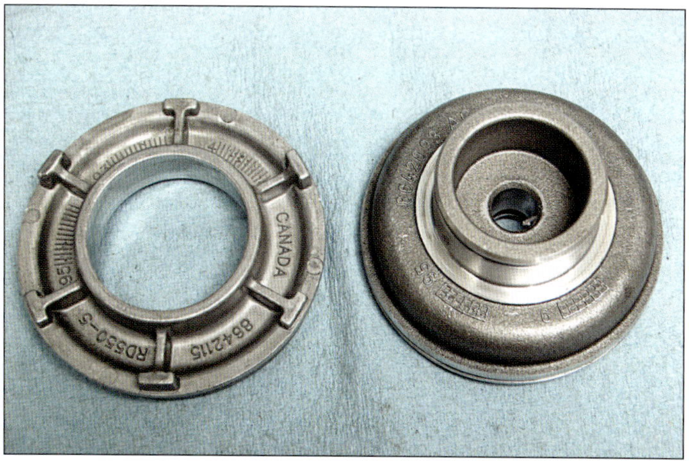

This is a typical C4 servo, which is the OEM's largest-volume second-gear apply servo. The Sonnax aftermarket second-gear super-hold servo kit utilizes O-ring sealing and increases the second-gear servo apply area by 18 percent over the OEM servo (part number 77911-03K).

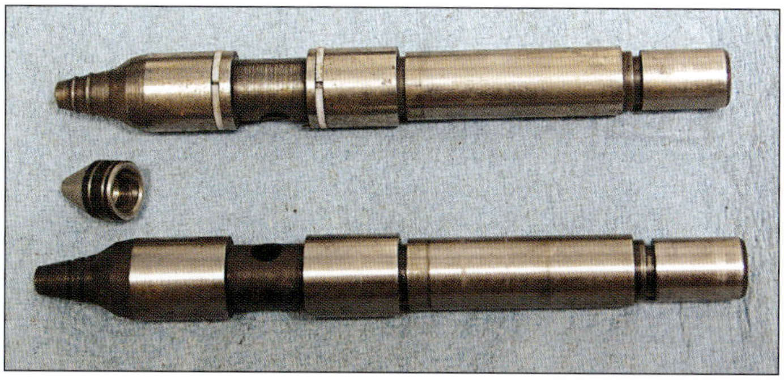

These second-gear servo apply pins were made in two versions: early and late. The top pin (early) has two scarf cut seals and was replaced by the smooth pin. The early pin with seals works better and prevents pressure leaks. They can be purchased separately, and most complete second-gear servo kits supply them. The cap in the middle is used to lengthen the pin and prevent excess band clearance. Follow the instructions carefully to avoid band damage caused by dragging on the reverse drum.

Corvette 700-R4 4L60 second-gear servos have the largest hydraulic apply area of any General Motors unit. Few aftermarket servos add more application area, and many boast Corvette replacement. Most that are advertised as billet replacements truly make a difference with larger piston area. After 400 ft-lbs of torque, consider a billet replacement to aid second-gear engagement. The same servo applies overdrive, which is not going to be much of an advantage. Few want the tires to break loose at 100-plus mph. Test procedures are provided with the servo installation that require internal access. Install the new servo while the pan and valve body are down.

Torque Converters

Proper converter selection significantly impacts drag/street performance. Determine appropriate stall speed by analyzing camshaft profiles and dyno-measured torque curves. The stall speed is the point of minimum internal converter slip, which is practically demonstrated during WOT brake-torque launches when the tires begin spinning. Different engines require matched converters. The 1985 models that produce peak torque at 1,200 rpm need lower stall converters, while 1992 models with higher-RPM torque curves require higher stall specifications. Be cautious because stall speeds that exceed 3,000 rpm significantly compromise street drivability and require elevated engine speeds for basic vehicle movement.

Converter costs increase dramatically with higher stall-speed capabilities due to heightened internal stresses and precision requirements. Torque-converter failures require a complete teardown of the unit and a thorough cleaning. Support bushings are scarred, and a complete valve-body disassembly for valve cleaning and polishing is required.

Always pre-fill the converter before installation. Standard units need 1 quart, while higher-stall

Centrifugal Governors

Centrifugal governors track road speed (output-shaft rotation) to regulate shift-valve pressure. They sense vehicle speed and not engine RPM, although they influence shift-point engine speeds.

Calibration involves counterbalancing weights against springs. Lighter combinations delay upshifts until higher speeds, and heavier setups produce earlier shifts. Numerous spring combinations exist, such as the B&M calibration kit (part number 20248). Replace governors that show tooth wear. ■

This B&M governor calibration kit (part number 20248) has plenty of shift speed options with the governor not included. If you find that your governor has worn teeth (like the one that is shown), it will require gear replacement.

The 1984–1993 700-R4/4L60 governor is under a dome-shaped cover on the passenger's side. A long, flat-blade screwdriver with small hammer works well to tap the cover out of its bore. The governor slides in and out with no retainer to remove.

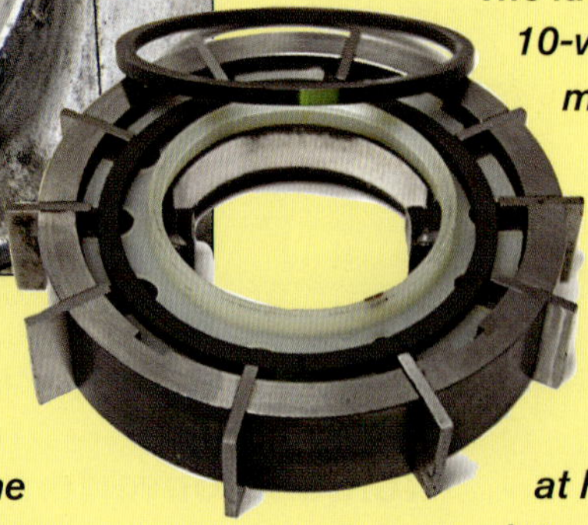

The late 700-R4 transmissions use a 10-vane pump rotor. Early 1984–1986 models may still have a seven-vane pump rotor and should be discarded. The black with yellow paint-mark rings maintain pump vane position. These should always be replaced with hardened guide rings. These rings tend to shatter at high RPM or if the transmission gets into a bind during installation.

(smaller diameter) versions require a minimum of 1/2 quart. Higher-stall converters generate increased heat and contain less cooling fluid. External transmission coolers become mandatory with performance converters. Units that exceed a 3,000-rpm stall require a minimum cooler size of 80 square inches mounted ahead of A/C condensers. Consult your builder for application-specific cooling recommendations.

There's a lot going on inside the torque converter. As RPM increases, it requires a precision unit to keep the pieces in place. Internal components (the aluminum pump vanes with steel reinforcements) risk contact at high RPM and create metal particles that contaminate the entire system. The stator (center of the photo) multiplies torque to maximize fluid transfer from the pump to the turbine. A one-way clutch prevents reverse rotation. When that fails, torque multiplication is severely limited.

This ATI Racing 10-inch lockup SuperStreet master torque converter (part number 708330) is ready for fluid to be poured into the hub area before installation. Let the converter sit for at least an hour for the fluid to disperse and avoid spilling fluid when you install the converter. (Photo Courtesy ATI Performance Products)

Transmission Removal and Installation Highlights

For 1984–1991 models, removing the distributor cap prevents damage during transmission lowering to access the upper transmission retaining bolts. Furthermore, distributor removal provides access to the upper bellhousing bolts without requiring a 24-inch extension and flex socket to remove the fasteners, which are often difficult to loosen. Removing the pan and filter and letting it drain overnight significantly reduces fluid spillage during removal. The 1992–1996 LT1/LT4 catalytic converter placement severely complicates access to the side transmission bolts. It requires specialized approaches, such as using customized 15-mm wrenches with material removed to navigate the converter support brackets.

When removing 1984–1993 transmissions, first disconnect the TV cable from the throttle body to allow valve actuator assembly disconnection at the transmission. When disconnecting the 15-mm nut to remove the shift lever, hold the lever with an adjustable wrench to avoid cable damage. Selector cable crimp failures allow dangerous shift-position misalignment (for example, believing that you're in park while you're actually in reverse). Some 1988 and all 1989–1996 models require starter removal to access the dust covers. Note that later aluminum gear-reduction starters use solid covers with access holes, unlike earlier slotted designs that permit service without removal.

The 1992–1996 models demand complete exhaust removal, which requires assistance due to the size of the assembly. Earlier L83/L98 models only require front-pipe and center-hanger removal. The LT1/LT4 catalytic converter placement severely complicates side transmission-bolt access and requires specialized approaches, such as like customized 15-mm wrenches with material removed to navigate converter support brackets.

Lower the transmission sufficiently to access the cooler lines,

The 1984–1991 L83/L98 models need only front-pipe and center-hanger removal to drop the transmission. Spray all of the exhaust-system fasteners with your favorite rust penetrant, preferably days before removal. The 1992–1996 LT1/LT4's exhaust system, which is one piece after the catalytic converters, requires complete removal.

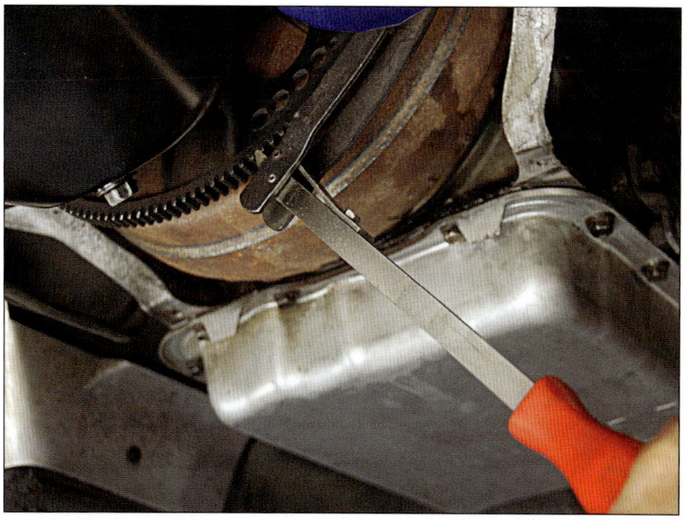

The 1988–1996 C4s require starter removal to drop the flexplate cover. Early units have a slotted cover to allow cover removal with the starter in place. This nifty flywheel holder helps remove the difficult-to-remove 15-mm hex-head bolts that retain the torque converter.

The two 10-mm, hex-head bolts retain the 1984–1991 exhaust system in the center and must be removed to access the torque-beam bolts. The 1992–1996 exhaust system uses a similar hanger with springs that must be removed. This exhaust hanger should not be omitted when building a custom exhaust system. It prevents exhaust leaks at the headers or manifolds.

When disconnecting the shift lever, hold the lever with an adjustable wrench when loosening or tightening the 15-mm nut to avoid cable damage. Cable crimp failures allow dangerous shift-position misalignment, which can lead to you believing that you're in park while you're actually in reverse.

Support the transmission (before removing the torque-beam bolts/nuts) preferably with a jack that is ready to lower the transmission. A short, 18-mm, box-end wrench holds the locknut during disassembly. This is an excellent reason to replace the nuts with the ZF Doc beam plates. Remove the front torque-beam bolt/nut at the differential and loosen the rear bolt/nut.

Once the torque beam is off the transmission extension housing, the unit is lowered to gain access to the upper transmission retaining bolts. A 24-inch-long, 3/8-inch extension and a good quality 9/16-inch swivel socket are required for bolt removal. Note all of the wiring on top of the bellhousing. Make sure that nothing is pinched during installation.

After the transmission bellhousing retaining bolts are removed, use a pry bar to push the torque converter back into the transmission and push the assembly off the engine.

As the transmission is lowered, the dipstick tube and throttle valve (TV) cable are removed. Next, the cooler lines are removed with the transmission on the jack and lowered slightly. Don't forget to remove the vehicle speed sensor (VSS) and electrical connector.

dipstick tube, and TV cable bracket, which uses a 10-mm fastener. After removing the retaining screw, pull the TV cable upward to disconnect it from its lever. Remove the dipstick tube during this stage. Reinstalling it during final assembly is significantly more difficult than installing it while it is in the lowered-position phase.

Flexplates

Factory flexplates feature three elongated mounting points. Performance applications utilize SFI 29.1-certified flexplates with six mounting points. SFI certification includes stringent safety standards that scale with power/speed increases that potentially require shields, blankets, and fluid-containment systems. Sanctioning bodies enforce specific requirements, so familiarize yourself with applicable regulations before track participation. SFI standards protect lives through engineering standards rather than arbitrary restrictions.

During installation, check the crankshaft pilot clearance and pump engagement. Proper converter installation should prevent a 3/8-inch rod insertion between the converter and the case. Verify the torque-converter rotation as the bellhousing bolts are tightened. Restricted rotation indicates misalignment that requires immediate correction. After torquing the bellhousing bolts to 45 ft-lbs, converters should rotate freely with 0.125- to 0.187-inch flexplate clearance. High-stall converters may require shimming to maintain the proper 0.125- to 0.187-inch pump engagement clearance and longer fasteners to ensure adequate thread engagement.

For the initial fill, add 9 quarts before starting to prevent dry-run damage. Final capacity varies by converter size: 9- to 11-inch converters require approximately 11 quarts, and OEM 13-inch units hold 12-plus quarts. Note that these transmissions disable overdrive when they are more than 1 quart low. Before testing, verify 1984–1993 TV cable adjustment to ensure full travel. During initial testing, shifts require several cycles to normalize. Mechanical systems (1984–1993) adapt quickly, while electronic systems (1994–1996) require extended adaptation periods. If any slippage occurs, immediately return under light throttle to verify the fluid level and the TV cable adjustment. Prompt intervention prevents catastrophic friction-material damage.

Manual Transmission Information and Options

Before examining specific transmissions, consider how operator technique significantly impacts longevity. Manual-transmission gear ratios enable skilled drivers to shift without clutch intervention when the RPM precisely matches the next gear ratio. As speeds increase, synchronizing internal ratios with engine RPM enables smooth transitions during upshifts and downshifts. In my 1991 6-speed, I primarily upshift without clutch disengagement and depress the pedal only when encountering resistance. Successful shifting requires precise timing between engine RPM (input speed) and road speed (output speed). Never force engagement when synchronization fails. This technique demands substantial practice and mechanical sensitivity.

Clutchless downshifting represents greater complexity and requires the engine RPM elevation to match the road speed. This demands even more practice, as forced engagement risks catastrophic synchronizer and gear damage. Extreme downshifts, such as shifting from fourth gear to first gear, for engine braking present particular dangers. Manual transmissions lack the protective safeguards of automatics and can potentially allow engine over-revving and wheel lockup during dramatic ratio changes.

The fundamental principle is that mastering clutchless shifting demonstrates proper speed matching, which reduces transmission stress—even during clutch-assisted shifting. Improperly timed shifts at high RPM overwhelm synchronizers, which are simple conical mechanisms with brass teeth that facilitate gear engagement. Mismatched speeds create extreme synchronizer stress to gradually wear their tapered engagement teeth and degrade shift quality.

Despite these techniques, never attempt clutchless shifting during competition or high-RPM operation! This is important.

Practice these techniques on expendable vehicles rather than on valuable 4+3 or ZF transmissions. Remember that excessive shift force invariably indicates gear clash. Developing the proper technique ultimately delivers smoother operation while dramatically extending component life.

Never remove a transmission for difficult shifting (particularly into first or reverse) without first verifying proper clutch disengagement. Symptoms such as difficult engagement or grinding frequently indicate a dragging clutch rather than internal transmission problems. The engagement of first gear remains easier than reverse because its synchronizer assists engagement between shafts rotating in identical directions, while reverse must halt and reverse rotation. Common causes include insufficient clutch master cylinder fluid, damaged pressure plates, or worn crankshaft pilot bearings. All prevent complete input-shaft rotation.

1984–1988 4+3 DNE Overdrive

This transmission suits Gymkhana, time trials, and short courses with stock powerplants. Its innovative push-button overdrive activation from second gear provides strategic advantages in torque-limiting scenarios. Although it's primarily designed for fuel economy, upshifting and downshifting the overdrive unit while in lower gears can benefit corner entry and exit.

The Doug Nash Engineering (DNE) overdrive employs counterintuitive engineering. It maintains direct drive (1:1) through spring-loaded clutch plates while engaging overdrive through the hydraulic pressure that releases these clutches. As with automatics, it requires dual holding mechanisms for output-shaft rotation, including a one-way clutch to secure the ring gear during overdrive. Its primary weakness lies in the front bearing assembly, which simultaneously manages radial loads and thrust forces from the holding clutch. Later versions incorporated improved bearings. Maximum torque capacity remains approximately 350 ft-lbs, which is a threshold that is easily challenged by high-traction tires.

The overdrive section utilizes Dexron III automatic transmission fluid for clutch operation and lubrication. Its output-shaft-driven pressure pump prevents first-gear overdrive engagement (ECM controlled) until sufficient pressure develops to completely release the direct-drive clutch. This configuration creates an effective 7-speed transmission. Early 1984 models featured console-mounted overdrive switches that complicated the rapid up/down shifting progression, while late-1984 and subsequent units incorporated shifter-mounted buttons to allow complete gear selection without removing your hand from the shift knob. Like the 700-R4/4L60, 1984–1987 models used throttle valve cables to increase hydraulic system pressure during wide-open throttle.

Internal Design and Common Weak Points

A telltale sign of overdrive failure appears when 75W-90 gear oil from the 4-speed section contaminates the Dexron III in the overdrive unit and necessitates a costly overhaul. Rebuilding presents several challenges. The rear clutch piston remains spring-loaded at rest and requires air pressure and specialized procedures (detailed in the factory service manual) to safely disassemble. In addition, the main carrier assembly demands precise indexing of multiple components to prevent lockup. This complexity makes professional rebuilding strongly advisable.

The BorgWarner 4-speed section proved robust until challenged by high-traction tires. Third-gear disengagement was the most common issue, which has been addressed through specialized synchronizer rings with angled internal splines that force inward gear retention. The underlying cause typically involved failing DNE units that created output-shaft movement during throttle transitions. For comprehensive service, Brian at S-K Speed Racing Equipment has extensive knowledge and component inventory for complete 4+3 transmission rebuilds.

Servicing

The overdrive incorporates radiator-mounted cooling like automatic transmissions that necessitate regular fluid maintenance, particularly following engine overheating events. Factory fluid pans utilized silicone sealant rather than conventional gaskets, although aftermarket filter kits often include paper alternatives. These paper gaskets frequently seal poorly due to distorted pan bolt holes. Silicone resealing requires hot, oil-resistant formulations that are

The often-maligned 1984–1988 4+3 automatic overdrive assembly couples to a BorgWarner T-10 4-speed manual transmission that can safely handle 400 ft-lbs of torque at best.

Loose-fitting gearsets and bearings require 75-90W non-synthetic gear oil for optimum operation and shifting. Slicker synthetic gear oils cause shifting issues because the synchronizer blocker rings are unable to slow down the upshifted/downshifted gearset.

The synchronizer's internal grooves and cuts allow the gear oil to be released as the ring pushes against the intended gear to be engaged. Note that the left has multiple vertical slots, the center has minimal slots, and the right ring has large slots. The larger slots allow lubricant to disperse quickly so that the ring grabs the gear and slows it down for gear engagement.

Use caution when removing the 4+3 front separator plate, as it is under extreme spring pressure. The recessed flat-head Allen screws are difficult to remove, and the rear spring plate must be contained before you attempt its removal.

This procedure contains the clutch plate spring pressure before disassembling the Doug Nash Engineering (DNE) 4+3 overdrive unit. Three 8-mm 1.25 x 45-mm-long bolts hold the spring plate, and a special tool is required to unload the captured spring plate after geartrain removal. This is why most C4 owners have professionals overhaul this unit.

This is a failed radial and thrust load bearing. The carrier assembly has been damaged from being pushed into the bulkhead separator plate. Ball bearings are missing from the radial thrust loaded bearing. When this occurs, fluid swaps between the overdrive unit and manual-transmission section of the assembly.

The 4+3 filter screen slips over the pump inlet, sealing to the tube with a rubber grommet. Make sure that the TV cable does not interfere with the filter after installation.

The shifter itself was decent quality with a reverse-lockout rod and an overdrive button on top of the shift knob for 1985-and-later C4s. The alignment tool (0.580-inch wide, 0.125-inch thick, and 2.00-inch long with a 0.750-inch tab) with the yellow paint mark is inserted into the shifter base. The driver-side console side cover must be removed to access the shifter for lubrication and adjustment of the shift linkage.

applied to alcohol-cleaned surfaces. Allow drainage for a minimum time period of 1 hour before applying sealant to prevent fluid contamination during reassembly.

Overdrive Operation and Controls

The 4+3 shifter represents a significant weakness since it's mounted to the transmission tunnel with exposed linkages. This arrangement is surprisingly archaic for the C4's otherwise-advanced design and depends entirely on drivetrain position stability, which contributes to gear disengagement during load transitions. Reverse lockout rods wear at the end, and eventually reverse engagement is capable without knob release. Throwback Automotive's 4+3 reverse lockout rod assembly is available for early and late 4+3 shifters.

Maintenance access requires removing the driver's seat and console panels for shifter service or neutral gate adjustment. Incorporating short-throw shift levers at the transmission may not have the expected outcome. Once installed, they require a labor-intensive neutral gate adjustment of all shift linkages. The shorter levers require more shift effort to engage all forward gear ranges.

First-Gear Switch Failures

The most common no-overdrive-upshift concern is the first-gear switch, which is located in the 4-speed section at the shifter shaft. The ECM requires gear-change input from the switch. If it does not receive an upshift into second gear, overdrive will not be enabled. First-gear switches were discontinued, and new old stock (NOS) parts may be available and costly. The switch can be bypassed by removing the harness connector and placing a jumper wire across the connector terminals. This circumvents ECM control to allow upshifting into overdrive in first gear if you're traveling at 20 to 25 mph. Under ECM control, as the vehicle speed drops below 25 mph, overdrive is disengaged and this too will be disabled.

ECM Bypass Options

Bypassing the ECM gives you complete control of the 4+3 overdrive unit.

For 1984, locate the overdrive relay, cut the tan/black wire approximately 6 inches from the relay, install an eye terminal, and ground this wire to bypass ECM control. For absolute control, additionally

Period-correct short-throw shift arms that reduce shifter lever travel for quicker shifts occasionally appear on secondary markets, such as eBay. The linkage pin can be moved up 0.750 inch using a 0.500-inch carbide drill bit. Add the shifter-bushing kit to provide shorter shifter travel and smooth shifting. Always hold the shift lever when tightening the shift-lever-shaft nut to avoid synchronizer damage.

The side cover rear of the transmission is where the first gear switch is located. The 1984 DNE units have multiple switches on both shift shafts. It also requires the same connector bypass installed.

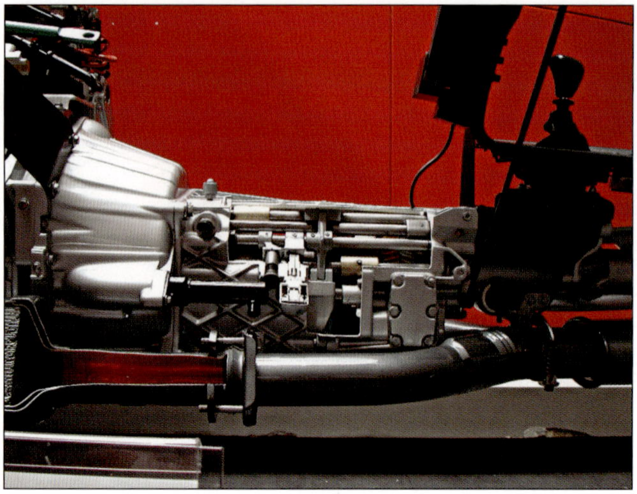

The 1989 C4 had a major breakthrough with the German-built ZF 6-speed transmission. The transmission had to be shipped overseas for repair, and repair parts were difficult to source. (Photo Courtesy Andy Bolig)

bypass the first-gear switch to enable overdrive engagement at any speed/temperature.

For 1985–1988, remove the black/light-blue wire from ECM connector C7 and the tan/black wire from position A7. Then, connect these wires together. Complete control requires an additional first-gear switch bypass.

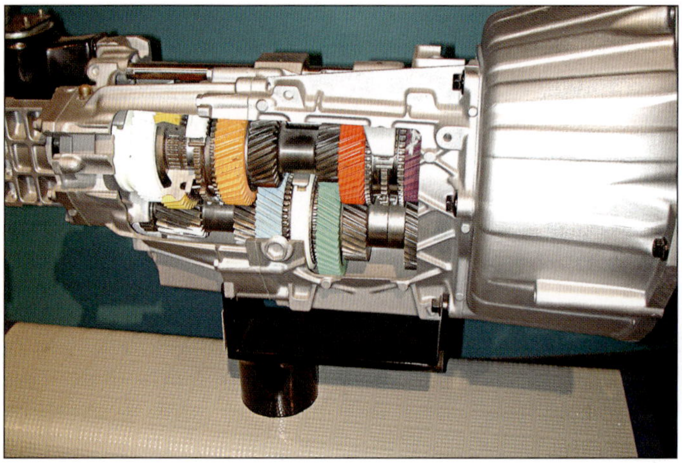

The ZF internal gearing is precise with robust shaft support (tapered and Torrington roller bearings). Specific gear oil is required due to the tighter internal tolerances. (Photo Courtesy Andy Bolig)

1989–1996 C4 ZF 6-Speed

The 145-pound ZF 6-speed's 2.68:1 first-gear ratio required grunt to get the typical 3,300-pound C4 rolling. Second gear was 1.80:1, third gear was 1.29:1, and fourth gear was 1.00:1. For overdrive ratios, fifth gear was 0.75:1 and the final drive was 0.50:1. Reverse was 2.50:1. All gear selections were synchronized. A purpose-built unit, ably handling 450-plus ft-lbs of torque, was a great fit for the C4 engine. The Corvette's first integral shifter was smooth and abrupt with no external linkage to be concerned with, and tight tolerances made them very reliable.

There are two ZF 6-speed input-shaft outer-diameter housings. The early ZF 6-speed (produced from 1989 to 1993 with a black tag on the case) has 1.375-inch input shaft–style release bearings that will be loose on the later 1.310-inch-diameter ZF 6-speed (produced from 1994 to 1996 with a blue tag on the case) input-shaft housing.

Computer-Aided Gear Selector and Bypass Options

Corporate average fuel economy (CAFE) standards mandated the computer-aided gear selector (CAGS) system, which forced first- to fourth-gear shifting patterns during light throttle operation to block a second- or third-gear selection. Aggressive driving prevented solenoid activation. CAGS bypass kits are available online, or you can be resourceful with a rubber cap or tape to prevent connector contamination. The 1996 C4s require a resistor on the wire-harness side to prevent an SES light. They are also available online. This is an off-road modification and not for street use.

Serviceability and Rebuilding Support

ZF ownership challenges persist due to parts and service scarcity. Initially, warranty work required units to be returned to Germany, as the ZF S6-40 was a low-production, Corvette-specific application. Currently, ZF Doc offers the best rebuilding support and parts sourcing. While later factory service manuals contain detailed overhaul procedures, early editions provide rudimentary ZF information.

Do-it-yourself rebuilding requires fabricating custom assembly fixtures and specialized tools, such as gear pullers. Given the intensive labor and expense involved, errors are extremely costly. This transmission specifically demands previous rebuilding experience and should never represent a novice's initial project, particularly with budget constraints.

Common Issue

The most common concern is countershaft gear rattle or a chucking noise (a noise that is rhythmic back and forth) at idle. This can be proven if the noise goes away when the clutch pedal is applied. Disengaging the clutch unloads the input shaft and countershaft gear. ZF Doc has a countershaft shim kit to tighten up the countershaft endplay to help this known phenomenon. This rattle is greatly accentuated with a replacement solid flywheel.

Remove the countershaft plug at the front of the transmission with a sharp pick to force it into the plug. Then, pry it out. The bearing retaining the snap ring is removed, and the thickest shim possible is inserted to allow installation of the snap ring. A light preload on the snap ring is acceptable, which means that it may require tapping into its fully seated position.

These are ZF Doc's upgrade components (minus the input shaft). The tungsten inert gas (TIG)–welded torque arm beam plates are well-made with self-locking nuts. Torque-beam alignment tabs are included. The countershaft shims and cover with the extension housing bushing and seal are shown.

Short-Throw Shifter Options

If you're in the market for a short-throw shifter, a few options are available, with Core Shifters and ZF Doc being the best. The Core Shifters all-new (no core required) 1.250-inch lower stick reduces the throw by 40 percent, which also increases shift

The 1989–1995 computer-aided gear selection (CAGS) solenoid white connector is disconnected to prevent ECM/PCM 1-4 intervention during upshifting. Plug kits are available to keep dirt out of the harness-side connector. The reverse-lamp switch at the top left corner is difficult to replace with the transmission in place.

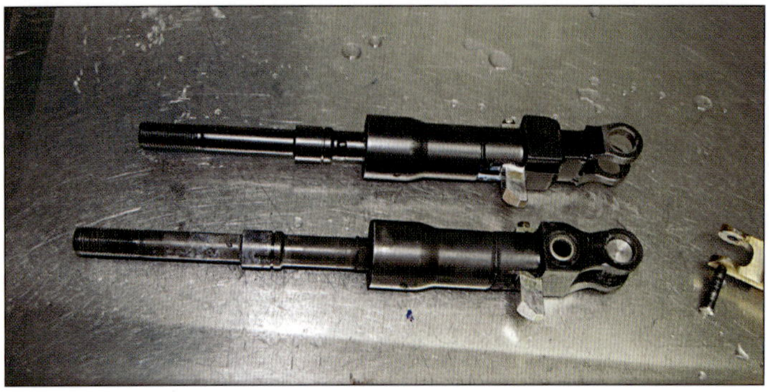

The ZF Doc modified shifter stick (top) is side by side with the original. The modified stick pivot bearing is covered with tape to prevent transit contamination. The longer lower portion of the stick's length shortens shifter travel and reduces torque to the shift application.

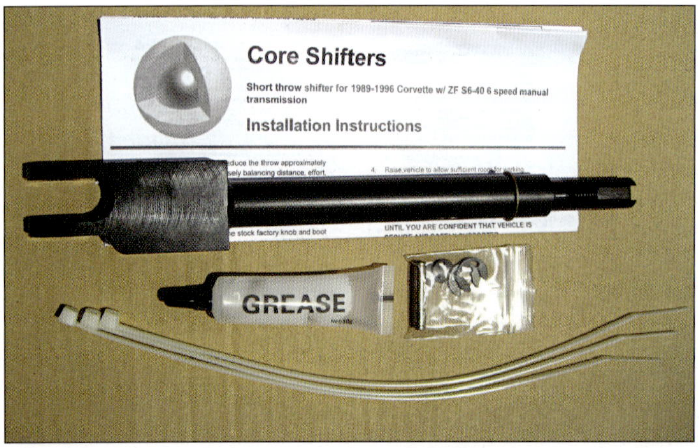

This Core Shifters piece is solid steel (two parts welded together), which eliminates the rubber isolator between the upper and lower parts. The lever is more rigid and precise, but it's harsher with no cushion to absorb the impact of shifting. There is a risk of noise and vibration transmitting through the lever, which is exacerbated when converting to a single mass flywheel. The short-throw ZF shifter stick comes with the attaching pieces and detailed installation instructions. (Photo Courtesy Chris Rinehart/ Core Shifters)

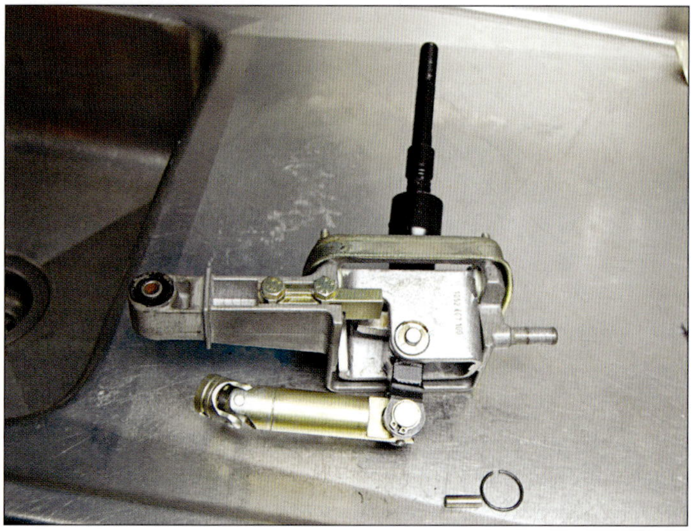

The ZF Doc modified short-throw shifter is ready for installation. The pin and ring retain the shift linkage onto the transmission's shifter shaft. The pin is installed with minimal effort, and the ring prevents the pin from coming out.

The 1989–1995 ZF 6-speed shifter requires this reverse lockout knob to be pulled up for reverse shifting. ZF Doc and Throwback Automotive have well-made replicas of this hard-to-find discontinued GM part.

effort. The ZF Doc shifter is shortened 1.100 inches at the top and lengthened 0.562 inch at the bottom. Shift effort is maintained at the pre-modification level. Shifter modification requires a core charge or sending your shifter in for service. Complete instructions are included with ZF Doc's short-throw shifter lever package.

Lubrication Choices and Aftermarket Alternatives

The ZF officially requires 10W-60 lubricant for all-climate shifting performance, and annual changes are recommended for seasonally stored vehicles to prevent condensation accumulation. My personal preference is to use Redline MTL 75W-80 GL-4. It delivers excellent all-around performance, although it requires additional shift effort below operating temperatures of 100°F. The specified 10W-60 optimizes cold-climate operation. When intact rubber boots protect the shifter mechanism, it should not require regular maintenance. For applications exceeding stock capabilities, the Tremec TR-6060 handles up to 650 ft-lbs, depending on the selected gear ratios.

Tremec Performance TKO and TKX 5-Speed

When evaluating 1984–1988 transmission replacement options, consider the true cost versus the advertised price. While Tremec swap kits appear expensive compared to used ZF units ($2,000-plus), the latter often require console/tunnel modifications and potentially harbor hidden synchronizer damage that can carry $3,000-plus repair costs. Factor in additional ZF-specific components, such as the bellhousing, slave cylinder, and hardware, and used installations often exceed Tremec conversion costs.

The Tremec TKX provides new components with warranty protection and engineered fitment. Importantly, both 4+3 and ZF transmissions utilize torque-beam support like automatics, which makes the TKX a more straightforward adaptation than T56 and TR6060 alternatives.

T56 and TR-6060 Swaps: Custom Work Required

The T56 and TR-6060 swaps demand fabricating custom torque-beam adapters that require substantial metalworking and welding capabilities. Critical considerations include maintaining proper driveline angles during adapter design and constructing offset shifter mechanisms. Realistically evaluate your fabrication skills and equipment access against purchasing engineered solutions, particularly when prototype iterations may be necessary. Reference the LS-swap section of this book (chapter 4) for detailed T56 and TR-6060 adapter guidance.

The Silver Sport Transmissions (SST) 1984–1988 4+3 to 5-speed TKX Tremec conversion kit has all of the pieces to make this a true bolt-in replacement. Upgrade clutch assemblies, bellhousings, driveshafts, and fluid are available separately through SST. The shift lever is in the original location for a seamless fit. (Photo Courtesy Silver Sport Transmissions)

Installation Tips: Torque-Beam Mounting, Alignment, and Torquing

Torque-beam failures frequently manifest as elongated mounting holes from loose fasteners, which is a condition that often goes undetected until it is a severe issue. While automatic-equipped C4s mask this problem (body-mounted shifters with flexible cables accommodate movement), manual transmissions immediately reveal issues through shifter-position changes during acceleration and deceleration. A proper repair requires replacement beams, which are increasingly scarce, or welding restoration with precise hole positioning. Avoid the common big-wrench solution of overtightening existing hardware.

The close proximity of fastener holes to the driveshaft support components inevitably leads to bushing-seal failures. Over-tightening frequently with an impact wrench will crack the extension or differential housings and distort critical seal and bushing surfaces. Always completely remove torque beams for inspection and thoroughly clean the factory white insulating paste. Apply polytetrafluoroethylene (PTFE)-enhanced thread sealant between the torque-arm and transmission/differential mating surfaces to prevent corrosion and galvanic activity.

Verify the replacement fastener's diameter. Aftermarket bolts frequently undersize critical dimensions. For optimal torque-beam security, consider ZF Doc's C4 beam plates that feature integrated self-locking nuts and reinforcement plates. These eliminate the awkward 18-mm/21-mm wrench positioning above the torque beam and ensure consistent fastener torque.

ZF Doc offers precision alignment gauges to ensure optimal driveline positioning. Measure directly above and rightward of the front U-joint yoke. Proper alignment requires maintaining 1.77 ± 0.236 inch of clearance between the support top and the underbody, with 1.1 ± 0.236 inch clearance from the support's right side to passenger sidewall. Torque the transmission-side fasteners to exactly 37 ft-lbs, which is a threshold that is easily exceeded even by low-power impact wrenches.

Clutches, Driveshaft, Axle Shafts, and Differential

All C4 Corvette clutch systems utilize hydraulic actuation with diaphragm (finger-style) pressure plates. The 1984–1988 models featured traditional flywheels with center-sprung clutch discs and employed hydraulic cylinders that pushed the clutch forks for disengagement. The 1989 models marked a significant design change with the introduction of pull-style, non-sprung center clutch discs for ZF 6-speed transmissions.

The ZF 6-speeds introduced magnesium bellhousings (1990–1995), while 1989–1990 models and 1990–1995 ZR1s had aluminum bellhousings. General Motors incorporated separator plates to isolate magnesium from dissimilar alloys. These components are frequently omitted during service. Pull-type clutch applications offer limited performance upgrades and no aftermarket flywheel options without total clutch replacement.

Flywheel-clutch selection involves some critical limitations. The 1988–1996 ZF bellhousings cannot accommodate 168-tooth/11-inch flywheels and require 153-tooth/10.5-inch alternatives. The 1984–1988 4+3 bellhousings accept larger 168-tooth/11-inch flywheels that may require input-shaft-mounted hydraulic cylinders. Serious competitors should prioritize SFI-approved bellhousings due to the potential danger zone for feet and legs during catastrophic failures. Higher torque capacity typically correlates with more aggressive engagement and increased pedal effort. Consult clutch suppliers with specific requirements.

The 1989–1996 ZF Doc performance clutch kits convert to a center-sprung, push-style diaphragm clutch. The original rubber-damped flywheel is replaced with a solid version with a transmission input shaft–mounted hydraulic clutch cylinder. The RAM Clutches spring-cushioned disc provides smooth, solid engagement. There will be a noise like a guitar string reverberating at low speeds as you accelerate. You can power through, accelerate quickly, and keep the cruise RPM higher. The ZF Doc countershaft endplay shim kit will help quell some of the solid flywheel's inherent reverberations.

The 6-mm cover bolt is rotated counterclockwise to reveal the 12-mm hex pivot ball that requires clockwise removal. The clutch fork can be forcibly removed during disassembly, and the installation requires pivot ball removal. Apply penetrant, wait, and apply more before attempting to remove stubborn pivot balls.

The ZF rubber-cushioned, damped flywheel provides smooth clutch engagement and eliminates the driveline drone and countershaft-main shaft chucking noise. The clutch plate side of the flywheel should not rotate more than 1.378 inches (35 mm) back and forth. All C4 flywheels should be torqued to a maximum of 74 ft-lbs to avoid rear main oil seal leaks.

The 1984–1996 C4 original clutch system had an external slave cylinder. This Lakewood bellhousing has an aftermarket replacement with a modified Lakewood boot. The -4 AN steel-braided line will be used for plumbing.

Eight damping springs help quell the inherent ZF low-speed throttle noises. The new Ram C4 conversion (part number 09-0810S) is a direct fit for the conversion. Clean the flywheel and pressure-plate surfaces with alcohol until the cloth remains clean after wiping.

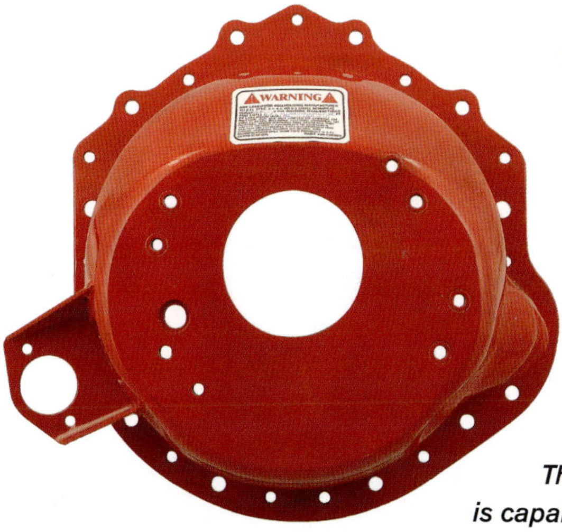

The Lakewood 15020SFI-certified bellhousing is a suitable replacement for the 1984–1988 C4 original aluminum bellhousing. The bellhousing is capable of housing the 14-inch, 168-tooth flywheel and retaining hydraulic clutch actuation. A 1993–1997 Camaro/Firebird slave cylinder and Earl's LS641001 adapter fitting allows the use of a -3 Teflon-lined, stainless-steel braided hose connection.

The C4 hydraulic clutch systems generally provide reliable service, particularly with regular use. However, moisture infiltration causes cylinder-bore corrosion and initiates minor leaks. Master cylinder piston leakage occurs hidden behind firewall insulation. Difficult reverse engagement often indicates hydraulic-system issues. If pumping the clutch pedal temporarily improves shifting, inspect for low fluid level and leakage points.

Driveshaft, Axle Shafts, Wheel-Bearing Hubs, and Universal Joints

Transitioning the power to the rear tires requires a knowledge that you have the right parts that take your right foot's input to the output of acceleration. A host of quality parts are needed to enact this process.

This Speedway Motors clutch air gap measuring tool, which costs about $70, checks for the required air gap of 0.150 to 0.200 inch for the best clutch disengagement and adequate release-bearing clearance as the clutch disc wears. The clutch release bearing must be fully seated against the input shaft. It is well worth the cost to avoid smoking a clutch.

This tool has 0.100-inch increments with an O-ring that records the distance. It takes practice to read properly, and you should measure twice. This extremely critical measurement will help to obtain maximum clutch life. The air gap is set by shims placed under the slave cylinder provided in the Ram Clutches comprehensive kit.

The Ram Clutches–provided stud replaces the lower input-shaft retaining bolt to prevent clutch-release cylinder rotation. Once installed, measure from the end of the stud to the clutch pressure plate fingers. Some setups require a shorter stud. Cut the stud if necessary and smoothen the cut area to ease the clutch cylinder installation.

The OEM ZF bellhousing with the Ram Clutches input shaft–mounted clutch release bearing is ready for the transmission. The provided clutch cylinder hoses are connected to the existing C4 clutch line or directly to the clutch master cylinder. Apply small dabs of Super Lube Grease (part number 21030) inside of the release bearing and align the stud clutch release-bearing slots.

There were two versions of the clutch master cylinder pushrod retaining feature: one is a spring clip and the other is a flat metal retainer. With the driver's seat removed, the easiest way to find this pushrod and retainer is lying on your back.

The race-inspired Tilton master cylinder from After Dark Speed is a true bolt-on kit with an adjustable pedal stop. The adapter mount allows you to bolt on the master cylinder with ease, and all of the hardware, the hose, and the fittings are included. Expect a shortened pedal travel with complete clutch disengagement on those high-RPM shifts. (Photo Courtesy After Dark Speed)

The 1989–1996 ZF 6-speed clutch master cylinder requires removal to bleed the system. When installed, the bleeder faces down. After removal, I hang it on the shield upside down and place the bleeder at the top. Carefully, install the cylinder by aligning the push pin and slowly pushing it toward the bellhousing. Torque the nuts to 20 ft-lbs.

Axle Shafts as Suspension Components?

The C4s feature an unconventional drivetrain-suspension integration where axle-shaft universal joints function as suspension pivot points. Worn universal joints directly affect alignment by altering camber and toe angles. Another unique design aspect involves differential drive yokes contacting the internal pinion-gear support shaft, which is a potential wear point. These side yokes rely on snap rings for proper positioning against the support shaft. Significant side-yoke wear typically emerges beyond 125,000 miles and possibly requires internal differential repairs to maintain suspension geometry.

Driveshaft and U-Joint Failure Symptoms

The C4 driveshafts experience minimal angle changes during torque application to create concentrated loading on specific bearing surfaces. Meanwhile, axle shafts undergo multidirectional movement throughout rotation. Universal joint failure indicators include rust trails that emerge from seals that are visible during inspection, clicking sounds during acceleration or cornering that progress to crunching noises, and any perceptible movement during wheel manipulation. Any detectable play warrants immediate replacement.

The factory universal joints omit grease fittings to reduce costs, and non-greaseable performance alternatives command premium prices due to their uncompromised structural integrity because grease channels inherently weaken joints. Always select replacement joints with an anticorrosion coating to prevent the galvanic reaction between steel joints and aluminum yokes. I recommend the Spicer 5-3613X (driveshaft) and 5-3615X (axle shafts). They are higher priced but are the appropriate components.

The use of U-joint removal and installation tools can be detrimental to an aluminum shaft. The pressure applied by the screw is difficult to feel, and the yoke end can be distorted.

Axle-Shaft Evolution and Upgrade Recommendations

The C4 axle shafts evolved throughout production to address noise concerns from the torque-beam suspension/driveline arrangement.

Rotate the differential side yoke to the 9 o'clock position. Remove the upper bolts at the differential side and the lower bolts on the knuckle (wheel) side. Rotate the shaft 180 degrees and repeat. After bolt removal, pull both U-joint cups from one side. The axle shaft can be removed without toe or camber link removal.

Universal joint cup alignment is paramount to avoid yoke material removal. The same goes for installation. The U-joint cap is tapped into place while holding the U-joint cross-shaft up to prevent displacement of the roller bearings. The cross-shaft must be held up until the shaft is rolled over 180 degrees. Then, repeat the procedure.

Make sure that the clips are fully seated into the groove and that the U-joint can be rotated by hand. The U-joint should have zero movement between cups once the clips are seated fully. Some U-joint cups may be loose enough to push out with your hand. At that point, the yoke or shaft should be replaced.

Final production versions incorporated cardboard sleeves with center holes to mitigate harshness. These axle shafts represent a relative weakness compared to driveshafts. My modestly enhanced 1990 L98 sheared one upon gaining traction. While the driveshaft diameter increases remain constrained by torque beam clearances, axle shafts can potentially accommodate 4-inch diameters (versus stock 3.5-inch diameters), although it can potentially interfere with coilover conversions. Maintain aluminum construction while increasing wall thickness, rather than switching to steel materials.

Steel driveshaft/axle-shaft conversions produce intolerable ringing harmonics that intensify with speed. While they are appropriate for competition applications, street installations require substantial sound attenuation equipment for acceptable operation.

Denny's Driveshafts & Driveline Parts (dennysdriveshaft.com) and Performance Shaft Technologies manufacture C4-specific driveshafts and axle shafts. When ordering custom-length components, precisely follow supplier measurement protocols. Incorrect specifications result in unusable parts with no recourse.

Wheel Bearing Hubs: Design and Service Life

The C4s utilize dual-row, ball-bearing hub assemblies optimized for reduced rolling resistance. While tapered roller bearings superseded ball bearings in the 1950s due to load-capacity limitations, modern vehicles have returned to large-diameter ball-bearing assemblies that offer minimal friction. These sealed, non-serviceable units eliminate messy repacking procedures and provide excellent durability.

Despite durability, these bearings eventually develop play that is detectable during inspection. Zero play is the only acceptable standard, as wear allows wheel movement that affects alignment and potentially brake operation. Bearing assemblies span a dramatic range in pricing. Suspiciously inexpensive sets (four for less than $200) suggest questionable quality, while premium units command $500 each. Reputable Timken front bearing assemblies for 1984–1990 applications are reasonable and cost approximately $250. The 1991–1996 front bearings command higher prices (in the $400 range) due to integrated antilock braking system (ABS) tone rings and sensors.

Rear Bearing Washer Confusion and Recommendations

Rear wheel bearings bring confusion concerning a thin steel washer (also known as a crush washer) placed between the rear spindle drive yoke and wheel-bearing assembly. Field observations show that not all C4s had the thin washers installed from the factory. They were not found in the 1984–1985 factory service manual, while part number 14076924 (a 58-mm outside-diameter washer) can be found in later factory service manuals and General Motors part manuals. I highly recommend reusing the washers. If yours are missing or you have a 1984–1985 C4, search the internet for a pair. They prevent the forward-reverse loading clicking noise. The clicking noise manifests most often in manual-transmission C4s.

High-Performance Bearing Solutions

Detroit Speed SKF X-Tracker racing wheel-bearing hub adapter kits are available. They stabilize wheel and brake-rotor movement and prevent caliper piston knockback. The

This seal, which is installed in 1984–1985 C4s, keeps dirt and grit off the wheel-bearing seals, which ironically have integral seals. I prefer to use them on all C4s to keep trash off the anti-lock brake (ABS) tone rings and sensors. They're available at Corvette Central, Zip Corvette, and other major Corvette specialty stores.

Apply high-pressure wheel-bearing grease lightly to both sides of the washer to keep the washer in place during assembly and prevent galling during torquing.

The Detroit Speed SKF X-Tracker racing wheel bearing hub adapters are torqued to 70 ft-lbs. This adapter and wheel bearing kit is specified by Detroit Speed for 1991–1996 Corvettes.

Regarding mandatory rear wheel-bearing installation procedures for long-term bearing life, a General Motors factory service manual stated, "the vehicle should not rest on the tires or be moved until the spindle nut is properly tightened." The spindle-nut torque is now 186 to 200 ft-lbs. You must do this, especially with manual-transmission applications.

This part is for use on 1988–1996 Corvette rear knuckles that mount in the stock bearing location with an integral X-Tracker bearing antilock braking system (ABS) sensor that provides wheel speed data. The Van Steel X-Tracker hub/spindle adapter kit begins with an American-made PoppySpeed Racing CNC-milled, 7075-billet, heat-treated aluminum hub adapter. An SKF Racing X-Tracker hub assembly with the double-row, angular contact ball bearing arrangement increases bearing capacity and hub stiffness by 50 percent over traditional tapered bearing units. Torque loading is handled by the Driveshaft Shop 30-spline 300M spindle to provide significantly increased torque capacity over the stock 27-spline unit. (Photo Courtesy Van Steel)

wheel hubs are in the factory location and do not affect wheel offset while retaining full functionality of the ABS system.

Differential Strength and Model-Specific Applications

The differential becomes a vulnerability when combining high torque with sticky tires. The 1984 manual-transmission C4s received Dana 36 units, which is the same differential used in all automatic-transmission applications through 1996. From 1985–1996, manual transmissions were upgraded to Dana 44 differentials that were better suited to withstand L98 and LT power output. While Dana 36 units tolerate extended burnouts in automatic applications, each instance of traction engagement progressively compromises their longevity.

Fortunately, automatic transmissions provide component protection through torque converter absorption, whereas sudden traction applied with spinning tires creates maximum differential stress. Dana 44 units adequately support road-racing applications without requiring additional driveline modifications to a point. Dedicated drag applications typically employ tube chassis with Dana 60 solid axles to accommodate extreme power-traction levels.

Differential gear-ratio terminology often confuses newcomers. Ratios that are numerically higher (4.10:1) provide quicker acceleration, while ratios that are numerically lower (2.59:1) require more initial torque for movement and a higher top speed. The proper ratio selection is one of the most critical project specifications that affects overall performance characteristics. Axle ratio "G" codes are noted on the console door placard. Missing placard information can be verified, such as marking the driveshaft and wheel and denoting when a full revolution has occurred. Rotate the wheel one revolution while observing driveshaft revolutions. If the driveshaft rotates 3.5 times per wheel revolution, you have a 3.50:1 ratio etc.

Selecting the Correct Ratio

Substantial ratio changes produce immediate perceptible driving dynamics. They are often more noticeable than expensive component upgrades. For automatic-equipped C4s with 2.59:1 or 2.73:1 ratios and a 0.069:1 final drive ratio, switching to 4.10:1 creates dramatic low-end improvement that is equivalent to adding 50 ft-lbs torque. However, it noticeably compromises highway driving. A 3.07:1 ratio often provides better balance with L98 automatic-transmission-equipped drivetrains. The 1992–1996 LT1 engine and automatic transmission combination, with its higher-RPM power curves, benefits from steeper 3.50:1 ratios to complement different torque characteristics.

Factory manual transmissions received numerically higher ratios than automatics: a 3.07:1 ratio for 4+3 models, a 3.45:1 ratio standard,

The Dana 44 rear axle yoke snap rings were available in eight different thicknesses. The Dana 36 units had seven possibilities. The target clearance between the pinion pin and axle shaft is 0.00 to 0.203 mm or 0.00 to 0.008 mm maximum. Quick Performance has an 0.085-inch-thick snap ring. Limit how wide you open the snap ring when removing (to avoid distortion).

Posi-Traction differentials (standard equipment on all C4 Corvettes) use metallic clutch plates to prevent wheelspin when one tire loses traction. High-tension steel-wave plates under the clutch packs load them to prevent wheelspin under most conditions.

The Eaton Detroit Truetrac Posi-Traction unit (part number 913A614) is an all-new replacement for the Dana 44 1985–1996 C4s. Truetrac uses a gearset to limit wheel-spin when slippage occurs, eliminating clutch plates that can wear.

and an optional 3.54:1 performance ratio for LT1 versions. Common Dana 44 upgrades feature 4.09:1 gearing for enhanced launches. This compensates for relatively tall first-gear ratios (4+3 overdrive: 2.88:1; ZF 6-speed: 2.68:1) and a lack of torque converter multiplication. The 0.050:1 final-drive gear ratio (sixth gear) does not affect highway cruising speeds.

Combined Differential/Transmission Ratios Matter

For spirited street applications, aim for 10.0:1 combined first-gear/differential ratios. Calculate this by multiplying the transmission first-gear ratio by the differential ratio. For example, for the 700-R4/4L60, take 3.07:1 (first gear) × 3.25:1 (differential) = 9.98:1 (combined). A 700-R4/4L60 with a 2.59:1 differential yields 7.95:1 combined, which is excellent for economy but underwhelming for acceleration.

Aggressive camshafts (270-plus degrees) paired with tall gearing (2.73:1/2.59:1) create particularly disappointing launch performance despite strong high-speed characteristics. Comprehensive planning must integrate camshaft profiles that affect effective compression, torque-converter specifications, and intended use. Proper gearing outweighs raw horsepower for short-course applications to improve acceleration and engine braking.

Understanding differential operation extends beyond familiar ring-and-pinion terminology. During cornering, axle shafts must rotate at different speeds, as the tires follow paths of different radii. The mechanism utilizes four small pinion gears: two idlers ride on the pinion shaft and two have both internal and external splines. External splines engage Posi-Traction clutch plates, while internal splines connect to axle-shaft yokes to transfer motion from the ring-gear carrier. These four pinions, housed within the carrier, enable differential axle-shaft rotation during turns and prevent road-surface scrubbing.

Ring-and-Pinion Setup and the Case for Pro Service

Ring-and-pinion replacement demands precise setup techniques. Critical adjustments include pinion

This pinion depth shim may require multiple bearing removals and installations to obtain the desired pinion-ring gear pattern. There are setup tools to verify the required shim thickness for a one-and-done bearing installation. Setup tools are costly for one-time use. The complete, ready-to-go unit makes more sense.

If these photos don't concern you, consider a ring and pinion replacement. Adjusting pinion depth requires carrier-side bearing removal for shim changes on both sides to obtain the correct (0.15 to 0.23 mm and 0.006 to 0.009 mm) pinion–ring gear backlash.

There are two methods for setting pinion-bearing preload. This earlier design uses shims between the outer pinion bearing and the pinion gear. Later D44s had crush sleeves setting the preload. Tighten the yoke nut until the required 10 in-lbs of pinion rotational torque is achieved. If rotating torque is surpassed, start all over again. The Dana 44 pinion yoke nut torque is 250 ft-lbs.

This Mac Tools bearing removal tool will remove all differential bearings and allows the bearings to be reused. The discs must be tight against the bearing to avoid bearing damage.

After the backlash check, final torque the D44 bearing caps to 63 ft-lbs. Apply Permatex 81182 sealer to the bearing caps and sealing surfaces. A 3/16-inch bead should be applied top to bottom on the bearing caps and around the outside of the housing. Torque the cover bolts to 35 ft-lbs.

depth to determine tooth contact patterns and operational noise. Improper depth settings cause progressive tooth wear (potentially to knife-edge profiles) and eventual catastrophic failure. Similarly, backlash (gear-to-gear clearance) requires precise setting to prevent clunking during load transitions. Specialized tools facilitate bearing removal during iterative shimming procedures. This operation specifically warrants professional service rather than do-it-yourself attempts.

For those avoiding specialized work, consider pre-built replacement differentials from Top Flight Automotive, Corvette Central, Zip Products, or RPI Designs. They all offer various gear ratios at reasonable prices, considering component and tooling costs. There are substantial core charges for Dana 44 units (refundable with acceptable core return) to reflect limited core availability. Budget approximately $200 for shipping both the replacement and core back to the supplier.

Pre-Built Differentials and Core Considerations

Professional rebuilding includes inspecting the Posi-Traction clutch plates, pinion gears, differential pinion gear shaft retaining pins, axle-shaft yokes, and the associated bearings/seals. Replace the components as needed. Due to supply limitations, verify Dana 44 ring-and-pinion availability before committing to the repair. Substantial ratio changes may require specific carriers or thick-ring gear adaptations. For example, 2.73:1 sets have more pinion teeth and require a larger-diameter gear than a 4.10:1 pinion gear. This can be addressed through thick-ring gear designs and eliminate the need for dedicated 3.45:1 carriers.

TECH TIP

Use the Right Sealant

For differential gear oil formulations, use Permatex silicone sealant (part number 81182). It is specifically formulated for that application.

Modern gear oils chemically attack conventional engine-oil sealants and typically cause leakage within 4 to 5 months after installation. GM's application of silicone between each differential bearing cap and the circumference of the housing increased structural rigidity and sealed the unit.

Various gaskets are available to replace silicone sealant, but that is not my preference. ■

Differential Maintenance

Regular fluid service is essential. Posi-Traction clutch plates generate fine metallic particles during normal operation and create a metallic-paint appearance in used fluid. These unfiltered particles circulate through the bearings and against the seals to accelerate wear. Differential fluids contain friction modifiers that facilitate clutch-plate operation and minimize wear. Use GL5-rated 75W-90

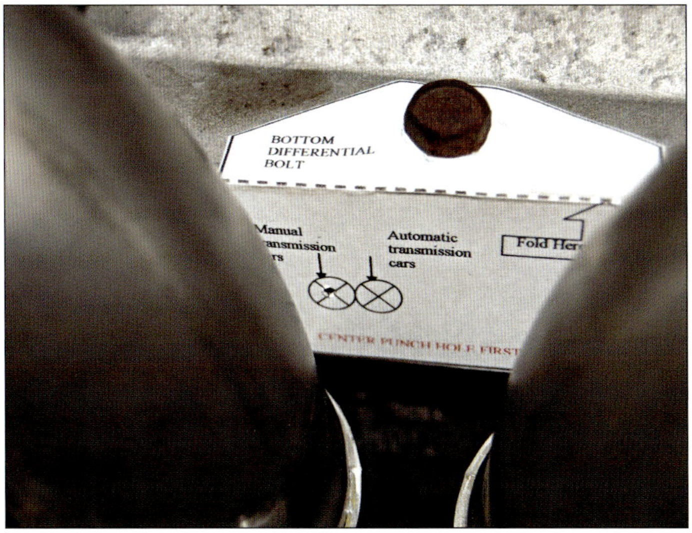

Throwback Automotive's differential drain installation kit for Dana 36 and Dana 44 differentials is shown. Place the template onto the lower differential-cover bolt and mark the appropriate hole using a sharp pin punch.

Next, drill the required 5/16-inch hole with the provided drill bit. Stops are added to all tools to protect the internal components. A large pry bar aids in moving the exhaust system toward the driver's side to allow straight-line drilling. Go slow as you approach penetration to avoid slinging gear oil.

gear oil, although verify the friction modifier content rather than assume its addition. For additional insurance, consider GM's proven Posi-Traction fluid additive (part number 88900330). Redline (part number 57904) provides the required friction modifiers and the appropriate GL5 protection for performance and daily applications.

The C4 differentials lack dedicated drain provisions and require fluid extraction via suction guns or pumps with dip tubes. While this approach leaves residual fluid and bottom sludge, it is the least invasive maintenance method when performed regularly.

The 1/8-27 NPT tap (provided) is used to tap threads into the differential housing. Brake cleaner can be used to flush the drill and tap shavings, accumulated sludge, and metallic particle buildup from the differential.

The provided internal hex plug with sealer applied is installed. Pump the Posi-Traction additive in first, followed by the GL5-designated differential fluid of your choice. Once the differential fluid is dripping and not gushing out of the fill port, install the 10-mm, internal-hex fill plug.

Suspension and Steering

The C4 suspension was a revolutionary advancement among American sports cars of the era, although there are notable generational differences. The 1984–1987 control arms (upper and lower) have shorter ball joint-to-pivot dimensions than 1988–1996 components to amplify geometry variations. Earlier models employ aluminum plates for shock/sway-bar attachment versus the more substantial direct-mounting approach of later designs. The 1988 redesign lengthened the control arms, increased spindle height, and enhanced positive caster for improved steering response. Rear suspension benefited from lowered trailing arm and camber mounting points to reduce geometry changes during suspension movement. Limited production numbers created a scarcity of 1984–1987 upgrade components and often necessitate conversion to 1988–1996 hardware at a significant cost.

Track C4s must be routinely checked for loose suspension pieces. With the steering wheel locked, pull inward and outward at the 3 and 9 o'clock positions and check for loose steering linkage. Wheel bearings are checked at the 12 and 6 o'clock positions. Pull up and down. No play should be felt. Loose differential yokes are found when aggressively moving the wheels at the 12 and 6 o'clock positions.

Check the lower ball joint for wear. A standard-diameter grease-gun coupler will be able to connect to the 90-degree grease fitting. If not, the ball joint is worn and requires replacement. The old school way is to place a jack under the lower control arm to unload the suspension, place a 36-inch-long bar under the tire, and see if the ball joint has any play as you pick up on the wheel.

Suspension Goals

Maximizing tire contact is the fundamental objective, despite irregular road surfaces that challenge ideal geometry. Every suspension system

To the left, a large frame hole provides spindle rod bolt clearance. Every time that these 18-mm, hex-head, spindle-rod bolts/nuts are removed, at least one of the nuts falls into the frame area. I suggest to remove the spindle-rod bracket with the rods to avoid wasted time.

This is a common sight: rubber- or urethane-bushed camber rods are damaged from twisting as the rods travel up and down. Camber rod assemblies should all have Heim joint rod ends to free up the suspension to avoid bushing damage.

has compromises. Certain conditions limit grip regardless of alignment specifications or component selection. Understanding basic terminology, including ride height, center of gravity (COG), caster/kingpin inclination, cross-caster, camber, toe, and thrust line, provides an essential foundation.

Ride-height considerations frequently prioritize aesthetics over handling dynamics. While a lower center of gravity theoretically improves performance, practical limitations—particularly ground clearance over irregular surfaces—demand balance. Even purpose-built race cars adjust ride height specifically for each track's characteristics. Consider Sebring's road course and its varied surface conditions. Weekend competitors should prioritize components that offer simple ride-height adjustability. Proper modification requires understanding that suspension systems function optimally at designed ride heights. Arbitrary lowering alters control-arm angles and overall geometry relationships.

Front-suspension rubber pivot bushings deteriorate as internal lubricants dissipate, which leads to drying and cracking. While traditional designs sandwich rubber between inner and outer steel sleeves, General Motors eliminated those sleeves and directly pressed rubber into aluminum mounting eyes. No suppliers currently offer OEM-specification rubber bushings, which necessitates denser replacement materials with reduced deflection characteristics. This sacrifices the original compliance that mitigated road harshness.

Available replacements include urethane and Del-a-lum designs. The latter combines aluminum sleeves with thin plastic liners and grease fittings to prevent squeaking. This is a common urethane issue, particularly during weather transitions. Installation techniques can minimize noise characteristics. Complete bushing replacement becomes necessary for most vehicles regardless of storage conditions. Interestingly, manufacturers confirm that regular

Rubber ball-joint boots are sealed to the joint and stud, and they burst when overfilled. Grease is everywhere and builds up in the wheel drum. Debris attaches to the grease, causing wheel imbalance. Use two pumps of grease maximum, and the replacement urethane boots allow grease to flow out, which requires cleanup after lubricating.

This two-jaw puller is used to break taper-fit suspension components loose. It's not a great idea to smack aluminum suspension components with a large hammer. Do not remove the shock absorber at the top or bottom until the lower control arm is supported.

Aluminum lower travel-stop plates have four 13-mm bolts retaining them to the crossmember. They allow upper and lower control-arm removal and shock-absorber replacement without unloading them. The 1994–1996 C4s do not have stop plates, so serious bodily harm can occur. The lower control arm must unload before control arms and/or shock absorbers are removed.

To remove the spring, remove the lower travel-stop plate, load the spring with the jack, and remove the shock absorber. After shock removal, lower the control arm slowly until the control arm moves away from the spring. Push your C4 off the lift or jack stands with reduced front-end weight. The floor jack must move and follow the control arm as it lowers. Dirt or debris can cause jack immobility.

The OTC Tools ball joint service tool is used for removal or installation of ball joints on or off the car. If the ball joint isn't going straight into the control arm, control-arm damage will be the result and take away aluminum if it was pushed in at this angle. A local machine shop should be able to handle the task if you don't feel comfortable doing it.

"exercise" rather than environment determines rubber longevity. Movement distributes internal oils to maintain flexibility and prevent non-use degradation. Front suspension pivots typically fail first.

Quality suspension components require greater investment and sourcing effort. Premium ball joints and tie-rod ends from manufacturers, such as Moog, TRW, and Precision provide essential safety margins to prevent

Cut all of the rubber protruding past the bushing's bore. This is crucial. If the bushing binds during removal, control-arm damage occurs. Some people burn the bushings out or drill the bushing until the material loosens up. Treat the pieces like aluminum (not steel) or find someone well-versed in bushing replacement.

Be careful when pressing the control-arm shaft out with a precut bushing. Stop frequently to check for shaft rotation. Stop and apply penetrant if it doesn't rotate. Use a metal bar or tube to stabilize the control arm and put the stabilizer next to the shaft.

If you find corrosion, lightly clean the area with a sanding roll. Take care to remove only the white powdery corrosion. Check the bushing fitment as you proceed to avoid a loose bushing. If the bushing goes in without any resistance, the inner diameter is too large and the component should be replaced.

Global West Suspension's smaller-outer-diameter bushing of the two blue upper control-arm bushings is installed first. It requires enough force to use a hydraulic press or a large arbor press.

The next step is to check the fit of the plastic Delrin washers between the control-arm pivots. Thick and thin washers are provided to make sure that there is no clearance.

catastrophic suspension and steering failures. Component separation typically results in a messy outcome in the best case, and an impact with an immovable object in the worst case.

Rack-and-Pinion Steering Upgrades

The C4's rack-and-pinion steering was a significant advancement that provides quicker response and eliminates complex linkage systems. The Z51-equipped models require 2¼ turns lock-to-lock versus 2¾ turns for

After the shaft with the selected plastic and steel washers is inserted into the control arm, push in the large-outer-diameter blue bushing holder into the control arm. A special 1¾-inch support tube is used to prevent control-arm damage as the bushing is pushed in. The support tube must fit tightly to avoid bending the control arm.

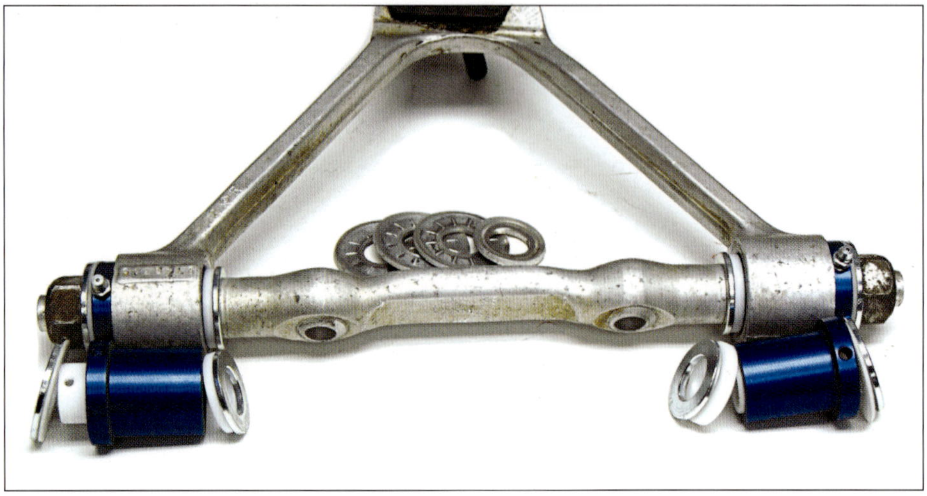

Rotation bushings were installed by lining up the grease-fitting holes before tightening the 30-mm hex nuts.

The corrosion between the rubber and aluminum impedes progress. Take it slow. The push tool should be slightly smaller than the aluminum bushing bore. If it's too small, it wedges in tight between the rubber and bore. If it's too big, bore damage occurs.

This is one pair of 1984–1996 upper control arms (part number 97190) from Specialty Products Company (SPC) with Delrin bushings and rebuildable ball joints. Multi-adjustability allows for complex changes in caster and camber. In addition, SPC offers extended upper ball-joint studs to lessen camber change. It's the ultimate race application.

Global West supplies 1/8-inch roll pins to retain the nuts. This is a very important step. Control-arm shafts can come out of the control-arm pivots if the nuts back off. This is ready for installation.

A bench vise easily pushes the sleeve with copious amounts of silicone grease applied into the bushing. The bushing should not rotate in the bore. The sleeve is the pivot point. Tight pivot points squeak more than usual and bind the suspension.

standard steering. Increased positive caster created greater steering-rack loads that necessitate power-steering coolers for 1987–1990 Z51 models. While 1990 FE1 models used simple 3/8-inch aluminum tubes, finned coolers proved to be the most effective. These coolers addressed noise, vibration, and shudder issues (documented in the 1990 technical bulletins) before becoming standard equipment in 1991. For early performance projects, we prioritized retrofitting 1990–1996 or aftermarket coolers whenever available.

The 1984–1990E (early, no power steering cooler) often has steering rack failure. At ambient temperatures, overheated and hardened sealing rings increase steering effort until the fluid warms up. The precursor is the fluid being full of metallic particles with a gray metallic shine as the fluid circulates. Metallic-laden fluid requires a flush and replacement of the steering rack, steering pump, and hose. The 1990L (late)–1996 power-steering-cooler-equipped C4s rarely have metallic fluid concerns. While power-steering pumps are theoretically rebuildable, replacement units are more economical due to internal-component scarcity.

Flushing the power-steering fluid every 2 to 3 years is recommended. Do it annually if your C4 is used extensively for track days. Steering rack-to-pinion preload can be adjusted without steering-rack removal. Applying a fresh coat of high-pressure grease after cleanup with proper adjustment tightens any steering-rack backlash concerns.

There are no 1984–1987 replacement steering shafts available to date, but Borgeson Street and Performance has options to make a replacement. The 1984–1985 steering shaft can be substituted with the later 1988–1996 shaft. The downside is that the steering wheel–centered clock position is off by 90 degrees. Repositioning the steering wheel places the turn-signal cancel cam out of phase. This is not a problem for race use. The 1988–1996 steering shafts have proven to be reliable. To date, universal joints have a good track record. The rubber isolators have been robust with no failures to date.

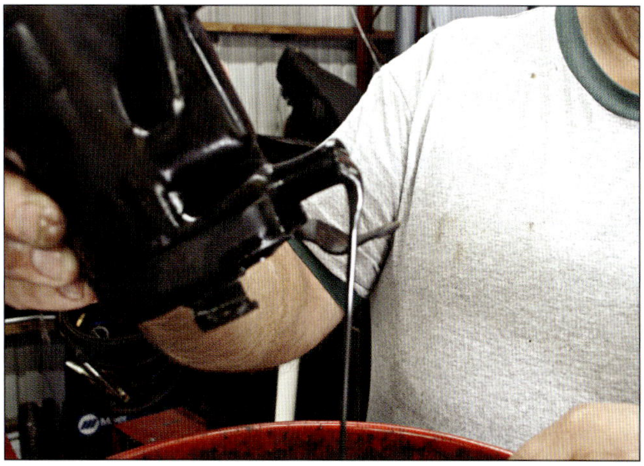

This gray metallic fluid tells the tale. A complete steering-system flush and replacement is next. Overheated, hardened seal rings have worn the aluminum steering-rack housing bore to allow pressure loss and increased steering effort.

Corrosion had built up around the bushing, and it took a lot of force to remove it. Take notice of the original rubber bushing's large outer-diameter steel sleeve minimizing movement. A cleanup of the bushing's bore with a sanding roll was required before bushing installation.

Steering Warnings

For 1984–1985 models, avoid steering with the engine off to reduce steering-shaft stress and extend component life. Consider urethane rack mount kits to minimize movement and improve steering precision. For

Steering rack-to-pinion adjustment is accomplished by loosening the outer segmented locknut. A 16-inch crescent wrench does a good job of loosening the locknut without damaging it.

1990–1996 models, always secure the steering wheel, preferably with straps, before shaft removal. Excessive rotation will damage the airbag connecting clockspring. Like a tape measure, this component has limited travel before failure and renders airbags inoperative if overextended.

Clean the rack's load-bearing surface and then apply high-pressure chassis grease to the concave rack contact surface. Use light force to tighten the adjuster plug clockwise until it bottoms. Rotate the adjuster plug counterclockwise 60 degrees. Check the steering-wheel return after cornering. If it's binding, back off the adjuster another 10 to 20 degrees.

The 1993 steering rack was in good shape. No metallic particles were in the fluid, and there were no leaks. With the new urethane bushing set installed, this is one sleeve that can go in tight to limit steering-rack movement.

The corroded metal tube was cleaned, and high-heat satin black paint was applied. Removal of the outer tie-rod end and boot is required for urethane cushion installation. If the tie-rod link falls under its own weight, chances are good that it's worn and should be replaced.

The power-steering cooler is removed for steering rack-and-pinion service. Hold onto the nut from the backside and torque the main rack bolt to 30 ft-lbs. Torquing the cushion strap bolts is tricky. Tighten them to 18 ft-lbs. Torque the pinch bolt for the steering shaft to 44 ft-lbs.

The factory-mounted C4 power-steering cooler is in place. Add a cooler if you don't have one. Setrab, Moroso, and Derale have suitable low-pressure oil coolers equipped with push-on hose and worm-gear clamps that are available to fit this location. Transmission coolers work equally as well for this application.

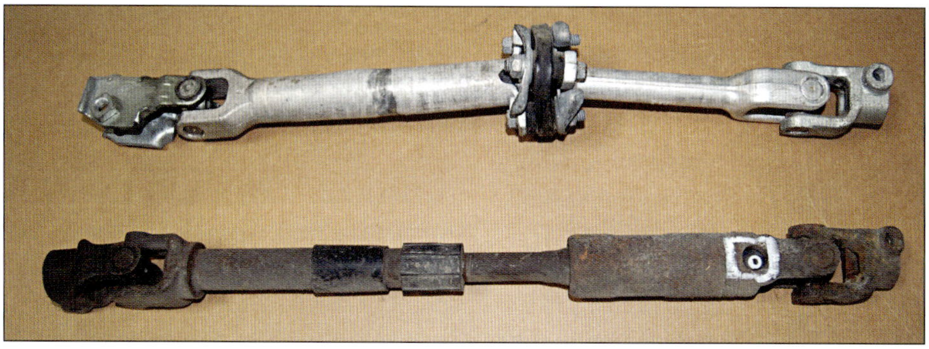

The 1988–1996 upper steering shaft with a centered rubber isolator was designed to deflect in a crash event. The lower 1984–1987 C4 steering shaft with a white square around an off-center safety pin denotes rubber isolator bond failure. The safety pin prevents total loss of steering control while allowing 3/8 inch of free play when the bond breaks.

Rear Suspension

C4s employ unequal-length spindle rods (trailing arms) to maintain rear knuckle caster control. These experience minimal rotational movement and allow OEM rubber bushings to accommodate stresses effectively. Camber control rods represent the most problematic rear components. As wheels pivot up and down in an opposing arc to camber transitions, bushings are torn apart due to design limitations. GM's evolution ironically worsened the situation. The early, thicker bushings provided greater deflection, while the later, thinner designs with reduced deflection accelerated rubber failure. Consequently, rear camber rod bushing deterioration became nearly universal among C4s.

Factory rear tie-rod assemblies reliably manage toe loads through ball studs and allow three-dimensional movement without rod twisting. Unfortunately, inner pivot wear necessitates complete assembly replacement. While some suspension wear manifests visibly, such as increased negative camber causing tire wear, toe-link deterioration creates particularly dangerous handling characteristics. Severely worn components cause dramatic directional changes during throttle transitions. Acceleration points the vehicle one direction, while deceleration redirects it unpredictably and potentially causes lane departures without driver input.

Specialty suppliers offer comprehensive rear suspension components, including urethane bushings, spindle rods, toe links, and camber rods. While urethane maintains linear movement well, rubber better accommodates multi-dimensional forces without transferring stresses to mounting points. Unfortunately, rubber components remain unavailable except as new old stock (NOS), which presents questionable reliability because rubber requires regular movement to distribute internal lubricants. Although rubber provides superior harshness isolation, it permits greater component movement.

The differential assembly is an integral part of the entire suspension system. Interestingly, General Motors used two differing rubber durometer (density) reading suspension cushions: one for Dana 36 rear axles and another for Dana 44 rear axles, with the same outer and inner dimensions. Today urethane is the only choice. This means that you may notice a harsher and/or noisier ride with the replacement cushions. In a reversal of all other urethane bushing installation procedures, differential rear-cover bushings require the steel sleeves to be removed. Push the rubber and inner sleeve out of the outer sleeve. Use a flat punch to push the outer edge inward and cut the outer sleeve out.

Place a jack on the metal spring reinforcement and slowly raise it to unload the spring. Once unloaded, remove the 21-mm nut from the spring height bolt. Some springs have a significant inward arc as they unload. Avoid jack contact with the composite spring material. Never place the jack directly on the composite spring. Gouges and small nicks cause damage that is not immediately apparent. Total spring failure can occur.

The lower bushing has a tear on the bottom left quadrant, and the bushing sleeve is off-center from torque loading. The large section of rubber bushing absorbs torque loading to provide balance for the Corvette owner who expects more road miles than track-event miles.

Unlike the front suspension, once the sleeve has been pushed out, these camber rod bushings remove easily with a screwdriver. Get under them and pop them out. Make sure that all of the corrosion has been removed from the bushing's bore if you decide to reuse the component.

These Heim joint ends are tricky to assemble. The boots must be installed over the very large rod end. Silicone does a good job of forcing them into place. Avoid pinching the boot with the rod-end sleeves as the rod ends are installed into the mount. It is easier to install the assembled rod ends into the spindle rod frame mounts and then bolt the assembly to the frame.

The wheel-bearing assembly requires removal to replace the knuckle-side spindle-mount bolts. New bolts are used for the correct spindle rod end fitment. Torque the spindle mount-to-frame bolts to 63 ft-lbs. Torque the spindle bolts at the mounts and knuckle to 140 ft-lbs.

The red Banski camber rods (bottom of photo) are simple to adjust and do not have a tendency to loosen like the Smart Struts that use urethane-bushed rod ends. Camber rods inherently twist as they move up and down. Over time, urethane-bushed rod ends work at loosening the nuts that are used to lock the rod's adjustment.

Differential-cover urethane bushings and sleeves are installed. Lightly apply silicone grease to the inner sleeve upon installation to avoid grit working its way into the bushing. There should be no movement or squeaks here, just support. Torque the support bolts to 89 ft-lbs.

This is the easiest way to replace your worn rear toe link. Van Steel has a 1984–1996 heavy-duty rear toe rod kit (part number RB-208). Your alignment technician will thank you, and your wheels will stay in a straight line under extreme conditions.

Banski Rear Suspension Links

Banski Motorsports produced exceptional rear suspension components that featured Teflon-lined rod ends that delivered frictionless articulation without greasing requirements. Although Banski Motorsports has discontinued production, it shared its manufacturing specifications publicly. Its designs primarily employed Omega-style clamps to facilitate rod-end centering and provide superior access during adjustment. These clamps require machined recesses and capture slots for proper rod-end retention.

Coleman Racing now supplies these specialized components. Traditional locknut designs present adjustment challenges. Proper Heim-joint function requires centered ball studs, which are critical to verify post-alignment. Off-center rod ends bind during articulation, which is a common issue with locknut designs due to difficulties maintaining rod position during tightening.

Build Your Own Rear Suspension Rods

Coleman Racing Products EZ-Just Suspension Link Rods (rods are 5/8-18 UNF thread with right- and left-hand thread) are available. Choose aluminum or steel.

Part	Number Required	Part Numbers
Upper spindle rod	2	• Part number 19008: 8.0 inches anodized aluminum • Part number 29118: 8.0 inches plain steel
Lower spindle rod	2	• Part number 19012: 10.0 inches anodized aluminum • Part number 29122: 10.0 inches plain steel
Camber rod	2	• Part number 19023: 15.50 inches anodized aluminum • Part number 29133: 15.50 inches plain steel
Tie-rod	2	• Part number 19029: 18.50 inches anodized aluminum • Part number 29139: 18.50 inches plain steel

For alternate EZ-Just suspension rods that use link rods requiring locknuts, subtract 0.500 from the overall rod length to accommodate the width of the locknuts.

Rod Ends Required

Eight right-hand-thread, 5/8-inch inner-diameter, Teflon-lined rod ends for spindle rods and the camber rods are required. In addition, you need eight left-hand-thread, 5/8-inch inner-diameter, Teflon-lined rod ends for spindle rods and the camber rods.

Cushioned rod ends are recommended to keep the rear suspension quiet. Metal-to-metal rod ends can be

TECH TIP

Progressive Rear Suspension Upgrades

Here are four levels of progressive rear suspension upgrades:

Level	Details
Level 1	• Urethane spindle rod bushings with original toe links and Heim-jointed camber rods
Level 2	• Heim-jointed camber rods and spindle rods with original toe links
Level 3	• Complete Heim-joint conversion (spindle rods, camber rods, and toe links)
Level 4	• Coilover shocks with comprehensive Heim-joint components • Regardless of intended use, Heim joint camber rods represent the minimum recommended upgrade to permanently address predictable bushing failures • Fundamentally, freely articulating suspensions deliver superior handling versus motion-restricted designs

noisy as they wear. Chromoly steel Nylafiber Matrix race rod ends from Rod End Supply are an excellent choice for high-static-load, do-it-yourself rod ends. The Nylafiber-lined rod ends will keep the suspension tight without any metal-to-metal loading and unloading noises. Speedway Motors is another source. Its polyurethane rod ends limit pivot angles with full rotation capabilities to prevent unwanted noise. The polyurethane rod end is thinner and makes it acceptable for rear camber rod use. Less material twisting occurs when the pivot direction changes.

Suitable spacers and fasteners are required to center the new control rods in their mounting positions. They can be found at McMaster-Carr or other industrial suppliers. McMaster-Carr has spacers available incrementally to avoid cutting your own from scratch. If you have a metal cut-off saw, round thick-wall stock can be used. Fasteners can also be found online or through McMaster-Carr.

The tie-rod assembly is a bit more troublesome. The inner mount at the differential was a custom piece and had to be made by a machine shop. The tie-rod assembly used 1/2-inch Teflon-lined left-hand-thread and right-hand-thread rod ends. Allstar Performance and Afco Racing Parts have tapered rod end studs to adapt the original tapered stud knuckle connector to the rod ends.

Banski will build your own rear suspension rod links and boots.

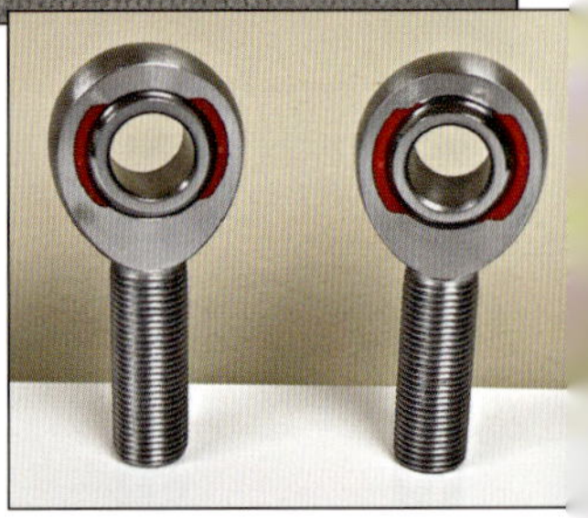

These are Rod End Supply's 5/8-inch male chromoly steel race rod ends with Nylafiber Matrix cushioning material. They provide unwavering suspension control and are quiet enough for street use.

Torque Specifications

Front Suspension	
Upper ball-joint stud nut hole	33 ft-lbs (tighten to first available cotter-pin hole)
Lower ball-joint stud nut hole	50 ft-lbs (tighten to first available cotter-pin hole)
Lower control-arm pivot bolts	82 ft-lbs
Upper control-arm shaft to frame horn	40 ft-lbs
Tie-rod end to knuckle front	33 ft-lbs (tighten to first available cotter-pin hole)
Anti-roll bar to frame	40 ft-lbs
Anti-roll bar link bolts	35 ft-lbs

Rear Suspension	
Shock absorber (coilover) to knuckle	89 ft-lbs
1984–1987 Shock absorber (coilover) to frame	63 ft-lbs
1988–1996 Shock absorber (coilover) plate to frame	22 ft-lbs
1988–1996 Shock absorber (coilover) stud nut	19 ft-lbs
Camber rod to bracket bolt/nut at differential	187 ft-lbs
Camber rod to spindle knuckle	107 ft-lbs
Spindle rod to knuckle	140 ft-lbs
Spindle rod to bracket	63 ft-lbs
Spindle rod bracket to frame	70 ft-lbs
Tie-rod to differential bolt	54 ft-lbs
Tie-rod to knuckle (tighten to first available cotter pin hole)	33 ft-lbs
Anti-roll bar to frame	18 ft-lbs
Anti-roll bar link bolt	39 ft-lbs

Maximum Cornering

A common complaint for the 1984–1987 C4 Corvette was a rough ride, which was due to high composite spring rates. It was common to see 1984 coupe bodies cracking at the corners of the rear hatch. The spring rate would not let the suspension travel away from the road surface and pushed the tire onto the pavement. While this may work well on a racetrack, where you're constantly pushing the vehicle into each corner, cruising local streets can be painful. My contention is that higher (stiffer) rate springs have a limit. If the spring rate is too high, even at the track, handling suffers as the tires oscillate and lose traction when skipping over road anomalies.

The General Motors RPO codes FE7 (heavy duty) and FE1 (soft ride) were the suspension spring options. As expected, the FE7 has a higher spring rate, so expect a rougher ride. RPO FE7 springs were used within RPO packages Z51 until 1990 and then in ZO7 packages until 1995 before they returned in the final Z51 package for 1996. The 1994 FX3 electronic selective ride and handling spring rates were lower and more manageable to allow cruising or better track handling with three adjustable options.

General Motors finally used the FE1 base suspension spring (code FSS) for model year 1996, and it proved to be a winner under all circumstances. The softer ride kept the tires from bouncing over the pavement, even

General Motors composite spring codes are shown on these springs for the front and rear locations. Compare the spring codes to the chart on page 144 for an idea of what spring you're working with. The spring codes can be used to determine spring stiffness.

If you have a missing front spring tag, you can find the code on the underside of the spring. The absence of a code indicates that the part is an aftermarket replacement. Aluminum height-adjustment shims are placed on top of the front spring pads. Typically, General Motors had two shims in place. Removing them will lower the front 3/4 inch. Wedges are required to drop the front end farther.

The original upper spring rubber pivot is removed, the surface is cleaned, and wedges are glued to the spring. This 3M weatherstrip adhesive keeps the lowering wedges in place. Allow a few hours for the adhesive to cure before installing.

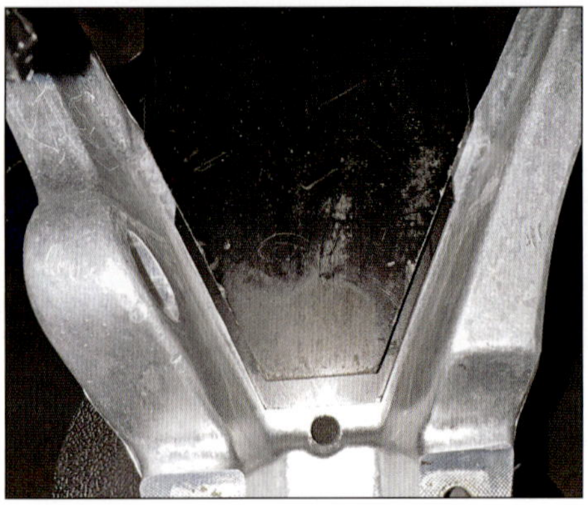

The rubber outer pads deteriorate on OEM springs, and there are no replacements. Corvette owner Brian Schuett shared this solution. A 0.250-inch-thick Delrin pad was configured and secured with silicone adhesive. The otherwise-useless front spring is now back in service. Delrin is available on many websites. (Photo Courtesy Brian Schuett)

These are the front spring retaining components. The two flat aluminum plates that are stacked together go between the spring pivot pad and crossmember. Early C4s had aluminum spring retainers, and the later used the stamped-steel pieces. You can shorten the aluminum spring retainer legs 3/8 inch or add a filler between the spring to retain the spring. The Van Steel red lowering wedges are ready to be glued to the spring.

in the harshest conditions. For new transverse springs, Van Steel is the best choice.

When ride-height adjustability is a concern for your performance level, these three options help considerably: a composite spring change, a factory spring modification, or a coilover shock/spring setup.

For a street-driven C4 that occasionally hits the track, OEM-type composite springs should be adequate. Factory composite transverse spring modifications allow minimal front lowering with wedges to replace the original rubber mounting blocks. Expect a 1- to 1½-inch drop. The 1988–1996 factory front spring will not directly fit in any 1984–1987 C4 due to spring width. Spring width

Isolator plates are stacked together between the spring's upper pad mount and the spring pad. Three or four plates make minor spring height changes and retain the spring. The stack can be moved to the bottom side to lower the back end.

Longer rear spring bolts are simple to install. Unload the spring using a jack. Do not allow the jack to touch the composite spring. Any nicks or damage to the composite material can lead to cracking and ultimately failure.

Hold the shock stud when tightening the nut to prevent internal shock damage. Center the cushions in the shock tower recess. The upper cushion has the correct bulge. Overtightening leads to cracking. Stud nuts should be self-locking or double nutted to prevent loosening.

A wire retainer holds the FX3 shock actuator in place. Do not force the actuator when reinstalling. Rotate the actuator slightly to engage the shock's drive gear. Note the position of the shock's toothed cup. Maintain the depth to engage the actuator's drive gear.

can be modified with a belt sander to accommodate the earlier C4. The outer edge of the spring end will be damaged if it lies on the aluminum control arm without protection.

Rear spring lowering is simple: install longer spring-hanger bolts. The OEM bolt length was 192.5 mm (7.750 inches) long (1984–1990) or 225 mm (8.850 inches) long (1991–1996). The bolt has a thread diameter and pitch of 14 mm x 2.0. However, the 9/16-12 thread x 9- or 10-inch-long bolts are easier to locate than 14.0 x 2.0 thread bolts. The 9/16-inch bolts and 14-mm bolts are the same diameter, so the 9/16-inch bolts are suitable substitutes. However, you must match new locknuts for the bolt thread that you chose.

Shock Absorbers

If you plan to keep your transverse springs, your shock-absorber choice is crucial to having balanced handling and ride comfort. A shock absorber damps wheel-assembly oscillations to prevent the wheel/tire from bouncing over road anomalies.

We typically recommend lower-end shocks for 1984–1987 Z51 C4s to smooth out the rough ride. Shock-absorber costs generally reflect quality and performance. KYB and Koni shocks offer great value with a good compromise for street driving with occasional track use. Bilstein shocks work well for weekend warriors, while QA1 shocks and coilover versions come with various adjustability options. Double-adjustable shocks typically indicate you're at the coilover level and seek maximum suspension performance.

One area of concern is worth repeating and involves the anti-roll bar coilover shock-absorber mounting on the 1984–1987 front lower control arms. General Motors revisited the removable-plate version and modified the 1988–1996 lower control arms with cast-in mounting points. Adding coilover shock load to the 1984–1987 lower control arm may be acceptable for street use, but not for sustained track use. Later 1988-and-up lower control arms are recommended, which means that an aftermarket upper control-arm change is necessary to allow proper alignment.

General Motors offered FX3 and F45 adjustable ride control shock systems to allow you to choose driving modes from the driver's seat. The 1989–1995 C4s had the FX3 option with Bilstein shocks and top-mounted actuators. The one-year-only 1996 F45 real-time damping package allowed shock adjustment based on wheel position. FX3 shocks are available intermittently, and you should expect to spend $1,000 for replacements. Actuator rebuilding services and small parts are available via Captain Z CNC and other Corvette parts suppliers to keep the system operating. The FX3 module mounted on the rear compartment wall between the ABS system and driver's seat can be disconnected to disable the system and extinguish the warning lamp. No other codes will pop up.

The 1996 C4 F45 shocks are discontinued, and NOS or used units will be costly. I've never heard a customer claim the ride-control settings made a remarkable difference in handling. Many owners with these packages eventually install OEM-style non-adjustable shocks. The 1996 F45 owners need shock simulators to avoid SES lights and speed limiting after installing different shocks. If you're serious about track days while enjoying weekend cruises, coilover shocks/springs at all four corners might be the answer.

Coilover shocks/springs allow an adjustable ride height and shock rate for ultimate control. The 1984–1987 C4 requires some engineering of your own, while 1988–1996 retrofits are available. Benefits include better handling, easy spring changes, and four-corner adjustability. With care, you can maintain a street setup and adjust for track days. Installation requires more labor than a simple spring/shock replacement. The front sway bar most likely needs relocation for spring clearance. At the front, coilovers don't significantly change suspension geometry or spring loading. I question the rear coilover's effectiveness. Retrofits use the OEM spindle-knuckle shock-absorber location forward of the original transverse spring.

Balance is critical for spring rates and shock settings. Road courses and highways have many anomalies that require different setups at every corner. Your adjustments must be a compromise to achieve the best overall performance. The advantage of coil springs is that changes are simpler and safer than transverse spring replacements. Serious competitors have several spring sets for specific tracks. Keep detailed notes of your track times with corresponding spring/shock settings and make incremental adjustments to the rebound and compression rates.

Coilover Suppliers

After Dark Speed, a company that is located in Mooresville, North Carolina, has numerous coilover kits for all C4 Corvettes. Its top-end JRI race kit features remote nitrogen canisters with 6 compression settings. The shocks have 30 low-speed rebound/compression adjustments and 12 high-speed rebound/compression settings. The 1984–1987 Corvettes are well covered, with top-end and street kits. After Dark Speed's commitment shows in its in-house-development 1994 C4 Corvette that is used to test suspension products.

Aldan American, a California-based company, offers American-

The reasonably priced front Viking coilover kit from After Dark Speed has single-, double-, or triple-adjustable shocks available with optimized spring rates for performance use. All coilover installation pieces are included. This C4 has its additional front sway bar relocation kit for adequate anti-roll bar-to-spring clearance with heavy-duty end links. (Photo Courtesy After Dark Speed)

The After Dark Speed rear Viking coilover kit complements its front Viking kit. Real-world testing on its 1994 C4 autocross car has optimized both kits. Custom spring rates are available. Front and rear kits are tuned for a 1- to 1½-inch drop and can be easily adjusted. It also has a JRI line of front and rear coilover kits available. (Photo Courtesy After Dark Speed)

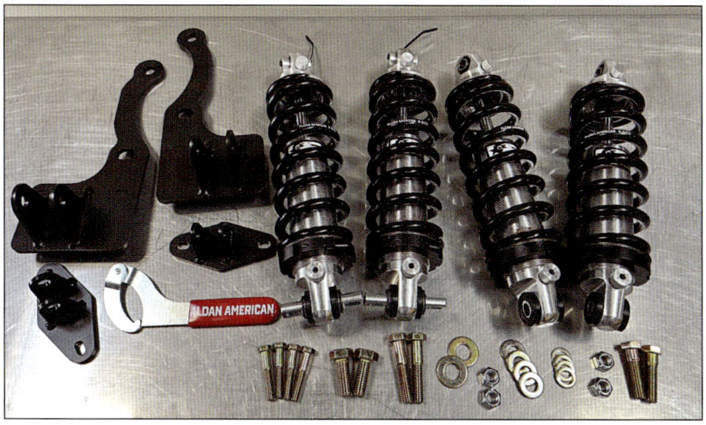

The Aldan American front and rear coilover kit allows up to a 2-inch drop. You'll need a sway-bar relocation kit for the front. The shocks offer 66 possible adjustments for rebound and compression. No kits are available for 1984–1987 C4s due to mounting differences. (Photo Courtesy Aldan American)

With concerns that the upper front coilover mounts would loosen, 0.100-inch-thick, moon-shaped pieces were cut out of a washer and welded into place. This ensured shock stability under adverse conditions. No other modifications were required beyond bolting on the kit pieces.

The Van Steel offset washer plate was substituted. Upper shock-mount load increased with the spring and shock absorber combination sharing the same support. The shock absorber's compression and rebound knobs are easy to access for quick adjustments.

Van Steel states that its 1988–1996 rear coilover kit will work with 1984–1987 applications. The stud was cut off the supplied 1988–1996 upper coilover mount adapter hardware, the spacing was perfect, and the original shock through-bolt was reused.

made coilover kits for 1988–1996 Corvettes as complete front/rear or individual kits. The rear mount uses a plate secured to the knuckle that positions the assembly in front of the rear axle shaft. It's not my preferred location, as it lessens leverage and shortens shock travel to reduce sensitivity during rebound and compression. Ideally, the spring load should match the original General Motors design location.

Doug Rippie Motorsports (DRM) pioneered C4 suspension development and campaigned race-proven C4s from its Waverly, Minnesota, location. Its affordable coilover spring kit utilizes original equipment-style shocks and fits 1989–1996 FX3 or non-FX3 C4s. The springs install on your existing or new replacement shocks. Ride-height can be adjusted via the provided spanner wrench. It's an excellent value.

Ridetech, which is based in Jasper, Indiana, offers the most comprehensive and expensive suspension kit that covers all suspension pivot components with coilovers and shocks for 1989–1996 C4s. Sway bars are included, and three shock options are available: single, double, and triple adjustable. The supplied

This lower rear coilover shock mount is how all aftermarket coilover shock kits are mounted. Each supplier has its own version. Minor material removal was required to the knuckle and adapter to fit the Van Steel version on the knuckle mounting point. Rebound and compression adjusters should be rotated 180 degrees from the photo. The idea was to adjust the shock from the wheel side if possible, but it didn't work out.

This coilover placement is closer to the original transverse spring connection point. My design to locate a suitable 16-mm, 12.9-grade bolt has been difficult. Spacers that have a 5/8-inch inside diameter are readily available. Frame modifications to locate the coilover at the top are required. This placement maintains the original spring rate with a longer lever to allow more shock-absorber sensitivity.

front sway bar works without relocation. This is the highest level of suspension improvement for serious enthusiasts. My only concern is that the rear coilover shock mounts near the original position, rather than at the knuckle's rear, which is where General Motors placed the transverse spring attachment.

Van Steel of Clearwater, Florida, with 40-plus years in the Corvette performance industry, has focused on suspension components. It covers all C4 Corvettes with its suspension products, including 1984–1987 models. The rear upper coilover shock mounts directly to the original mount with no adapter needed. It offers specific kits for 1988 Corvettes and dedicated 1989–1996 kits. The coilover options include street single-adjustable, advanced street, and race versions with double-adjustable shocks. Appropriate spring rates complement each kit. Van Steel provides coilover installation kits for all 1984–1996 C4s to accommodate various setups. The rear coilover lower mounting uses a machined adapter over the existing shock-mounting eye to place the shock inward like Aldan American and Ridetech.

Sway Bars/Anti-Roll Bars

Sway bars or anti-roll bars work in conjunction with the spring rate. Selecting the correct bar isn't as simple as choosing the largest diameter. They come in tubular or solid forms, with the solid being heavier with less twist. As with the spring rate, this is a science. Both work together to keep the tires in contact with the road and prevent body roll. In most C4 applications, you can use a lighter spring rate with a larger anti-roll bar to improve handling while maintaining ride quality.

The challenge is to force the anti-roll bar end-link bushing over the 90-degree sharp edge without tearing the bushings. A half-round metal file will taper the inner edge to help ease in the bushing. Coaxing the bushing into place with a dull flat-blade screwdriver helps. Heated bushings are pliable but collapse under pressure.

If slip-joint pliers won't insert the sleeve, start over. Old material or corrosion is likely causing a bind. Keep the silicone grease flowing and always coat the inside of the bushing and the outside of the sleeve.

Larger diameter isn't always better. Too much stiffness can reduce pavement contact. Consult your spring supplier for recommendations to avoid conflicts. The links are as important as the bar itself. At minimum, fresh urethane bushings will tighten up both front and rear suspension anti-roll bar links.

Do not remove the outer metal sleeve. They are not included in urethane bushing kits. Push out the inner metal sleeve and remove as much rubber as possible. Apply just enough heat to break the rubber's bond from the outer sleeve with a propane torch. Small wire brushes work well to remove the heated rubber pieces.

The outer anti-roll bar bushing goes over the inner end of the anti-roll bar metal sleeve to prevent loss of the bushing. The belt sander removes material to level the face of the bushing's surface. This allows uninhibited bushing movement within the anti-roll bar link.

Van Steel has this ready-to-go anti-roll bar kit with solid mount Heim joint end links in 32-mm and 35-mm diameters. Rear anti-roll bars are available in a 25.4-mm diameter with the same solid mount end links. Their front anti-roll bar relocation kit makes the bar and coilover kit installation simple. (Photo Courtesy Vansteel)

At a minimum, there should be 1/8 inch from the coilover spring to anti-roll bar end. This project required moving the anti-roll bar pivot point. Other projects required a simple opening up of the pivot mounting holes to an oval for adequate clearance.

The repositioned mount point holes are drilled for Rivnut installation. The 10 x 1.50 mm steel Rivnuts will handle a 5,000-pound upset load. Rivnuts are available on the internet in a multitude of sizes. Ribbed Rivnuts hold better and prevent rotation when tightening.

Reduce the Flex

The C4 Corvette was a significant departure from earlier generations with front frame rails integrated into a unibody structure to reduce weight and theoretically minimize flex. Three front-rail variations exist: the coupe (1984–1986), the late coupe (1986–1996), and the convertible (1986–1996) with additional underbody X-frame crossmember support. Without roof-rail connections, the structure lacks upper bracing beyond the door latches and metal frame that connects the front and rear pillars at the roof corners. The composite roof offers marginally better rigidity than its acrylic counterparts. Convertible models received additional underbody X-frame bracing to make them (particularly with hardtops installed) the least-flexible configuration.

Frame rigidity concerns vary by location. Harsher northern road conditions accelerate structural fatigue and generate squeaks and rattles while roof-to-frame bonds are stressed. This flexing compromises cornering stability and overall chassis integrity. All C4s benefit from convertible-style underbody bracing. We frequently install OEM convertible bracing on coupes that are destined for performance applications.

The wheels are off the ground with no suspension load. Note the shim count and respective placement. Loosen the rear control-arm-shaft nut just enough for front bolt removal to avoid shim loss. Remove the control-arm shaft-to-frame nuts on both sides for brace installation. The 10 x 1.50-mm self-locking shaft nuts require replacement if they spin freely during removal and installation.

Install the cupped washers toward the control-arm shaft as the bolt passes through the brace and shaft. Previously removed shims are installed between the inner cupped washer and the cross-member's upper control-arm mount point. Masking tape may be used to retain shims until the control-arm bolts are tightened.

The cupped side of the washer must be against the control-arm shaft. If that is not the case, control-arm shaft damage and shim loss will occur, and vehicle stability will be jeopardized. Torque the shaft nuts to 37 ft-lbs.

Standard alignment shims may be required to obtain a snug fit. Place them between the cross-member frame horns and brace. Alignment will be affected if there are gaps between the camber brace and frame when tightening the upper control-arm nuts.

Underbody Brace

The 1986-and-up convertible X-frames or stiffener kits enhance all C4 coupe chassis rigidity. The 1984–1986 coupes lack the front X-frame mounting points that General Motors added to all of the frame rails by 1987 with robust reinforcement. I prefer GM's X-frames, which may be found at swap meets, for the best reinforcement. An alternative is Vette2Vette's Gordon Killebrew–designed, stiffener kit for all C4s. The No Flex Frame Stiffener Bar system comes as SKU NF86L-96, with SKU NF84-86E for 1984–1986 models. While it's effective, it's second-best to a General Motors X-frame. These stiffeners run parallel from the front to the rear wheel without diagonal support. Their advantage is that they don't interfere with underside components, which is unlike the X-frames that can cause exhaust rattles with 3-inch pipes.

Lift-arm placement is crucial for X-frame removal. Refer to chapter 1 for lifting your C4 and rear jackstand placement to avoid the X-frame. Four aluminum spacer blocks keep the X-frame at the correct height. Often misplaced, the parking cable is captured in a cutout area between the X-frame and spacer block.

Four studs pass through a floor reinforcement to secure the X-frame to the metal section of the floor. The Vette2Vette frame stiffener does not have the crucial X-frame or strengthening floor attachment. High-center road anomalies damage the X-frame, while floor and exhaust component protection is enhanced.

The 1986 convertible frames received additional reinforcement and X-frame mounting panels. The 1987-and-newer C4 frames had the additional panel. Field reports suggest that a few early 1987 coupes do not have the panel. The X-frame mounts to the rectangular bolt pattern at the bottom of the panel. The significant bump on the frame rails tightens up available LS conversion header clearance.

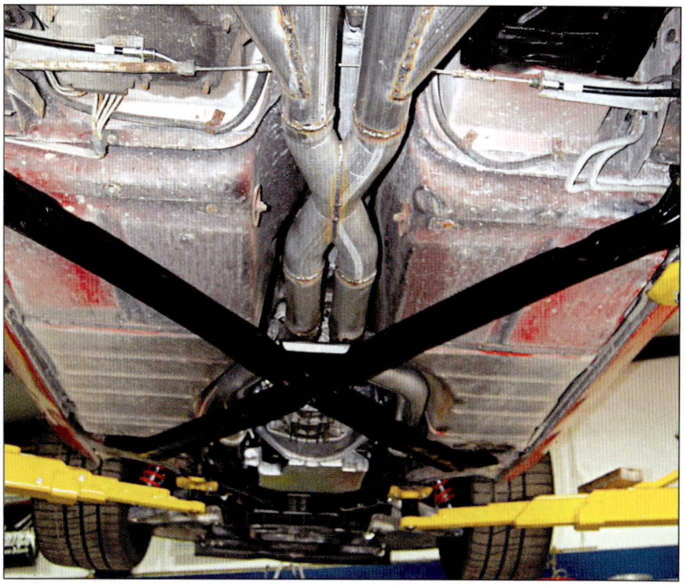

This 1993 coupe is retrofitted with a General Motors swap-meet X-frame that was added for frame stiffening. If the X-frame scrapes, a warning is given that the electric exhaust cutouts will be next. Hopefully, more X-frames and hardware can be found on eBay or at swap meets.

This X-frame supplier has moved on to other endeavors. It was an attempt to replicate the General Motors X-frame. No intersection bolts were used, which lessened overall structure stability versus GM's version. Ground clearance was reduced with the 1 x 3-inch rectangular tubing. The idea of adding reinforcements at the 1984–1986E front frame mounts was stellar. A niche product entrepreneur is needed to supply a robust C4 X-frame that ties in all four corners and the floor.

Vette2Vette's frame stiffener's longitudinal tubes provide relief from frame flex. Two options are offered: early 1984–1986E and 1986L–1996. Early kits require welding and nutsert or Rivnut installation. This front frame-stiffener mount positions the stiffening rod above floor level with no ground-clearance issues added.

The rear connection of the Vette2Vette frame stiffener is above floor level. The locknuts at both ends are loosened to extend or shorten the adjustable bars. Clear instructions are provided on installation and adjustment.

Alignment: Driving Techniques

For alignment, I prefer waiting until after you've driven 25 to 50 miles at low speeds so that the chassis settles into typical ride height. Any ride-height change requires an alignment check. With modern alignment machines, some technicians don't necessarily understand suspension geometry. While it's adequate for typical vehicles, your custom specifications may confuse them. Other technicians are well versed in all aspects of suspension and alignment technique. Find an old-school shop that understands suspension and steering systems for performance alignment decisions. For track C4s, build a relationship with your alignment shop. You'll visit frequently until you dial in your setup.

Caster critically affects high-speed stability through weight distribution across the spindle. Visualize this by placing a straightedge between the upper and lower ball joints. Proper geometry positions the upper joint rearward of the lower for positive caster. As the upper control arms shift rearward, positive caster increases to create greater front tire loading. Beyond 3 degrees, positive caster significantly enhances stability and increases steering effort. Seven-plus degrees necessitates power steering and accelerates outer-tire-edge wear. During full steering inputs, positive caster creates lifting forces that momentarily reduce contact patches. This geometry provides essential self-centering characteristics.

Optimal settings target 7 to 9 degrees of positive caster to balance high-speed control with reasonable steering effort. Cross-caster (side-to-side differential) compensates for the road crown and typically reduces driver-side caster by 0.5 degrees to minimize steering pull. Since road design varies geographically, local alignment specialists typically configure the suspension for regional conditions rather than universal specifications. The same holds true for race conditions. Increased left cornering will benefit from increasing driver-side caster.

Most roads incorporate banking for practical reasons. Flat corners reduce tire contact, while centrifugal forces promote outward movement. Camber significantly influences handling characteristics, particularly on winding roads. Negative camber (inward tilt at the top of the tire) increases the cornering grip but requires careful balancing against tire wear considerations. Competition applications typically employ increased negative camber, despite accelerated outer-edge wear, especially on courses that combine corners with extended straightaways.

Toe alignment refers to parallel relationship of the wheels/tires to forward travel. Imagine pointing your toes inward (toe-in) or outward (toe-out). Measuring across tire centerlines typically reveals that front measurements are narrower than rear to indicate toe-in. Most specifications recommend approximately 1/8-inch toe-in for high-speed stability, while toe-out enhances turn-in responsiveness at some cost to stability. Improper toe settings accelerate inner- or outer-edge tire wear, which is another performance/longevity compromise. Incorrect settings create hazardous handling characteristics, and loose components cause dynamic toe changes (particularly in the rear), producing unpredictable directional behavior.

Racetracks have banking changes, dips, and anomalies that your suspension must navigate. For track days, proper alignment and components are crucial. Develop a simple method to switch between street and race setups. With careful documentation, you can change setups without alignment machines by marking adjustments and counting turns. After any incident, have the suspension checked immediately.

Study alignment terms and how they affect your C4. Understand understeer (steering input makes no difference and impact is imminent) and oversteer (the rear tries to pass the front). What works for one driver may not work for another. Every great racer has lost control pursuing faster lap times. There's a razor-thin edge between grip and spinning. While driving school may bruise your ego, the instructor's goal is to make you safe and fast. You'll drive your C4 better, recognize problems earlier, and evaluate improvements objectively. Controlled power, whether it's 185 or 1,000 hp, delivers the ultimate lowest lap times.

GM Front Spring Codes

Soft Ride Option FE1

Years	Code	Ride Quality
1984	BMA, FHU, HMR, HLA	Harsh despite "soft ride" designation
1985	FJY Harsh despite "soft ride" designation	
1985–1989	HKX, HMP, HMN	Improved; less harsh than earlier soft ride springs
1992–1995	FHA, FHC, FSM, FSS	Good; better ride quality, reduced harshness
1996	FSS	Excellent; best ride quality of all options

Heavy Duty Ride

Years	Code	Ride Quality
1984	BMB	Extremely harsh; "kidney belt required"
1985	FHU, FHB, HMR, HLA	Slightly better than BMB; still very firm
1990–1996	AA	Improved over predecessors
1991	FHA	Note: Confusing designation; same code was used for a soft spring in 1990

GM Rear Spring Codes

Soft Ride

Years	Code	Ride Quality
1984	BMF	Very harsh, though not as severe as HD version
1986–1996	RCA	Improved over 1984; still firm
1989–1990	NYR	Moderate improvement

Heavy Duty Ride

Years	Code	Ride Quality
1984	BMH	Worst of all; teeth-rattling ride
1985–1996	NYU	Slight improvement over BMH, still very rough

Alignment Modifications for Maximum Positive Caster

The objective is to reposition the 1984–1985 upper control-arm spacers to provide maximum caster.

There's no need to remove the wheel/tire assembly. It is best if you support a 1984–1985 Corvette with the front tires lightly touching the work surface. Jack up the front of the Corvette so that the tires are barely touching the ground. This allows the spacers to be removed without disassembling the entire front end.

Swap the spacers as shown in the diagram. Keep the shims in the same position until an alignment is performed. Thick spacers at the front of the upper control-arm shaft increase positive caster. For those who question the validity of the benefits, General Motors installed the spacers as shown from 1986 onward during factory assembly.

Factory alignment specifications were updated to add 3-plus degrees of positive caster. Use the alignment specifications provided.

Alignment Specifications 1984–1996		
Front		
	Left	Right
Caster	6½ degrees positive	7 degrees positive
Camber	1/4 degree negative	1/4 degree negative
Toe	0 to 1/16 out	
Rear		
	Left	Right
Camber	1/2 degree negative	1/2 degree negative
Toe	0	

These slightly modified alignment specifications provide the best possible road feel at speed and during cornering. The specifications are suitable for high-speed interstate, gymkhana, and autocross events. This setup will enhance high-speed feel with the most front tire load while still being able to handle low-speed parking-lot maneuvers.

For the racetrack only, as speeds increase, front suspension negative camber can be increased an additional 1/2 degree for ultimate handling, Caster can also be increased another 1 to 3 degrees to eliminate cross-caster variation, depending on the particular track design. The additional camber and caster adjustments are not recommended for any public roadway.

Outer-edge front tire wear is to be expected as positive caster and camber adjustments increase. The outer tire edge scrubs from the severe turning angle.

Alignment Modifications for Maximum Positive Caster (1984–1985)

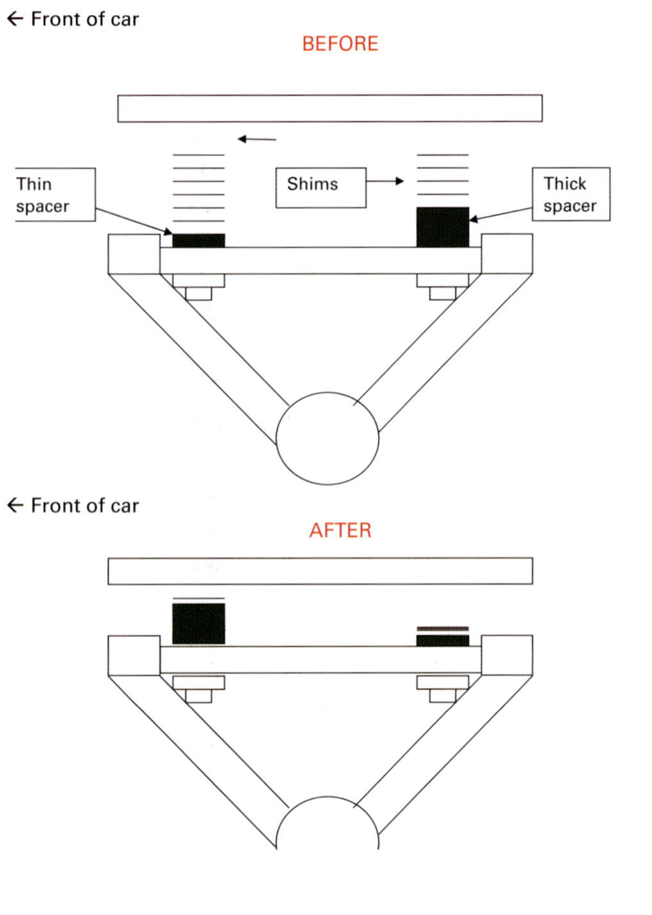

Performance Brake Kits

Many owners invest heavily in performance upgrades but neglect the braking system. Brake upgrades serve multiple purposes: control, safety, and aesthetics. Braking depends on vehicle balance. More braking is needed where weight is concentrated. The C4 Corvettes have 51- to 54-percent front and 49- to 46-percent rear weight distribution, depending on options and fuel load. For track events, experienced drivers use the brakes to set up corner entry and exit. Dedicated racers weigh each corner to determine the optimal caliper size, rotor dimensions, and braking bias. They fine-tune with adjustable proportioning valves and monitor heat with infrared guns.

Consider the rear tire width and grip when upgrading to larger rear calipers. There's sufficient rear weight for additional braking. The stock rear calipers and rotors are inadequate. This upgrade requires an adjustable proportioning valve. Adjustable bias helps at different tracks, as some corners need more rear or more front brake power for stability. Waiting longer to brake while going into the corners decreases lap times but requires optimal balance. The core issue is system integrity. Small rotors, tiny calipers, and pads fail during repeated high-speed braking, and they generate excessive heat, which subjects the brake fluid to extreme temperatures and boiling.

Standard Brakes

The C4 Corvette brake systems departed from the C2/C3 17-year run of cast-iron fixed-caliper design. The 1984–1987 C4's two-piston, floating, 2.126-inch-diameter, aluminum brake calipers with 11.50-inch-diameter, 0.740-inch-thick rotors performed poorly under extreme braking. The 1984 C4 calipers have a 1-year-only mounting pad area, and there are 1984 brake caliper adapters. This raises a question: If General Motors changed the mounting area, why should you add braking power to an already-weak design? It is better to update your 1984 spindles to a 1985–1987 version for improved braking.

The 1988–1996 C4s with standard brakes used two 1.496-inch outside-diameter caliper pistons on the front for increased clamping power. These models had 12.009-inch rotors (still 0.740-inch thick) that performed better in city driving but lacked repeated, stable, high-speed braking capability. These brakes had larger disc pads for more clamping force.

From 1990–1995, the ZR1-option C4s (including 1990 Z51 manual coupes) and Z07 models came with 12.990-inch-diameter, 1.100-inch-thick, directionally cooled rotors. The 1996 Z51 and Z16 Grand Sport C4s also featured these rotors. The large disc pads, with 38-mm calipers on 13-inch rotors, allowed better high-speed stopping and provided more confidence in extreme conditions.

Parking Brake

General Motors began the C4 with a standalone parking-brake system. By 1988, it switched to a compact rear brake caliper with an internal parking-brake mechanism. The standalone system proved to be more reliable than the 1988–up integral units. The 1988–1996 street/track cars benefit from upgrading to the 1984–1987 parking brake to allow multiple brake-component upgrades. Baer and Wilwood offer solutions to the integral parking brake. All C4 rear calipers used the same undersized, single, 1.575-inch (40-mm) piston with compact car–sized pads.

Transmission Brake

The 4+3 and ZF 6-speed manual C4s had an advantage because transmission braking was available. However, using any transmission for braking risks drivetrain damage, engine overrevving, and rear wheel lockup. Racers use this technique after extensive practice in competition. They can afford mistakes that you might not be able to. Remember, engine speed isn't controlled during downshifting, whether accelerating or braking. Exceeding the rev limit can destroy an engine.

Basic Upgrades

Every C4 owner should consider three inexpensive upgrades: a brake bias spring, stainless-steel brake hoses, and a complete system flush. Stainless-steel hoses with Teflon/polytetrafluoroethylene (PTFE) tubes and steel mesh reduce expansion for a firmer pedal. All aging C4s need this replacement. The original rubber hoses can't match the performance of stainless. Aging rubber balloons under pressure and softens pedal feel, while deteriorating inner liners restrict fluid flow in both directions and possibly cause components to overheat.

When flushing the brake system, fluid selection matters. The DOT5 or DOT5.1 brake fluids aren't recommended for C4s, due to higher viscosity and incompatibility with ABS modulator valves.

The brake fluid dry boiling point exceeds the wet boiling point. Focus on wet boiling points. The DOT3 and DOT4 fluids are hygroscopic and immediately absorb moisture when they are exposed to the air. Once opened, tighten the cap on the containers and discard them after a month. As fluid absorbs moisture, the wet boiling point drops and creates bubbles during heating that cause a spongy pedal. This happens

A turkey baster works well to remove the discolored/contaminated brake fluid from the reservoir to begin cleaning.

Replacing the master cylinder bias spring is an inexpensive upgrade. The spring on the left is the original, and the heavier wire spring (right) is the replacement. Upgraded bias springs have been tested under race conditions, and they make a difference. Many suppliers offer the upgraded brake bias spring.

The Federal Motor Vehicle Safety Standard 106 DOT specification is required for street legal-use hoses. Non-DOT-designated hoses are considered off-road (race) use only. Every improvement has drawbacks. Stainless-steel hose mesh coverings cut through objects that it rubs against. Dust and grit pass through the stainless mesh over time and work a hole into the hose's Teflon or polytetrafluoroethylene (PTFE) liner.

This sludge will slowly make its way to the antilock braking system (ABS) controller and cause many issues before it reaches the brake calipers. Use a cloth soaked with brake cleaner or alcohol to wipe out the sludge at the bottom of the reservoir.

Cleaning the reservoirs will keep the 1986–1991 antilock braking system (ABS) controller modulator valve assembly's small orifices clear of debris when pressure bleeding the system.

The 1992–1996 C4 master cylinder reservoir is held in place with a pin that can be removed for cleaning. The reservoir can be cleaned with brake cleaner using the supplied straw. Bend the straw at various angles to remove as much contamination as possible. The best policy is to let the reservoir dry out for an hour before adding new fluid.

after extended braking sessions. Until flushing is possible, bleeding provides a temporary fix.

Brake Fluid Testing

With traditional bleeding methods, water enters the system whenever the master-cylinder cap is removed. Despite taking precautions, moisture penetrates the seals and the vent system. As anticorrosive inhibitors deplete, copper is released from the corroding steel lines. Test strips can be used to detect copper, or you can simply flush every two years to extend caliper life. If you participate in gymkhana or track events, flush more frequently, and flush immediately if you boil the brake fluid.

For racing with hard-braking corners, flush before each event. For racing or spirited driving, reliable brakes are critical. A fluid flush costs far less than an accident. Follow your caliper manufacturer's fluid recommendation, especially for warranty purposes. I use Wilwood EXP 600 DOT4, which has boiling points of 626°F dry and 417°F wet. Baer's DOT4 fluid, which has boiling points of 608°F dry and 383°F wet, is also excellent.

Brake bleeding options include speed bleeders with check valves that release fluid when they are partially opened. These require a tight bleeder thread-to-caliper fit to prevent air ingress during pedal release. They function until the thread coating wears off but it can help in emergencies. Vacuum bleeders lose suction when the bleeder valve opens due to thread leakage and creates a mess as fluid drips around valves.

Manual bleeding is the least desirable. It requires an assistant and careful monitoring of fluid levels. If the master cylinder runs dry during the bleeding process, restart the process. A time saver is to crack bleeder valves just enough for the fluid to dribble out. Pump the pedal and watch fluid levels until you see fluid at each caliper. Find an assistant for the next step. During the bleeding process, once the brake pedal is at the floor, have the assistant hold it down until

As old, discolored fluid leaves the calipers, clear fluid emerges and it's time to move on to the next bleeder. Take a second lap around to check that the bleeder screws are tight before wrapping up the flush. It is very important to relieve brake bleeder system pressure. Once system pressure has been released, shut off the fluid-supply valve and disconnect the master-cylinder supply hose.

you tighten the bleeder valve to prevent air entry. If the pedal is released while the bleeder valve is open, air will be ingested.

Pressurized brake-fluid tanks are the best way to bleed and flush the hydraulic braking system. Brake fluid that is pressurized in an airtight tank eliminates moisture intrusion and forces out air and fresh fluid throughout the system. This is the best policy at the racetrack. With a quick connection, one person can perform a complete fluid change within 15 to 20 minutes.

A standard practice is bleeding the caliper farthest from the master cylinder first. In 1986–1996 C4s, this is counterintuitive. The right front caliper is the farthest away. Fluid routes through the controller behind the driver's seat before reaching calipers to place rear calipers closer. I recommend this sequence: right front, left front, right rear, and then left rear.

Brake Maintenance

Disc-brake pads are available from many suppliers. Here are two key facts to remember: 1) street pad compounds lose grip after repeated hard braking, and 2) race compounds perform poorly until they are heated. All options involve tradeoffs. Metallic pads wear rotors according to their grip level and compound, but they handle heat better than ceramic pads. Quality pads use edge codes to indicate friction coefficients from C (least aggressive) to H (most aggressive). The ZZ codes denote unclassified and typically aggressive materials. EBC Brakes and Hawk offer formulations that range from street to track use. Brake kits include manufacturer-recommended pad sets for their rotors.

When changing disc pads, never push caliper pistons back without loosening the bleeder. Debris in the bore can be forced into the antilock brake modulator valve and restrict flow. Fill the master cylinder before pumping the pedal after the pad installation. Ideally, flush the entire system.

General Motors recommends replacing the 8-mm guide-pin bolts on all 1984–1987 front and all rear upper guide pin caliper mount applications. Torque them to 22 to 25 ft-lbs. Torque the 1988–1996 lower guide-pin bolts to 16 ft-lbs. Specialty suppliers stock them as "C5 Corvette front caliper mount bolts."

Stable rotor thickness ensures smooth braking. Overheating creates high and low spots that cause pedal pulsation that worsens with each heat cycle. Machining only temporarily fixes this problem, which returns faster each time. As the rotors get thinner, they become more susceptible to heat distortion. If rotor machining occurs, thoroughly wash the surfaces with a degreaser and water to lift the metallic dust and debris from the surfaces.

Clean the wheel hub surfaces with a Scotch-Brite disc pad, wire wheel, or a hub cleaner–specific pad. Local auto part stores have wheel hub cleaners available that allow complete corrosion removal around wheel studs. High spots cause rotors to wobble at high speeds and caliper piston kickback, resulting in a low brake pedal.

Install five lug nuts to keep the rotor in place. Use a dial indicator to check rotor parallelism, which is a huge concern with fixed calipers. OEM C4 calipers are not fixed and move with the rotor as the rotor moves in and out.

Mark the high spot on the rotor and denote the closest stud to the high spot. Place the shim on the stud 180 degrees from the high spot. Shims are used between the rotor and hub to correct rotor parallelism runout concerns. Fixed calipers should maintain 0.004-inch-and-under parallelism.

Caliper Distortion

When choosing a simple pad replacement with a fluid flush or rotor upgrade, be aware of potential OEM C4 caliper issues. The calipers reportedly bow outward under pressure. The machined U-shape spreads at the outer pad surfaces to cause uneven wear and sticking pistons from misaligned pads during hard braking.

Floating (OEM) caliper runout becomes a concern at 0.050 inch and more. Sometimes two shims are required, depending on how close the high spot is to the stud. It can be tricky to determine where shims should be placed. The first attempt may take multiple efforts to find the sweet spot. Shims are available from web suppliers. The brass shims were made from locally obtained 0.005-inch shim stock.

Caliper distortion measurements are taken at the inner and outer disc pad machined surfaces. This 1991 caliper measures 2.367 inches at the inner pad surface. "Inner" and "outer" refers to the rotor surface to which the caliper applies pressure.

The outer measurement of 2.382 inches of the same caliper shows there is a 0.015-inch difference, which is due to casting variances. The spread (distortion occurs as the piston forces the outer section of the caliper outward) would be greater if the caliper was due for replacement. At 0.050 inch and above, at the outside measurement, caliper replacement is required to avoid caliper piston binding.

Corvette Factory Upgrade Options

The C4 Corvettes have several upgrade options. The most affordable is converting to C5 calipers with 1.614-inch (41-mm) pistons and 12.990-inch directional cooling rotors. Suppliers, such as Corvette Central, Top Flight Automotive, BDE Systems, Ecklers, Motor City Vettes, and TPS, offer kits for 1985–1996 C4s. Van Steel provides front C5 upgrade kits and/or adapter brackets. All include remanufactured calipers with new rotors, pads, hoses, and hardware. Resourceful owners might source components separately to save money or upgrade to better rotors. Note that C5 rear brake-caliper kits aren't widely available.

Multiple aftermarket brake options exist for C4 Corvettes. Rather than covering every company's offering, I'll focus on rotor variations and treatments. Many replacement calipers and upgrade kits are available.

Rotor Choices: Street to Racetrack

Several driving methods can optimize rotor life under extreme conditions. The simplest approach—avoiding extended braking—isn't practical for track events. Cryogenic treatment and thermal cycling are available options. This treatment tempers rotors for more stable thickness. The claims that it helps rotors run cooler seem dubious. While the molecular structure changes, the mass remains the same and cannot dissipate heat faster. Cryogenically treated OEM rotors last longer but aren't ideal for high-performance stopping power.

Slotted rotors help vent hot brake gases without the cracking issues of drilled rotors. All drilled competition rotors eventually develop cracks around the holes. Ball milling creates rotor slots and improves durability through heat reduction. The slot pattern (circular or straight) design matters less than its function: venting pad gases and cooling the friction surface. Slotted rotors work well for street driving and weekend track use with modest power upgrades that offer longer life and better security.

Cross-Drilled Rotors

Cross-drilled cryogenic rotors provide maximum venting and heat reduction. They will crack around the holes when pushed to their limits, but it isn't problematic for track users, who regularly inspect their brakes and consider rotor replacement routine maintenance. These premium rotors are the most expensive option. Race teams keep multiple backup sets ready. Avoid bargain cross-drilled rotors made from inferior materials without proper heat treatment. There's no such thing as an inexpensive race-ready rotor.

Aftermarket Brake Kit: Wheel Choices

Before installing an aftermarket brake kit, verify the inner wheel clearance. Don't assume that stock C4 16- or 17-inch wheels will clear all aftermarket calipers. Most upgrade calipers are six-piston fixed designs with three pistons on the outside, which adds substantial material. Maintain a minimum 0.100-inch clearance everywhere to prevent caliper-to-wheel interference. While spacers can provide clearance, they add stress to wheel studs and are not ideal. After installation, check the clearance of all rotating components before road testing. Most upgrades require new wheels to accommodate the larger brakes properly.

Baer, Ceika, and Wilwood dominate the C4 braking upgrade market. Select calipers based on your needs. The Z51 calipers may suffice for street driving and occasional gymkhana events. I've seen 1996 Z51 C4 owners with severely worn pads and rotors from daily interstate driving. For example, on Interstate 75, which goes through Atlanta, drivers frequently exceed 80 to 90 mph and brake hard to avoid traffic or police. This wears out even premium brake systems quickly.

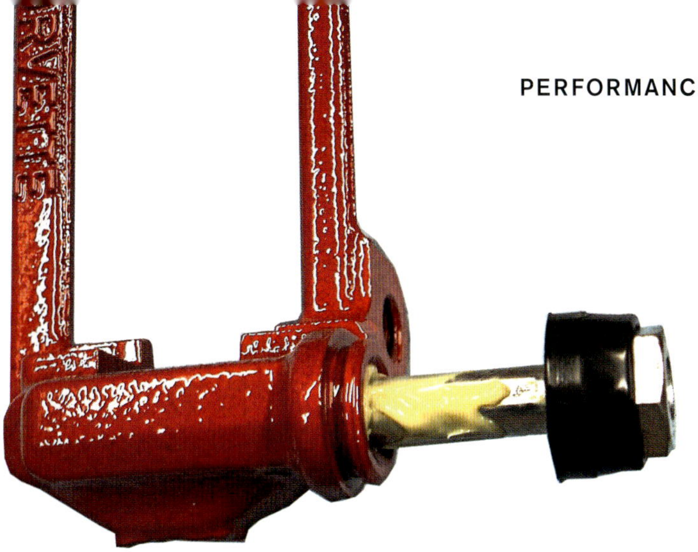

Floating-caliper slider pins should be serviced during pad changes. The caliper slider pin seal holds lubricant to keep water, dirt, and debris off the slides. Remove the slider pins and clean the pins and the caliper bracket pin holes. Install new seals and apply extreme-temperature caliper lubricant to the pins before assembly. Slider pins that stick and rotor runout guarantee a low brake pedal.

Remove the caliper brackets for rotor replacement. Clean and blow out the mounting bolt hole threads. Clean the bolt threads and apply blue Loctite for a street application and red Loctite for a race application. Torque the 1985–1987 front caliper bracket bolts to 133 ft-lbs and the 1988–1996 bolts to 166 ft-lbs (plus or minus 15 ft-lbs). Torque the 1984–1996 rear caliper bracket bolts to 70 ft-lbs.

Remember the difference between occasional panic stops and repeated high-speed braking. Expect to invest a minimum of $2,500 for upgrades, and costs approach $5,000-plus for top-tier components.

Aftermarket kits typically feature fixed calipers instead of OEM floating calipers. Fixed calipers apply equal pressure to both sides of the rotor, while floating calipers press one side and then slide to compensate for pad wear. Fixed calipers can have rotor parallelism issues. If the rotors aren't perfectly perpendicular to the pistons, the pads wear unevenly and may drag. These calipers must be precisely centered on the rotor for proper pad installation and to prevent dragging.

Baer offers massive 14-inch rotors and calipers to provide extreme braking for high-powered C4s. They offer three performance levels: Track4 (not available for rear brakes), Pro+, and Extreme+. Its six-piston fixed calipers deliver maximum clamping force without risking caliper

This 1985 has C5 Corvette front brake calipers and Hawk HB247F disc-brake pads with slotted rotors. New stainless-steel caliper slides, pins, and fasteners from Zip Corvette Products are installed to avoid disc pad drag. Apply a thin film of extreme-temperature caliper slide grease on the metal disc brake pad shield surface to prevent the brakes from squealing.

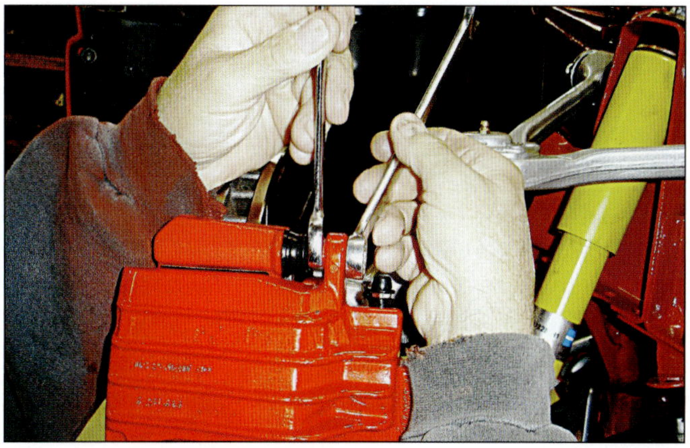

Corvette specialty suppliers have one-use, 8-mm bolts available under "C5 caliper hardware." Hold the caliper pin with a thin wrench and torque the replacement bolt to 22 to 25 ft-lbs. The stainless-steel brake pad anti-rattle retainer at the center of the caliper should also be replaced.

separation during extreme braking. The substantial cross-drilled and slotted rotors resist warping even after repeated high-speed stops. The Pro+ and Extreme+ versions feature hat-style rotors with the friction surface fastened to the hub, unlike the Track4's one-piece design. All components feature color coatings for corrosion protection and aesthetics. Kits include performance pads, hoses, and hardware.

When installing Wilwood rotors on their hats, check for line-up marks (if used), align them, and torque them. Install safety wire and follow the same twist pattern and end wrap. Baer provides its two-piece rotors ready to install. Check the recommended rotor rotation. Stamped arrows on the pad surface denote the Wilwood rotor rotation. Baer has information on its instruction sheet.

Clean all of the rotors with Dawn dish soap or alcohol until the cleaning cloth does not discolor. Avoid using brake cleaner. While brake cleaner degreases, it takes away any coating, paint, powder coat you might want to preserve. Removing surface machining particles, residual oils, and grease will help to prevent pad residue buildup and the inherent squeaks that occur.

Temporarily install the calipers on the support. Check for centering and distance from the outer rotor's edge. Note that the shims are required and their position. Apply a small dab of 3M yellow adhesive to each shim to keep them in place. Install the caliper supports with the shims in place using the supplied bolts and red Loctite 271. Torque the bolts to 65 ft-lbs.

This six-piston Baer caliper is fitted. Check for equal distance from the rotor surfaces to the brake pads. Shimming is similar. The caliper pistons bind if the rotor is not rotating parallel to the disc pads. The disc pads should be at the outer edge of the rotor and allow full disc pad-to-rotor surface contact. It may seem obvious, but always make sure that the bleeder screws are at the top of the caliper.

All Wilwood C4 caliper offerings allow disc pad replacement without removing the calipers. A self-locking nut with a through-bolt and sleeve retains the pads and saves time on the racetrack. Baer brake calipers require caliper removal on all versions, which is no fun when exchanging pads after a hot lap. Caliper bracket removal is not required when servicing Baer or Wilwood rotors. At the track, this is a major advantage over OEM factory brake upgrades for C4 or C5.

Rear brake stainless hose applications require a banjo bolt to keep the hose off the rear suspension pieces. Banjo bolts require two sealing washers (copper or aluminum) on either side of the bolt that passes through the hose end. All straight-cut threads require a washer to seal fittings. National Pipe Thread's (NPT) tapered threads rely on thread pressure for sealing. Always put a light bead of red Loctite on the NPT threads to prevent leaks and fitting movement.

With the Wilwood "Forged Narrow Superlite 6R" calipers, the piston diameter increases as the rotor enters the caliper to provide balanced and stable high-heat braking. Install the caliper with the small-diameter piston at the bottom. The arched, stainless-steel brake hose goes toward the frame and connects to the hard line. The hose must not touch any rotating pieces. This should be checked with the wheels loaded on the ground and as the steering wheel rotates lock to lock.

Parking Brake

Baer includes a standalone emergency-brake assembly with Pro+ and Extreme+ rear kits that outperforms the 1988–1996 integrated caliper emergency brake and enables more rear brake options. You'll need to install 1984–1987 parking-brake cables to complete the upgrade.

Wilwood supplies 1985–1996 C4s with 12.88- or 14.00-inch drilled and slotted rotors and up to 6-piston calipers in various colors. It also provides rear kits with a standalone parking brake for 1988–1996 models. This approach pairs larger rear calipers/rotors with a compact parking-brake assembly that has its own pads, which allows use of your existing parking-brake system. Note that 1984 Corvettes need 1985-and-newer front spindles for these options to fit.

Ceika offers custom-built fixed caliper and rotor systems for 1988–1996 C4s. Its rotors range up to 15.94-inch diameter in drilled, slotted, or wave-cut designs. Systems with up to 8 large pistons are available for 20-inch wheels. Measure carefully before purchasing. Pad compounds range from street to pro-race formulations. Multiple caliper/rotor colors and finishes are offered. Its philosophy is to maximize braking power within your wheel constraints. Note that 1984–1987 C4 kits or replacements aren't offered for the 1988–1996 integral parking brake.

Wilwood's lever-operated parking-brake caliper allows rear rotor diameter and caliper piston count increases. OEM parking brake cables are coupled to Wilwood-specific cables. Specific stainless-steel brake hoses are also required. The upside is that the easy-to-service, mechanical parking brake calipers have great vehicle restraint. The downside is that it's one more thing to remove when rotor replacement is required.

Upon inspection, the C5 Corvette's triangulated bolt pattern was similar to the C4's rear bearing pattern. Elongating the C5 parking-brake back-plate mounting holes permit the use of C5 parking-brake and rotor components. The C5 parking-brake plate assemblies are relatively simple to find used. Shoes and hardware are available to bring the assembly back to new condition.

An issue arose when fitting the assembly to the caliper support mount (bracket) plate. An aluminum-end mill cutter was used to remove 0.150 inch from the mount. Structural integrity in this area is not a concern. Providing enough clearance for the cable mount is the main objective. Any C5 factory service manual covers the parking-brake assembly in detail for proper overhaul and servicing.

This is another version with a modified OEM cable mount. The original parking-brake assembly and hardware are fitted with Dale's oversize parking-brake shoes. This upgraded the 1986 C4's tiny rear brakes to C6 Corvette Z51 or J55 13-inch rotors and calipers. The functioning parking brake keeps the Tremec 5-speed-equipped competitor in check when parking.

The C5 or C6 rear calipers can be mounted using brake adapter plates from Dale Griffith of Dale's Corvette Parts. Save a few bucks and add an excellent parking brake while upgrading the rear brake calipers and rotors. The parking-brake mounts are the C5 Corvette version. The mounts require minor trimming for proper fitment. The 1984–1987 C4 modified (shortened) cables are required.

These are Ceika brakes with scalloped, drilled, and slotted F1-style rotors. Huge six-piston calipers clamp the two-piece brake rotors. (Photo Courtesy Ceika)

This later C4 features Ceika drilled and slotted rotors with six-piston calipers for a more modest approach. If you dream it, Ceika will put together a brake kit for you. (Photo Courtesy Ceika)

Master Cylinder Proportioning Valves

Examining the 1984–1991 master cylinder reveals that the front port has a smaller bore than the rear, which creates higher front pressure. Changing the master cylinder's brake bias spring increases rear pressure, but major bias changes require a new master cylinder with single front/rear ports, plus an in/out adjustable proportioning valve for complete system control. OEM master cylinders have a 15/16-inch bore. Replacement aftermarket units from 15/16-inch to 1.00-inch are acceptable. When upgrading master cylinders, always check pushrod-to-master cylinder piston clearance. This adjustment is crucial. Without enough clearance, brake lockup occurs. If there is too much clearance, it's a low brake pedal. Aftermarket replacement master cylinders may require machining material off the brake booster's pushrod or welding to increase the length.

When upgrading to larger calipers and rotors, an adjustable proportioning valve allows fine-tuning of the front-to-rear brake balance. The 1984–1985 C4s lack ABS, 1985–1991 models have basic ABS, and 1992–1996 versions include ABS with a prime pipe that connects the master cylinder to the control module. This prime pipe isn't pressurized. It supplies fluid to the acceleration slip regulator (ASR) portion of the electronic-brake traction-control module (EBTCM).

Baer, Wilwood, and I do not officially endorse these modifications. They haven't tested universal products in these applications. While the principles are sound, use common sense and thoroughly test the system before road use. Installation requires new lines from the master cylinder to the proportioning valve, and the original lines connect to the valve. You'll need adapters (C4 lines use metric bubble flares, while proportioning valves have 3/8-24 female threads) and flaring and cut-off tools. Follow the proper flaring procedures and check all of the connections for leaks under pressure.

Wilwood offers a 1-inch-bore master cylinder (part number 260-8555) and a proportioning valve (part number 260-8419). (The part in the photo is similar but is not the 260-8555 master cylinder.) The cylinder requires minor round file work to open up the mounting holes to fit the C4 power brake booster. The downside is all of the screws that are required to remove and replace the cover. A flat-plate bleeder adapter works fine when pressure bleeding. (Photo Courtesy Wilwood Engineering)

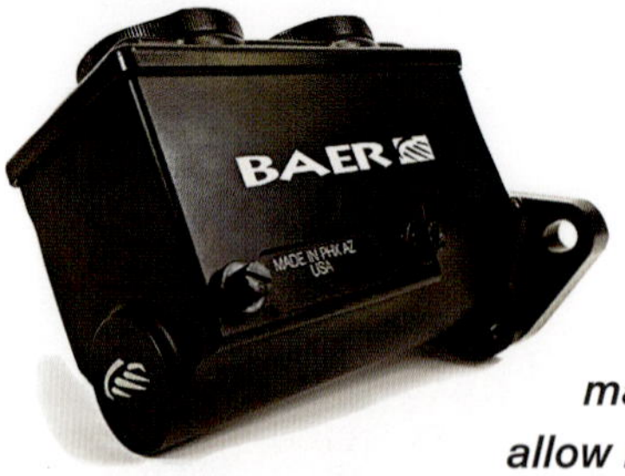

Baer's Remaster master cylinder (part number 6801272LP) has a 15/16-inch bore, which is like the General Motors OEM master cylinder. The master-cylinder mounting holes are already oval to allow multiple stud mount widths. Two filler caps ease fluid level checks. A two-top pressure bleeder adapter is difficult to locate. It comes in multi-colors. (Photo Courtesy Baer Brakes)

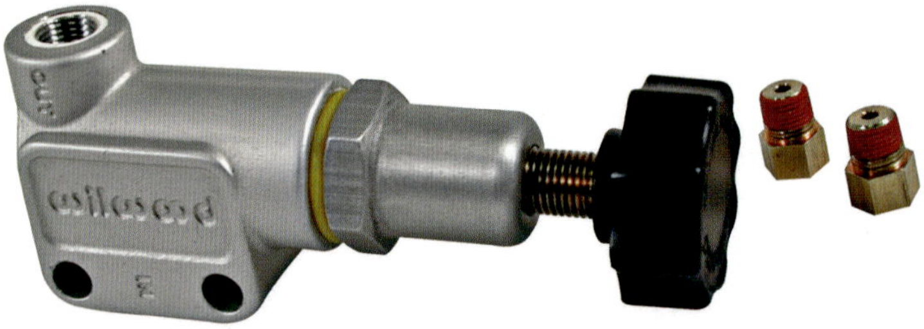

Wilwood's universal in-out rear-only adjustable proportioning valve (part number 260-8419) requires 1/8-27 NPT male-to-female flare adapters to connect the rear brake lines and master cylinder. (Photo Courtesy Wilwood Engineering)

Baer's general fit proportioning valve (part number 2000035) requires 3/8-24 male tube nuts for line installation. The lines require double flaring when using steel tubing or a single flare with stainless-steel tubing. (Photo Courtesy Baer Brakes)

Power Brake Boosters: ABS/EBTCM

The C4 power brake boosters rarely fail. Since they're composite, consider adding reflective shielding if you use race headers that generate excessive heat. Testing is straightforward. Run the engine a few minutes, shut it off, and then apply the brakes. You should get two vacuum-assisted applications. Alternatively, deplete the vacuum with multiple pedal presses, maintain pressure, and then start the engine. You should feel the pedal soften as vacuum assist engages. No pedal assist indicates an internal leak.

The 1986–1991 ABS and 1992–1996 EBTCM prevent wheel lockup by modulating brake pressure based on speed, which functions independently from the primary brake system. The 1984–1991 ABS uses two front brake lines but only one rear line. If either rear wheel locks, both receive the same modulation. The 1992–1996 EBTCM adds traction control (applies the brakes during wheelspin) and uses two rear lines for independent four-wheel control. While these systems prevent lockup regardless of master-cylinder pressure, they function more efficiently with proper front-to-rear brake balance. This minimizes ABS/EBTCM intervention.

Brake Cooling

One cost-effective way to improve your stock brake system is to add cooling ducts. Performance and race cars direct cool air onto the calipers and rotors to handle the increased demands and extend rotor life. While specialized ducted lower spoilers are sometimes available, a simpler approach uses Howe Products cooling ducts attached to the existing spoiler. Connect the ducts to 3-inch hoses that are routed to the frame ahead of the rotors. Position the hoses carefully for optimal cooling and check for clearance by turning the steering from lock to lock. This system works best at highway speeds and on road courses. It's less effective for Gymkhana events with brief acceleration/braking cycles. After such events, a gentle drive helps stabilize brake temperatures.

Final Thoughts

High-level competition requires investing in quality components. Inspect the brake and suspension systems before each event and plan for frequent fluid changes. After any major brake work, pump the pedal several times to ensure firmness and confirm the pads are contacting the rotors. Once the pedal is firm, begin road testing with low-speed stops to bed the pads. Start with three moderate stops from 50 mph, allow them to cool, and then repeat that process. Follow your brake supplier's specific break-in procedures carefully.

Your upgraded brake system should inspire significant confidence. For car-show enthusiasts, stock C4 rotors and calipers look underwhelming behind open spoke wheels. Decorative caliper covers aren't fooling anyone, and they actually impede cooling airflow and contribute to higher fluid temperatures and potential boiling. Beyond appearances, brake upgrades can be lifesaving. They deliver shorter, more balanced panic stops that protect you and others on the road and in competition.

WHEEL AND TIRE COMBINATIONS

Wheel preferences widely vary. My focus is maximizing rubber on the road. A 315/30ZR18 tire on an 18x11-inch wheel with a 50-mm offset fits under the front and rear fenders on 1988–1996 C4s. Front tire turning clearance is not limited and allows brake-duct routing. These tires sit at the fender's outer edge, but most racecourses don't generate enough suspension movement to cause rubbing issues. Cray Corvette Wheels offers five designs online, although I only found one with exact fitment specifications. The company's specialty is hub-centric wheels. Note that 1984–1987 C4s have a 1-inch hub-to-hub offset difference that requires a minimum of 0.500-inch spacers when using 50-mm offset wheels.

For overall handling, more rubber at all corners results in better grip. Drag racers benefit from thinner front wheels and tires to reduce friction while maintaining 18x11-inch wheels in the rear for traction. The sidewall height affects comfort and performance. Taller sidewalls improve ride comfort but reduce the cornering capability by acting as air springs. Considering the C4's stiff suspension, 18-inch wheels provide the best balance for street and track use. While 20-inch wheels may look appealing, they're only suitable for tracks with minimal surface irregularities. Otherwise, they're too harsh on the driver and the suspension. Having both 18- and 20-inch wheel sets provides another tuning variable that effectively changes what the spring rate should be.

While tire compounds remain proprietary, manufacturers share important usage concerns. Many track tires crack when they are exposed to temperatures below 20°F. After cold exposure, they need 24 hours at temperatures of at least 40°F before any flexing, inflation adjustment, mounting, or vehicle loading. Tires with cracks (sometimes called "checking") should never be used on roads or tracks. Track events prohibit the use of any damaged tire, including previously repaired tires with plugs.

Tires are rated using uniform

This direct bolt-on 18 x 11-inch x 50-mm offset Forgestar wheel with a 5 x 120.65-mm bolt pattern completely fills the 1993 C4's wheel well. The 315-30 x 18 BFGoodrich Rival S Extreme Performance summer tires have adequate clearance for suspension movement in the front and rear. You won't like these tires when the road is wet or if the temperature is below 40°F.

The 50-mm offset wheel and 315-30/18 tire just make it under the front wheel well. There was no concern with fender rubbing while turning the steering wheel from lock to lock or over major track anomalies. This 1993 model can be driven to the track and reach track speeds of more than 150 mph.

The 1996 Grand Sport C4s had rear fender chevron flares for the factory-recommended 315-35/17, 11.3-inch tread width tires on 11 x 17-inch wheels. You can stuff 12.10-inch 335-30 x 18 tires under the rear fender flares and still not be too far out from the fender. Motor City Corvette Parts has the rear fender flares and extensions for a factory appearance.

The five-spoke 1996 Grand Sport wheels are popular with a chrome or black finish, and Top Flight Automotive sells several versions. They are staggered: a 17 x 11-inch x 50-mm offset in the rear and 17 x 9.5-inch x 56-mm offset in the front. Adding more sidewall height than the 18-inch examples makes street driving more comfortable with minimal tradeoff in handling from sidewall flex.

Tire sipes and grooves determine how well they shed water and prevent hydroplaning. Slick tires do not grip well. They are only for all-out competition on dry surfaces. This is why worn tires do not grip well on wet surfaces. Decreasing the sipe and groove depth diminishes grip on wet surfaces.

tire quality grade (UTQG) standards through manufacturer and third-party testing. Tread-wear grades aren't particularly reliable because the wear varies by driver and vehicle. For track use, avoid tread wear ratings above 300, as those tires typically provide insufficient grip.

Tire brand preferences typically develop from personal experience. Serious weekend racers often maintain separate track-day tire sets if they drive their C4 on the street. High-grip tires wear rapidly due to their sticky compounds, and track alignment specifications accelerate wear. Store track tires properly. They should be off the ground, away from concrete/asphalt, out of the sunlight, and preferably covered.

A significant concern with aftermarket wheels is their center hub

Performance driving schools prep you for wet- or dry-surface roads or racetrack events. Sipe patterns can make a huge difference in their ability to push water out of the grooves. Many road courses do not shut down the track unless there is a deluge, so competitors change to rain (grooved) tires.

Check the tire sidewall ratings and recommended pressure before purchase. Traction ratings use an outdated alpha system (AA is the highest and then it goes A and B, and C is the lowest), which is useful but not crucial. The temperature rating is critical. You must have an "A" rating for speeds above 115 mph to make sure that the tire can dissipate heat. Speed ratings are essential for track driving: H (up to 130 mph), V (149 mph), Z (168 mph), and Y (over 186 mph).

diameter. Most use universal sizing to fit multiple vehicles, which makes them too large for the C4's 70.3-mm hub diameter. This creates looseness at the mounting area, which is a risky situation where wheel studs must center the wheel. To solve this, use hub-centric rings that fit over the C4 hub and fill the gap in the wheel's center bore. Another alternative is tire truing—if you can find a tire dealer that has a machine in working order. Once the process is complete, the tires will be perfectly round until a wheel is removed or loosened and retightened.

I generally avoid wheel spacers, especially on performance Corvettes. Even thin 0.125-inch spacers compromise lug stud engagement, and 0.250-inch spacers require longer wheel studs. For 1984–1987 C4s, 0.500-inch spacers allow 9.5- or 11.0-inch-width wheels up front, which is necessary due to the shorter control arms. Some suppliers offer 0.100-inch spacers to make 1988–1996 wheels fit earlier C4s, but most of them that I've seen aren't hub-centric and limit wheel choices. Given their cost plus the required hardware, these adaptations rarely make economic sense.

If spacers are necessary, US Wheel Adapters is recommended for its hub-centric options. It can customize spacers for the common mismatch between C4 hubs (70.3-mm

Tire date codes are important. This tire date of 2607 (late June 2007) indicates that it should never be driven at highway speeds but is good for rolling around the shop. Tires dry out as manufacturing oils evaporate and cause cracking and tread separation. Unmounted 3- to 5-year-old race tires are usable when stored in a cool, dark, and dry location. The survival rate for ultraviolet (UV)-exposed tires is less than a year. The shelf life of used, heat-cycled tires drops to 9 months.

Hub-centric rings are important for high-speed road courses and interstate travel. I prefer aluminum hub-centric rings over plastic or composite rings. The rings can fall off during wheel or tire service. A bit of weatherstrip adhesive will keep them in place.

diameter) and aftermarket wheels (often using BMW's 72.6-mm diameter). The spacers include integrated hub-centric rings with custom configurations built in 3 to 7 business days at reasonable prices. Its technical resources are also excellent.

Never underestimate the importance of proper wheel studs and lug nuts for vehicle safety. Use manufacturer-recommended lug nuts torqued to specification. Default to 100 ft-lbs if no specification is provided. Be aware of whether your wheels require flat- or tapered-seat lug nuts. Flat-seat applications typically need washers to prevent wheel surface damage during torquing. For

Wheel spacers such as these are trouble. There is no way to center them, which causes wheel/tire balance issues. Lug-nut stud purchase is diminished, which makes them unsafe on any roadway. Wheel studs should protrude a minimum amount of 0.750 inch past the wheel-lug contact area.

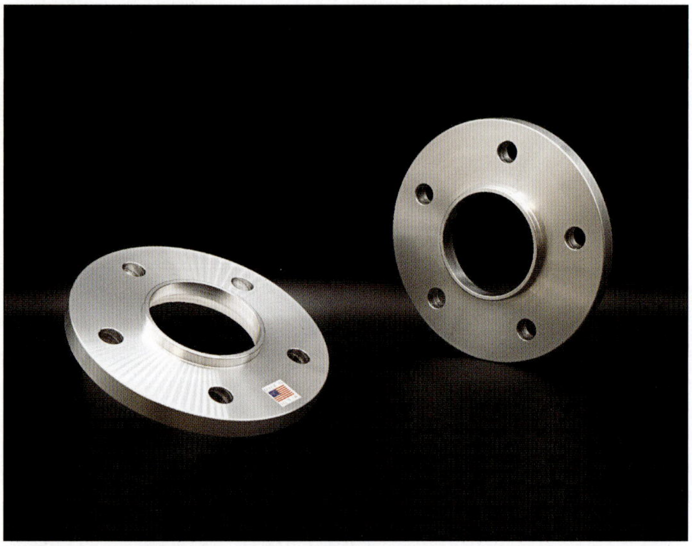

US Wheel Adapters has purpose-built, direct-fitment wheel adapters with hub-centric, wheel-mounting surfaces. It stocks bolt-on and slip-on versions for 1.50-inch spacing. Slip-on spacers require longer wheel studs. (Photo Courtesy Cole Higgins/US Wheel Adapters)

Front wheel studs can be replaced quite easily. At the rear, hub removal is required to access the stud. The stud-specific remover tool (OTC part number 4295) pushes out studs similarly to the ball-joint remover tool that is shown. Shocking the bearing and distorting the hub with a hammer may work, but it defeats all of the precautions to ensure parallel rotor and wheel runout.

A Lisle tool (part number 22800) pulls studs straight in without thread damage. Before use, always apply oil via the tool's outer-perimeter lube ports.

tapered seats, ensure the lug nuts fully cover the wheel's tapered area. Studs should extend at least 1 inch beyond the fastening area for secure thread engagement. Watch for covered lug nuts that might bottom out before achieving proper torque. Racing applications and spacer use require longer wheel studs.

These details may seem trivial, but wheels are frequently damaged or come off the wheel hub due to seemingly minor oversights.

Race tech inspectors expect to see the lug studs protruding through the lug nuts for tech check-in. These long race studs have been installed by Van Steel. They are excellent for track use. They are heavy duty and have plenty of length to let the tech inspector know that you are serious.

Interior Modifications and Race Preparation

Although it may seem that the words "interior" and "performance" don't fit well together, your life may depend on them meshing. Always be prepared for the unexpected while you're in the driver seat. Will you have to put out a fire or help someone else put out a fire? If you're held in your seat and feel safe, lap times decrease as your confidence grows. Driveline monitoring gauges that are easy to read and distinguish can save you thousands of dollars.

Fire Safety

Fire extinguishers are essential for any vehicle, particularly composite-bodied C4 Corvettes. The C4s' fuel-injection systems can spray pressurized fuel onto hot engines and create difficult-to-control, catastrophic fires. A portable extinguisher can help contain a fire until emergency services arrive. Serious race C4s feature button-activated fire-suppression systems that target key areas. These systems must meet race sanctioning body requirements regarding fire retardant types and maintenance intervals. Remember that safety inspectors enforce the regulations for everyone's protection, including yours.

With underhood fires, the C4's heavy hood causes access challenges. Our shop's 1990 Corvette experienced this when a fuel leak ignited after years of neglect by its previous owner. The intense fire melted the hood release cables and forced firefighters to cut both hood corners for access. Although the firefighters quickly extinguished the blaze, it still destroyed the A/C evaporator, melted the windshield, and severely damaged the firewall. In a rural area without prompt emergency response, the Corvette would likely have been a total loss.

Opening the hood during a fire increases the risk of releasing a dangerous fireball of flames and hot liquids. When you detect burning odors, immediate action is critical. After approximately 2 minutes, a fire typically

Fire extinguishers can be mounted at the front of the driver's seat for quick access. Before competing, check the fire extinguisher annually (at a minimum) to ensure that it has a full charge and is not past its expiration date. ABC-rated units are recommended for overall protection. Handheld fire extinguishers rated A and C will not handle flammable liquids, which is the major fire-control concern.

The installation of an alternate auxiliary hood-opening-cable kit is highly recommended for emergencies. The first step in making sure that the hood will open in an emergency is to have the hood pins or catches adjusted (if required) to allow smooth hood operation. Auxiliary cables will be little help if you fight the hood to open it.

Another option is the C4 hood-opening tool. It takes some training to get the hang of using it. It is not recommended if you're in a panic situation unless you practice using it daily. The tool is inserted between the hood and door pillar. Then, a counterclockwise twisting motion pushes over the latch.

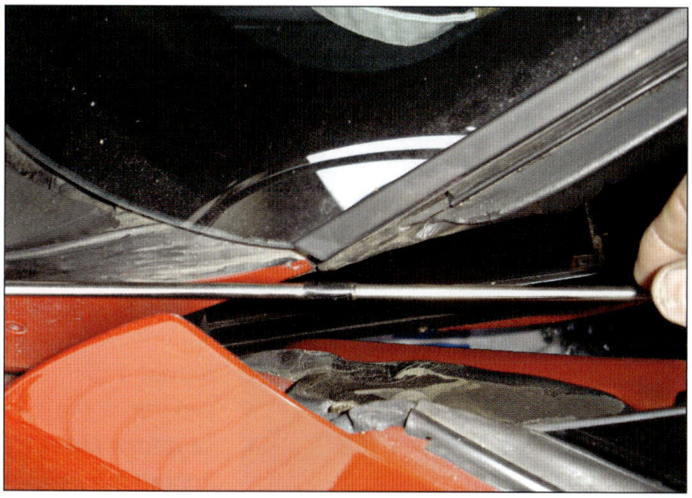

The black wrap of tape on the tool's long portion of the rod should stop near the windshield pillar trim. This tool relies on an easy-opening hood. The best policy is to practice this a few times and take an annual primer on the operation. Hood-opening tools and auxiliary cable kits can be found at all major Corvette suppliers online.

exceeds a handheld extinguisher's capacity. Never open the hood if the flames are visible underneath. Call 911 and move to safety immediately.

Interior Performance Enhancements

Proper seats and seat belts are crucial during extreme driving maneuvers. Body movement compromises control and safety. The 1984–1993 seats were moderately form-fitting and nicknamed "butt funnels" by some owners. Sport seat options were available with adjustable kidney bolsters and an inflatable lumbar support. These performed adequately for most driver sizes. The 1994–1996 seats accommodated wider bodies with increased seat-bottom room, while the sport versions featured stability-enhancing bolsters.

Aftermarket race seats, including those from Braum, Corbeau, Cipher, DFX, Next Level, Procar, and Sparco, provide reduced weight and superior body control under high G-forces. These seats feature pronounced cushion and seatback bolsters as well as crucial shoulder guides for harnesses. Installation requires adapting existing seat tracks or fabricating new mounts, as the rare 1984–1986 manual tracks are difficult to source. Proper seat positioning is important. If you're straining to reach the steering wheel or work the pedals, it can be hazardous to your health or someone else's.

Seat belts are critical for control and safety. Your C4's belts have endured decades of stress. GM's cinch-button feature tightens retractors to prevent extension during high-speed maneuvers. The supplemental inflatable restraint system

This full set of race seat belts controls body movement and improves your driving. The lap belts can piggyback on the original seat-belt studs. The shoulder belts are secured to the roll bar's crossbar. Always check with your race sanctioning body for proper installation. (Photo Courtesy Gary Bitner)

(SIRS), introduced in 1990, works with seatbelts in a specific sequence. The belts absorb the initial impact before the airbags prevent forward movement toward the steering wheel. Never drive an airbag-equipped C4 without functional seatbelts. Belt failure places your head dangerously close to the wheel during airbag deployment.

Road-course racing demands proper racing harnesses for optimal vehicle control. These come in five, six, or seven-point systems with dual shoulder belts, lap belts, and anti-submarine straps that prevent submarining under the harness. Many sanctioning bodies require anti-submarine belts. Before competing, obtain and thoroughly review your racing association's rulebook regarding acceptable restraint systems and installation specifications.

The C4 floor is a hybrid—it's composite in the front with a steel seat platform. The submarine seat belt in the center of the seat requires drilling a 0.500-inch hole into the floor reinforcement. A thick, large-diameter washer is required to ensure seat belt security.

Factory seat belts have this cinch button to tighten the seat belts and hold you in place for performance driving. Move the seat back a bit, hit the cinch button, and let the belts retract a click or two. Move the seat forward to tighten the belts. The belts must be fully retracted to disable the feature.

Consider harness fastening mechanisms when selecting racing belts. Cam locks allow sequential belt attachment that is similar to standard vehicles. Latch-and-lock systems require connecting all belts to a central point before securing the latch. This is more time-consuming but often more secure. Mounting options include direct bolting to the floor/pillar, loop-and-latch systems with eyebolts and spring latches, or wraparound mounting on roll-bar crossbars that are positioned below shoulder height. Race inspectors will verify that all of the mounting points can withstand crash forces.

Quality racing harnesses provide confidence to the driver during aggressive driving maneuvers and keep you properly positioned. The SFI Foundation establishes the safety standards for harnesses and other racing components. Note that SFI certification expires after two years, after which belts are considered potentially compromised. Replace any harness that shows even slight webbing damage. The cost of new restraints is insignificant compared to preventing injuries or fatalities.

Four-point roll bar installation requires the removal of all rear-compartment trim, carpet, and insulation before starting. The rear support bars mount to the top of the rear frame rails, and fabricated aluminum covers keep burning rubber out. The 4 x 6-inch, 0.025-inch-thick plates retain the main hoop to the floor and were welded by a local race shop. Later versions offer a diagonal brace to avoid hoop collapse in a rollover event. The crossbar allows shoulder seat belt mounting.

Roll Bars/Cages

Installing effective C4 roll protection is challenging due to the lack of a traditional frame. The main hoop and reinforcement bars require secure mounting to floor and rear deck areas with proper reinforcement plates. Many owners mount the harness bars below the main hoop to make proper installation literally life-critical. Roll bars need at least four mounting points to provide meaningful rollover protection. Two-point floor mounting can cause more harm than help. Full racing cages (6-, 8-, or 10-point designs with side-impact bars) require interior gutting and extensive fabrication. Always have certified welders with racing experience construct these safety systems. Never compromise on materials or construction quality. The consequences could be fatal.

This is the driver-side rear quarter panel with the inner fender liner removed to show the top of the frame rail. The rear roll bar supports must be attached to the top of the rail. The rear compartment must be cut out for the roll bar to pass through it. The access hole must be large enough for the mounting plate that you choose to attach to the frame rail.

Sanctioned racing events enforce specific safety requirements. You must comply with the sanctioning body's roll bar, seat, and other regulations. Inspections become increasingly

A roll cage is installed in this track-proven 1986 C4 Corvette. The owner enjoys this C4 on and off the track. (Photo Courtesy Gary Bitner)

stringent as vehicle speeds increase to protect all participants. Always obtain the sanctioning body's rulebook and follow it precisely to ensure a smooth technical inspection and maximize your track time.

Gauges

The 1984–1989 digital gauges present significant drawbacks for performance driving. Their main limitation is requiring two toggle switches to cycle between auxiliary gauges instead of displaying them simultaneously. While General Motors programmed the automatic display switching for critical engine issues, this gauge system demands excessive attention during track driving. The 1985 update offered bolder displays with improved sunlight visibility. The 1986 dash cluster repositioning reduced glare, but neither achieved true performance car functionality.

The 1990–1996 models returned to a more practical layout with four analog gauges, a digital fuel gauge, and a hybrid speedometer. This configuration better suited performance driving, although the coolant-temperature gauge remained difficult to decipher. The 1992–1996 clusters added digital readouts to supplement analog displays. Today, numerous aftermarket options exist to update gauge clusters. Precise instrumentation serves dual purposes. It prolongs engine life and optimizes track performance by allowing drivers to monitor speed and RPM at corner entry and exit points.

New Vintage USA offers more refined analog options with a standard speedometer and tachometer along with four auxiliary gauges. Its Performance II package features chrome accents with black and CFR Blue faces, while the Aviator package uses all-black backgrounds with high-visibility orange needles. Both utilize stepper motor technology for precision and red backlighting for night visibility. Notably, New Vintage offers 1990–1996 gauge clusters with near-complete instrument visibility from the driving position, blue backlighting, and programmable speed-sensor inputs.

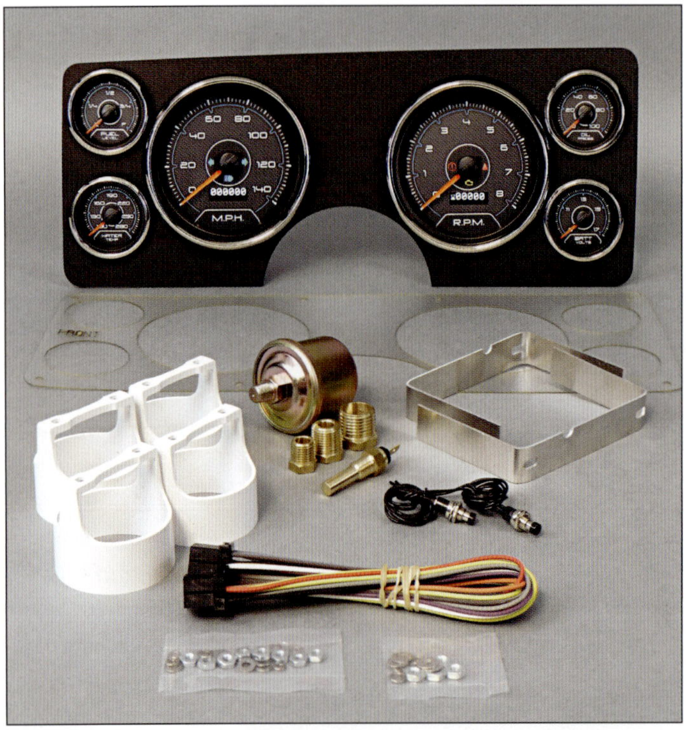

New Vintage USA's CFR-series instruments are shown. A textured inner dial with colored accents and bold numbers will make your dash stand out. Topped with waterproof glass lenses and stainless bezels, the high-tech design sets the bar for dash design with the CFR-series instruments. Four additional gauge clusters are available with black- or white-face gauges.

This New Vintage USA's 1990–1996 CFR-series C4 gauge cluster is based on its Phoenix platform with user-selectable inputs, organic light-emitting diode (OLED) screens, and stepper motor technology that were all made in the United States. All 6-gauge kits with OLED screens feature Phoenix Direct Drive technology, which is by far the easiest way to wire up a 6-gauge kit. It is LS swap and Holley Terminator-X Max compatible.

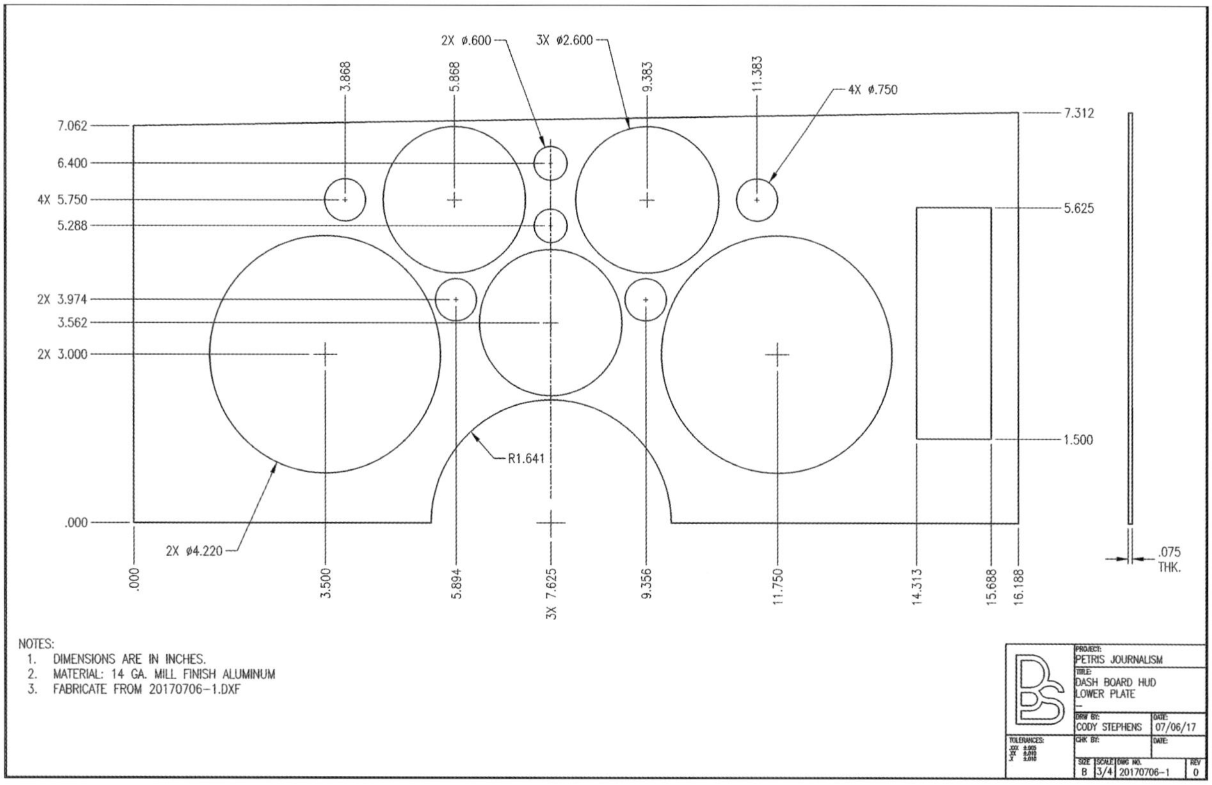

Throwback Automotive's 1984–1989 custom gauge plates are made to mimic a factory gauge panel. Water-jet cut front and rear plates sandwich gauges between them and eliminate the protruding bezels of aftermarket gauges. The back plate houses Speedhut gauges to be used in conjunction with the next drawing. (Drawing Courtesy Michael Urquhart/Throwback Automotive)

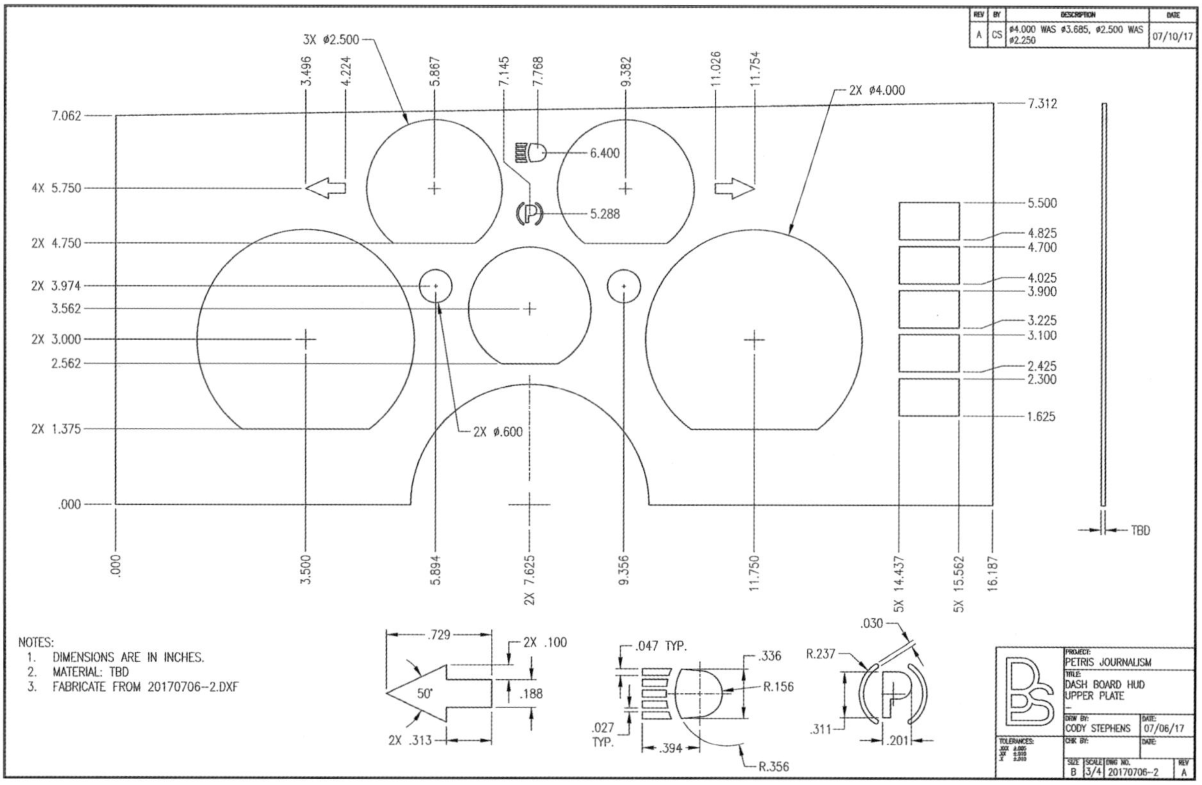

The 1984–1989 plate two (front plate) has warning-lamp icons water-jetted into the plate to enhance the true custom-gauge panel appearance. The vertical stack of five rectangular boxes on the right house's warning lamps was removed from the existing C4 center-gauge warning panel. The two 0.600-inch-bored holes between the tachometer and speedometer are the shift light and coolant overheat/low oil-pressure warning lights. (Drawing Courtesy Michael Urquhart/Throwback Automotive)

This is ready to install and easy to read at speed with a factory-gauge-pack look. We used green, blue, and red acetate panels for the warning lights. It takes trial and error to achieve the correct LED brightness. Resistors are used to trim the LED warning-light-level output and the vertical stack of warning lights, including the fasten-seat-belt light, service-engine-soon light, low coolant level light, etc.

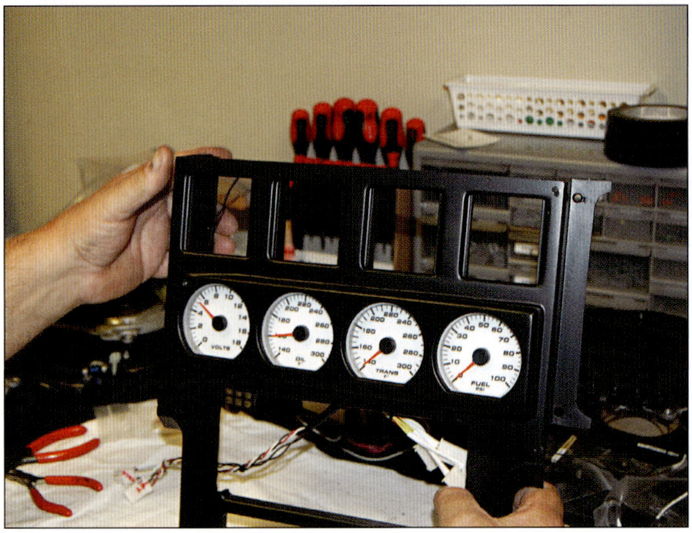

The sister panel to the main gauge cluster has plenty of information to monitor. The owner of this panel competes in Sports Car Club of America (SCCA) events and is an instructor. He preferred 2.125-inch-outer-diameter Speedhut gauges. Throwback Automotive designed and fabricated the four-gauge panel for direct fitment into the center cluster.

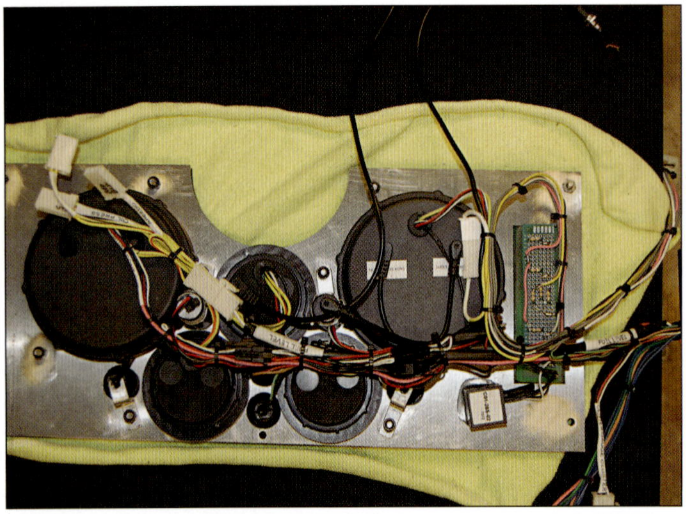

This shows the nerve center of the two-plate gauge cluster. These Speedhut 1.500-inch-thick gauges leave plenty of room for wiring. Speedhut's daisy-chain wiring connects the back lighting, gauge power, and ground. The Throwback Automotive circuit board was custom designed for the light-emitting diode (LED) vertical warning light display. You must use Speedhut's provided gauge backlighting rheostat to control after-dark lighting.

This is one of my first designs using AutoMeter gauges and a single plate. The warning lights are simple push-in 12-volt lamps. It works well, although the smaller gauges aren't as easy to read. The original dash control switches are removed to install the center cluster gauges. Being able to monitor the fuel pressure and air-to-fuel ratio at a glance can help you save your engine when you're at wide-open throttle (WOT) on a long straightaway. It gives you an idea of the possibilities, and there are plenty of options over the ready-to-go gauge pack.

This is another Throwback Automotive exclusive: a 1990–1996 custom gauge cluster with two plates and AutoMeter Phantom gauges. Throwback Automotive has these plates in stock and ready to ship with or without gauges. Gauge choices are available for a true custom look for your C4. (Photo Courtesy Throwback Automotive)

New Vintage USA incorporates all factory warning lights and indicators. A notable limitation is the absence of an oil-temperature gauge in standard offerings, although the company provides custom gauge services to address this. Retaining cruise control in 1984–1989 models requires installing and wiring a 1990–1996 C4 cruise-control module into the existing dash harness. All gauge packages come with proprietary sensors and wiring harnesses.

These aftermarket gauge systems accommodate Gen III LT or LS engine swaps and use metric-to-NPT adapters for sensor installation.

For custom builds, we prefer Speedhut and AutoMeter gauges. Our packages typically include all factory instrumentation (a speedometer, tachometer, oil-pressure and oil-temperature gauge, coolant-temperature gauge, voltmeter, and fuel gauge), plus additional performance gauges, such as the fuel-pressure, transmission temperature, and exhaust-gas temperature gauges. This approach maximizes the available dash space but requires significant technical skill. Speedhut offers extensive customization options, including faceplate colors, needle styles, bezel finishes, backlight colors, and custom graphics. Its stepper motor technology and precision sensors deliver superior accuracy.

Performance driving necessitates proper pedal covers with grooved surfaces. Rubber covers provide limited grip, especially when they are wet.

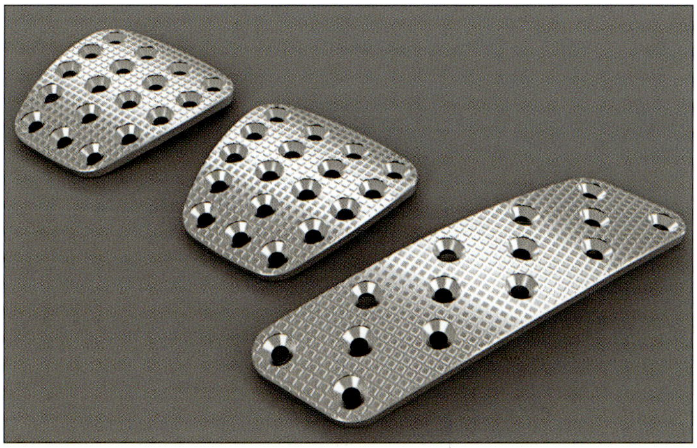

Ultimate Pedals offers complete sets, including dead-pedal options for enhanced stability during cornering. Top Flight Automotive provides various color choices. Installation requires attention to detail. Always use threaded screws with locking nuts (rather than self-tapping screws) and ensure that they have been tightened with the proper torque. A loose pedal cover creates a dangerous driving situation.

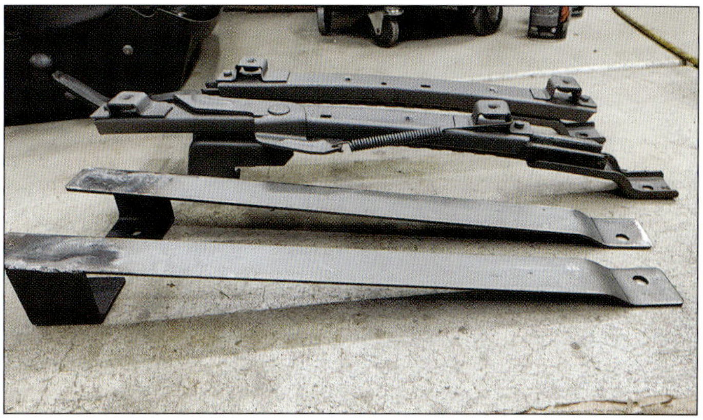

Molten Metal Racing's low, fixed-mount seat brackets eliminate the six-way power seat weight and drop you lower in the seat. The drop is about 1.5 to 2 inches lower than stock on manual sliders. (Photo Courtesy Molten Metal Racing)

FEATURE: GARY BITNER

C4 Corvettes are to be enjoyed—carving through mountain passes (at the posted speed limit, of course) or at wide-open throttle on road courses. The C4's low-end torque also served the 3,200-pound sports car well at the drag strip.

This was the path that Gary Bitner took. At an early age, he could be found at Cecil County Dragway, pushing his reflexes to obtain the lowest possible ET. Naturally, when he purchased his first Corvette (a stock 1986 model), he frequented Orlando Speed World to test and tune it.

When Bitner realized the joy of pushing his 1986 C4 through the corners, he became an avid fan of the Sports Car Club of America (SCCA) events. He became an SCCA member, racing regularly, thriving on the challenge, driving with precision, and enjoying the camaraderie. Bitner especially loved pushing his Corvette and his driving ability on iconic racetracks, including Sebring International Raceway and Daytona International Speedway, where he became a familiar face.

When I met Bitner, I was the shop service manager at Eckler's Corvette Service Center in Titusville, Florida. He came by and asked for my thoughts about adding power to his 1986 C4. He was always polite (never pushy), and it was easy to spend time with him in his quest for more grunt under the hood. After some bolt-on pieces were added to increase power output, we discussed the next steps to make his C4 competitive.

He decided to replace the engine, and the replacement wasn't just any engine, it was a Chad Golen 383 stroker. Knowing that Bitner's 1986 Corvette was a work in progress, we decided to replace the archaic GM ECM with a FAST fuel-injection control system. This proved to be an excellent plan, which allowed him to match fuel and ignition requirements for street and track events. Long straightaways at wide-open throttle produce high under-hood heat that can be controlled to some degree by leaning out the air-fuel ratio at maximum RPM.

One thing led to another, and before the project was finished (they never really are), the automatic transmission was replaced with a performance piece, the braking system was updated with C6 ZO6 Corvette brake rotors and calipers, and the suspension was upgraded with Van Steel coilovers. I fabricated a custom exhaust to tuck inside the C4's transmission tunnel with an X-pipe to balance the system. Then, the custom Speedhut gauge cluster, seven-point seat belts, and a roll bar were installed.

While the project was in the works, Bitner generously shared his innate skills as a driving instructor at SCCA events. He mentored up-and-coming drivers at Florida International Rally and Motorsports Park (FIRM) and helped them learn with his patience and enthusiasm.

One of Bitner's favorite pastimes was working with young students from the Tire Rack Street Survival School through the SCCA. Thankfully, he passed along his racing knowledge to help the next generation of drivers become safe and confident.

Bitner was not boastful; he was just the opposite. He was a good listener who wanted to help. This trait made him a natural teacher. Despite being in the passenger's seat of a new student's car that was totally out of control, he would stay calm and provide guidance without raising his voice. When he was on the racetrack, his throttle application was the same—deliberately smooth to avoid wheel slip while accelerating as fast as possible out of a corner. Control is paramount, and Bitner had that mastered.

When Bitner picked up his C4, I knew that the automatic transmission was going to be replaced. After his drag racing days were replaced with corner carving, there had to be a manual transmission behind the 383-ci engine for engine braking. Not too long afterward, the plan was made to install a Silver Sport Tremec TKO600 5-speed manual transmission. The plan also included switching to a 3:45 differential gearset in a Dana 44 housing. Now, Bitner was able to go around the Daytona road course and up on the oval, listening to the sweet sound of his 383.

As I mentioned, you're never really finished with any project. Next, we were talking about how to increase the horsepower for the long straightaways on large oval tracks. The plan was to replace the restrictive L-98 long-tube intake runners with a new old stock (NOS) TPIS Mini Ram intake manifold. This would allow the 383 to stretch its legs with additional airflow at the top end of the RPM band.

Sadly, Bitner had a medical issue and passed away recently, leaving his supportive and loving wife and two daughters. He will be missed by many people who he helped along the way. Bitner was a prankster I was told, and he was never anything but a gentleman to me. He will be missed by my family and the SCCA racing community.

Gary Bitner stands next to his drag-race-ready C4 Corvette. Bitner drove his C4 frequently and always drove it to and from the drag strip.

Gary Bitner's 1986 C4 Corvette is shown at the Daytona International Speedway after the 383-ci engine replacement and 5-speed manual-transmission conversion. At this point, the coilover suspension and C6 brake components had been installed.

Gary Bitner drives his 1986 C4 at Daytona International Speedway after the automatic-to-manual transmission swap. The manual transmission works well on corner entry and exit—you always must be aware of gear selection. If you drop from fourth to second gear, you may lose traction or create wheel hop, breaking differential pieces or, worse yet, stuffing the C4 into a retaining wall.

I designed the R4-to-Sanden 706 adapter supports for Gary Bitner's C4. Note the silicone heater hoses that ensure longevity under extreme conditions. The Golen-prepped engine pulled the car past the 140-mph mark with ease on long straightaways. A custom aluminum radiator from Brice Thomas kept the high mark of the temperature below 220°F under wide-open throttle.

Fasteners and fastening points are major concerns for a true race car. I decided to utilize a grade-8 through bolt and self-locking, fine-thread nut for the upper coilover mount. The longer-than-necessary bolt ensures that the shock eye mount is on the bolt's shoulder (not on the threads). While an adapter is supplied with most coilover kits to convert the cross-bolt to a pin mount, this makes more sense to have a secure bolt (as the shock was designed for).

Gary Bitner opted for the QA1 double-adjustable shocks and the SPC fully adjustable upper control arms. The adjustable control arms allow you to change to 1.0 degree of negative camber for the road course and then go back to an acceptable 0.5 degrees of negative camber for the drive home. Increasing the caster to 8 or 9 degrees positive is also possible for a rock-steady feel at 100-plus mph.

Advance Adapters
4320 Aerotech Center Way
Paso Robles, CA 93446
800-350-2223
advanceadapters.com

Aeromotive
10955 Mill Creek Rd.
Lenexa, KS 66219
913-808-2376
aeromotiveinc.com

Accel
2445 Nashville Rd.
Bowling Green, KY 42101
866-464-6553
holley.com

AFCO Racing Products
977 Hyrock Blvd.
Boonville, IN 47601
800-632-2320
afcoracing.com

After Dark Speed
283 Cayuga Dr.
Mooresville, NC 28117
704-340-1896
afterdarkspeed.com

Air Flow Research
28611 Industry Dr.
Valencia, CA 91355
877-892-8844
airflowresearch.com

Aldan American Suspension
2675 Temple Ave.
Signal Hill, CA 90755
310-834-7478
aldanamerican.com

American Racing Headers
120 Riverstone Dr.
Stanfield, NC 28163
631-608-1986
americanracingheaders.com

ARP (Automotive Racing Products)
1863 Eastman Ave.
Ventura, CA 93003
800-826-3045
arp-bolts.com

ATI Performance Products, Inc.
6718 Whitestone Rd.
Gwynn Oak, MD 21207
410-298-4343
atiracing.com

Auto Accessories of America (Top Flight Automotive)
100 Classic Car Dr.
Reedsville, PA 17084
833-486-7354
topflightautomotive.com

AutoMeter
413 W. Elm St.
Sycamore, IL 60178
866-248-6356
autometer.com

Baer Brakes
2222 W. Peoria Ave.
Phoenix, AZ 85029
602-233-1411
baer.com

Bailey Engineering
bailey-eng.com

BBK Performance Products
3060 Performance Cir.
DeLand, FL 32724
386-624-0025
bbkperformance.com

Bilstein
8685 Bilstein Blvd.
Hamilton, OH 45011
513-881-7600
bilstein.com

BluePrint Engines
2915 Marshall Ave.
Kearney, NE 68847
308-236-1010
blueprintengines.com

Bosch Auto Parts
1 Tower Ln., Suite 3100
Oakbrook Terrace, IL 60181
888-715-3616
boschautoparts.com

Bowler Performance Transmissions
10885 May Chapel Rd.
Lawrenceville, IL 62439
618-943-4856
bowlertransmissions.com

BRP Hot Rods (Muscle Rods)
770-751-0687
brphotrods.com

Callaway Cars
3 High St.
Old Lyme, CT 06371
866-927-9400
callawaycars.com

Canton Racing Products
232 Branford Rd.
North Branford, CT 06471
203-481-9460
cantonracingproducts.com

Captain Z CNC
N2261 Frommander Rd.
Fort Atkinson, WI 53538
Email: aaron@captainzcnc.com
captainzcnc.com

Ceika Brakes
877-378-3004
ceika-store.com

Chevrolet Performance
P.O. Box 33170
Detroit, MI 48323
800-222-1020
chevrolet.com

Cold Hose
3611 NW 27th Ave.
Ocala, FL 34475
800-223-7167
coldhose.com

Comp Cams
8649 Hacks Cross Rd.
Olive Branch, MS 38654
800-999-0853
compcams.com

Core Shifters
core-shifters.com

Corsa Performance
140 Blaze Industrial Pkwy.
Berea, OH 44017
440-891-0999
corsaperformance.com

Corvettes at Carlisle
1000 Bryn Mawr Rd.
Carlisle, PA 17013
717-243-7855
carlisleevents.com

Corvette Central
13550 Three Oaks Rd.
Sawyer, MI 49125
800-345-4122
corvettecentral.com

Dale's Corvette Parts
717-965-4477

Denny's Driveshafts & Driveline Parts
1189 Military Rd.
Kenmore, NY 1417
800-955-1872
dennysdriveshaft.com

Derale Performance
14722 Anson Ave.
Santa Fe Springs, CA 90670
562-404-0488
derale.com

Detroit Speed & Engineering
185 McKenzie Rd.
Mooresville, NC 28115
704-662-3272
detroitspeed.com

Dewitts Radiator
29988 Anthony Dr.
Wixom, MI 48393
517-548-0600
dewitts.com

Doug Rippie Motorsports
412 Pacific Ave.
Waverly, MN 55390
763-658-6109
dougrippie.com

Earl's Performance Plumbing
2445 Nashville Rd.
Bowling Green, KY 42101
866-464-6553
holley.com/brands/earls

Eckler's
600 N Cedar Hollow Rd.
Paoli, PA 19301
877-305-8966
ecklers.com

EFI Connection, LLC
1110 Chestnut St.
Erie, PA, 16501
814-566-0946
eficonnection.com

Energy Suspension
1131 Via Callejon
San Clemente, CA 92673
949-361-3935
teamenergysuspension.com

Engineered Cooling Products
1900 N. Austin Ave.
Chicago, IL 60639
773-599-3067
ecp-radiator.com

FiTech Fuel Injection
12370 Doherty St., Suite A
Riverside, CA 92503
951-340-2624
fitechefi.com

Forgestar
6600 Stadium Dr.
Kansas City, MO 64129
800-788-9353
forgestar.com

Fuel Injector Connection
3482 Keith Bridge Rd.
Cumming, GA 30041
fuelinjectorconnection.com

General Motors
P.O. Box 33170
Detroit, MI 48232
800-462-8782
gm.com

Global West Suspension
655 S Lincoln Ave.
San Bernardino, CA 92408
909-890-0759
globalwest.net

Golen Engine Service
17 Dracut Rd. #C
Hudson, NH 03051
800-591-9171
golenengineservice.com

Gorilla Automotive Products
6131 Knott Ave.
Buena Park, CA 90620
323-585-2852
gorilla-auto.com

Hawk Performance
920 Lake Rd.
Medina, OH 44256
800-542-0972
hawkperformance.com

Holley
2445 Nashville Rd.
Bowling Green, KY 42101
866-464-6553
holley.com

Hooker Headers
2445 Nashville Rd.
Bowling Green, KY 42101
866-464-6553
holley.com/brands/hooker

JW Performance Transmissions
1826 Baldwin St.
Rockledge, FL 32955
321-632-6205
racewithjw.com

Koni
1961 International Way, #9526
Hebron, KY 41048
859-586-4100
shop.koni-na.com

Kwik Performance
9683 N. Cedar Valley Ln.
Fair Grove, MO 65648
417-955-1467
kwikperf.com

KYB
2625 N Morton St.
Franklin, IN 46131
630-620-5555
kyb.com

Lakewood Industries
2445 Nashville Rd.
Bowling Green, KY 42101
866-464-6553
holley.com/brands/lakewood

Lane Culver Automotive Specialties
203 McCutcheon Loop Rd.
Laceys Spring, AL 35754
256-882-2450
culverautospecialties.com

Lingenfelter Performance Engineering
1557 Winchester Rd.
Decatur, IN 46733
260-724-2552
lingenfelter.com

Littelfuse
6133 N. River Rd., Suite 500
Rosemont, IL 60018
800-323-2480
littelfuse.com

Mac Tools
5195 Blazer Pkwy.
Dublin, OH 43017
800-622-8665
mactools.com

Matco Tools
4403 Allen Rd.
Stow, OH 44224
866-289-8665
matcotools.com

Meziere Enterprises
220 S Hale Ave.
Escondido, CA 92029
760-746-3273
meziere.com

Michelin
1 Parkway S.
Greenville, SC 29615
866-866-6605
michelin.com

Mishimoto
1515 Garnet Mine Rd.
Garnet Valley, PA 19060
877-466-4744
mishimoto.com

Mobil 1
22777 Springwoods Village Pkwy.
Spring, TX 77389
800-662-4525
mobil.com

Molten Metal Racing
429 N. Weber Rd., #285
Romeoville, IL 70725
747-666-5836
molten-metal-racing.com

Monster Transmission
2600 Lakepointe Pkwy.
Odessa, FL 33556
801-383-0023
monstertransmission.com

Moroso Performance Products
80 Carter Dr.
Guilford, CT 06437
203-453-6571
moroso.com

Moser Engineering
102 Performance Dr.
Portland, IN 47371
260-726-6689
moserengineering.com

Motor City Corvette Parts
342 Hudson St.
Wyandotte, MI 48192
844-323-8388
motorcityvettes.com

MSD Ignition
2445 Nashville Rd.
Bowling Green, KY 42101
866-464-6553
holley.com/brands/msd

New Vintage USA
21840 Wyoming Pl., #1
Oak Park, MI 48237
248-850-5482
newvintageusallc.mybigcommerce.com

Pegasus Auto Racing Supplies
2475 S. 179th St.
New Berlin, WI 53146
800-688-6946
Pegasusautoracing.com

PennGrade 1
801 Edwards Dr.
Lebanon, IN 46052
317-923-5321
penngrade1.com

Performance Distributors
2699 Barris Dr.
Memphis, TN 38132
901-396-5782
performancedistributors.com

Performance Shaft Technologies
1717 N. Overbrook Ave.
Clearwater, FL 33755
888-575-7888
pstds.com

Permatex
6875 Parkland Blvd.
Solon, OH 44139
877-376-2839
permatex.com

QA1
9574 217th St. W.
Lakeville, MN 55044
952-985-5675
qa1.net

Quick Performance
515-232-0126
quickperformance.com

RAM Clutches
201 Business Park Blvd.
Columbia, SC 29203
803-788-6034
ramclutches.com

Red Line Oil
2331 City West Blvd.
Houston, TX 77042
707-745-6100
redlineoil.com

Remflex Exhaust Gaskets
P.O. Box 170
Mineral, WA 98355
866-641-7325
catalog.remflex.com

Ridetech
350 S Saint Charles St.
Jasper, IN 47546
812-482-2932
ridetech.com

Rod End Supply
1128 S Payne St.
Olathe, KS 66061
800-284-2902
rodendsupply.com

Scoggin-Dickey
5901 Spur 327
Lubbock, TX 79424
800-456-0211
sdparts.com

Setrab
24 S Clayton St.
Centerburg, OH 43011
740-625-6228
setrabusa.com

Silver Sport Transmissions
2250 Stock Creek Blvd.
Rockford, TN 37853
865-609-8187
shiftsst.com

S-K Speed Racing Equipment
1075 Route 109
Lindenhurst, NY 11757
631-957-9427
skspeed.com

Sonnax
2 Imtec Ln.
Bellows Falls, VT 05101
802-463-9722
sonnax.com

Spal
2445 Nashville Rd.
Bowling Green, KY 42101
866-464-6553
holley.com/brands/spal

Specialty Products Company
4045 Specialty Pl.
Longmont, CO 80504
800-525-6505
spcalignment.com

Speedhut Custom Gauges
649 Innovation Cir.
Payson, UT 84651
801-221-1460
speedhut.com

Speedway Motors
340 Victory Ln.
Lincoln, Nebraska 68528
800-979-0122
speedwaymotors.com

SPELAB Auto Parts
spelabautoparts.com

Stainless Works
10145 Philipp Pkwy.
Streetsboro, OH 44241
800-878-3635
stainlessworks.net

Strange Engineering
8300 N. Austin Ave.
Morton Grove, IL 60053
847-663-1701
strangeengineering.net

TCI Automotive
8649 Hacks Cross Rd.
Olive Branch, MS 38654
800-999-0853
tciauto.com

Throwback Automotive
809 W. Willow St.
Scottsboro, AL 35768
256-259-2400
throwbackautomotive.com

Top Flight Automotive
100 Classic Car Dr.
Reedsville, PA
833-486-7354
topflightautomotive.com

Torqhead
113 Gaylord Rd.
St. Thomas, ON
N5P 3S3, Canada
226-289-3369
torqhead.com

Tremec
46643 Ryan Ct.
Novi, MI 48377
248-859-6500
tremec.com

Tunercat
38 Water Oak Dr.
Sea Pines Plantation
Hilton Head Island, SC 29938
tunercat.com

US Wheel Adapters
1322 N. King Ave.
Lubbock, TX 79403
877-823-2787
uswheeladapters.com

Van Steel
12285 West St.
Clearwater, FL 33762
800-418-5397
vansteel.com

Vette2Vette
1109 N. Bloomington St.
Streator, IL 61364
815-673-6200
vette2vette.com

Wilwood Engineering
4700 Calle Bolero
Camarillo, CA 93012
805-388-1188
wilwood.com

Wurth Industry
598 Chaney Ave.
Greenwood, IN 46143
877-999-8784
wurthindustry.com

Zip Products
8067 Fast Ln.
Mechanicsville, VA 23111
800-962-9632
zip-corvette.com

ZF Doc
5612 E. Almeda Ct.
Cave Creek, AZ 85331
602-319-6575
zfdoc.com